How to Build a Human

What Science Knows About Childhood

EMMA BYRNE

First published in Great Britain in 2021 by Souvenir Press,
an imprint of PROFILE BOOKS LTD
29 Cloth Fair
London
EC1A 7JQ
www.profilebooks.co.uk

10 9 8 7 6 5 4 3 2 1

Typeset in Freight Text by MacGuru Ltd
Designed by Barneby Ltd
Printed and bound in Great Britain by Clays Ltd, Elcograf S.p.A.

A CIP record for this book can be obtained from the British Library

ISBN: 978 1 78816 491 7
eISBN: 978 1 78283 673 5

Dedicated to Catherine, who helped me find the courage to embark on this wild and wonderful experiment

Contents

Introduction: The Only Advice You Need

I spent the first couple of weeks of my daughter's life waiting for the grown-ups to arrive.

Not many generations ago, I'd have been part of an extended family. I'd be among multiple generations, from siblings near my own age, aunts and uncles a little older than me, and possibly a full set of parents and grandparents who were still young enough to be actively raising children. There would have been this unbroken chain of experience, a whole team of people ready to pitch in with ideas and practical help, and whose own kids I would probably have already helped to raise. A bunch of people would owe me babysitting favours, a tribe of curious kids would have wanted to spend time with this baby, someone would have been cooking for us, and everyone – and I mean *everyone* – would have an opinion on parenting.

That's not how many of us live now. Some 50 per cent of the world's population lives in towns and cities. In the US and Northern Europe, around 10 per cent of us will have moved house in the previous twelve months, and the vast majority of us live at least an hour's travel from our parents. With the cost of living in major cities skyrocketing, generations are spread out in space. With people starting their families ever later, we're getting more spaced out in time too. We're surrounded by comparative strangers by the time we start families.

When my daughter was born I spent a subjective eternity feeling dangerously incompetent. That's not a comfortable feeling for someone like me. It's probably not a comfortable feeling for you either. Forgive me for leaping to conclusions about you on such scant data but, if you've picked up a book about science and parenting I'm going to infer that a) you like to know stuff, and b) you're either about to be, already are, or know someone who is a parent. If you've picked this up and you're currently mid-panic, red-eyed from weeping or sleep deprivation, wondering why the hell they let you come home from the hospital with this utterly dependent thing who you just can't seem to make happy for more than a few minutes at a time, allow me to give you the only useful bit of parenting advice ever committed to print. Take a deep breath, and memorise it ... Ready ...?

DON'T PANIC

I confess to plagiarising that from *The Hitchhiker's Guide to the Galaxy*. Any time you're tempted to pick up a parenting book I strongly suggest that you put it down, and pick up a copy of *Hitchhiker's Guide* instead. In all honesty, it's about as scientific as most of the baby 'manuals' out there, and has the added benefit of being funny.

But if you *do* have the energy for something that's factual, that's focused on raising children and also has the added benefit of occasionally being funny, then read on.

The art of parenting like a scientist

What we used to have, when we had an extended family instead of Amazon Prime, was a variety of voices, with a variety of experiences, all weighing in. New parents soon learned to try all these different things and then to keep doing whatever seemed to work for a specific child. Contrast that with the often evangelical fanaticism some parenting manuals provoke – to the point where parents, discovering that sleep training or baby-led weaning or phonics just doesn't seem to work for their particular child, assume that the book knows best, and double down on their efforts, making everyone miserable.

Thankfully, by the time I'd become a parent, I'd had the perfect training for feeling like I hadn't got the faintest bloody clue what was going on, for incessantly trying things I felt sure would work only to see them fail, for meticulously preparing for hours only to see things go wrong in an instant. In short: if you want to learn what it's like to feel stupid, frustrated, baffled, stressed *and* bored at the same time, please can I recommend a career in scientific research?

Because science *as it is done* is very different from science *as it is written*. That's the dirty little secret that gets distilled away: first when cleaning up the narrative for journals, then when telling that story through the press. Science looks like a neat rack of answers when actually it's a writhing mass of questions. Science is less about control and more about curiosity. Science isn't pristine lab coats, exact measures, predictable outcomes. Science, and scientific parenting, is about asking why.

Or more often it's about asking '*WHYYYYYYYYYYYYYYYYYY?*'

So here's the most important thing I want to share about the art of parenting like a scientist: it's mainly the art of getting comfortable with uncertainty. Of learning to not panic. And that's not easy, because the stakes are so high! What we *want* is to be *certain* we're doing the right thing by this tiny, dependent creature (or this gangling, awkward creature, depending on the stage you've reached). But parenting is all about uncertainty – you're learning as you go. Even if you've parented before, or have been parenting for years, this child in front of you *right now* is unique and unknown. In the face of the unknown, there's an art to staying calm, creative and above all *curious* about the children in our lives.

Whenever we're disappointed, scared or confused, there's money to be made. Parenting manuals are clutched like lifebelts, NCT WhatsApp groups light up with 'Is anyone else's baby grinding their gums/banging their head/eating pebbles?' The first few months can become a frenetic charting exercise of sleep and feeding intervals, Wonder Weeks, regressions and milestones. There is a sense that out there, somewhere, there's a key to it all: a routine or trick or a secret that will elevate you to being a Good Parent of a Perfect Little Baby.

Here's something you need to know: babies aren't born to be content. They're born to *need*. They need food, comfort, connection and safety, and they cry. That's not a bug – it's a feature. The same way that fussy toddlers, argumentative tweens and sullen, withdrawn teenagers are all stereotypes for a reason. Babies who didn't raise hell when they were hungry, afraid or cold were not babies who lived long enough to become your ancestors.

I felt insecure in the earliest days of my daughter's life even when she wasn't crying. I once ran into the nearest clothes shop to try to find a fleece all-in-one for my three-week-old because a total stranger commented that it looked like she had a cold neck. In retrospect I realise that it was a warm spring day, she was under a blanket and – oh yes – *we were inside a café at the time*. But anxious parents are phenomenally vulnerable. There's a double whammy of fear: first, of failing this person you're responsible for, and second, of shame that other people seem to know better than you do. Faced with broken sleep, fussy eating, tantrums, bed-wetting, withdrawal, risk-taking and rebellion, it's easy to feel like a failure, rather than seeing these things as natural consequences of a child's brain in an adult-designed world.

It's little wonder that we so often look for certainty when it comes to raising children. We want an authority to tell us how to do it right. If there's an allegedly 'scientifically proven' method, whether it involves controlled crying or self-control in the face of marshmallows, we can't be judged for doing it wrong, right? Science made us do it.

Why all parenting manuals are wrong

There's a joke (it's a long one and not brilliant, so please hang in there), and it goes like this.

A theoretical physicist gets caught in a terrible storm while she's driving home across the Pennines. The roads become impassable so she abandons her car and sets off on foot towards a farmhouse she can see in the distance. She knocks at the door, and a woman answers.

'Aye, love?' says the woman in the house.

The physicist explains that she's stranded and needs a place to stay for the night.

'Aye, cummon in lass,' says the woman, 'but tha'll have to take us as tha finds us. It's lambing season an one on t'ewes is breech. Tha dun't know aught abaht lambing, does tha?'

The physicist says she doesn't but that she's happy to try to help.

'Cummon dahn to t'barn, then,' says the sheep farmer.

In the barn, the sound of the ewe's bleating is frantic. The farmer is elbow-deep, trying to turn the lamb, while the physicist gets out a pad and pencil and starts making complex calculations.

'What's tha doin', lass?' asks the farmer. 'I thought tha was going help?'

'I've got an idea,' says the physicist, 'but it only works with a spherical sheep in a vacuum.'

If you want a bigger joke than that – and who wouldn't? – try any book that pretends to give you the formula for potty training without tears, or the secret for getting your one-year-old to eat like a Parisian toddler, or the recipe for a considerate and responsible teen. By their very nature, parenting manuals assume a perfectly abstract child – a spherical baby in a vacuum.* It is astronomically improbable that your particular child at any given moment in their first two decades bears more than a surface resemblance to the kids in those books. Those kids are fictions.

Distinctly not average

Remember when you were taught about averages in school and how they'd been designed to smooth out scientific observations? That's not untrue, but it's not the whole truth either. When you have a single object or phenomenon to observe – a star, say, or the boiling point of water – and a range of variably accurate instruments, taking the average of their measurements should get you closer to the 'truth' that is being observed. At least assuming that the error is normally distributed – some thermometers measure a little hot and some a little cold, for example. Adding together lots of noisy measures lets you get a good idea of the underlying signal.

But humans are most definitely not a single, stable phenomenon. We're not trying to discover the 'true' nature of 'Baby' in the way we might determine the 'true' boiling point of water.† There is no

*Sorry for that horrifying image.

† Why am I still using scare quotes around 'true'? Because the pedantic among you will already be pointing out that the boiling point of water

single Platonic Baby against which all others should be measured but research is often reported this way. What you'll see with your child is the *variance* – all the ways in which your child is unique. In this book I've tried to uncover as much as I can about the variety of experiences of parenting, of growing up, and of becoming human as I can. But there is no one way to get things right. You just need to keep trying, to stay calm, curious, and creative in the face of all this uncertainty. Because the research on parenting is pretty WEIRD.

Blame it on the WEIRDMOMS

There's a famous experiment on the link between a child's ability to delay gratification and their future success.[1] The researchers in this 1970s study reported that the kids who could wait a few minutes to receive a second marshmallow, rather than eating the one marshmallow they already had in front of them, seemed to be more successful, do better at school, and even have better health outcomes than those who found it hard to wait for the larger reward. But the study was small, and recruited only those kids at the nursery at Stanford University: not exactly a representative cross section of society. That didn't stop a 2014 book based on the research (*The Marshmallow Test* by Walter Mischel) from spawning a slew of parenting blog posts, TED talks and educational approaches.

But it's the spherical baby in a vacuum problem again. Compared to *your* child, compared to *your* family, compared to the circumstances you're in *right at this moment*, what happened in a baby lab in Stanford may have only the slightest relevance. Not only is your child unique, the children in these studies tend to be drawn from a fairly limited sample that has its own specific quirks. The kids in most of these studies are WEIRD.

It's a long-standing issue that almost all psychological studies

---

changes at different atmospheric pressures. The truth is rarely pure and never simple.

are carried out on WEIRD populations – that's to say, groups of people from societies that are western, educated, industrialised, rich and democratic. Almost all the studies that we know of relate to a way of living that is experienced by only 12 per cent of the world's population. In child development studies, the sample gets narrower again. The subjects of these experiments tend to be kids whose caregivers a) know people in university labs, and b) have the time and motivation to participate in these experiments. As a result we're really looking at kids in WEIRD societies with parents who happen to be motivated, open-minded, and scientific – or WEIRDMOMS. The kids who were volunteered for these sorts of experiments were a pretty homogeneous lot. And even if your child happens to have a WEIRDMOM, as mine does, these studies aren't likely to be that much help in your day-to-day life.

That's because the reductionist processing of these kids' behaviour into a simple correlation between the number of seconds they can wait for a treat and their eventual IQ vastly oversimplifies whatever mechanisms may be at work. Trying to get your kids to have a better life by focusing on teaching them to resist sugary treats, as if you were obedience-training a dog, is never going to work. In these studies, it's likely that the kids who were privileged enough to have learned that delayed gratification paid off were also those whose parents were privileged enough to have the time and resources to consistently fulfil promises they'd made. Kids who grab the first marshmallow may have learned that promises can't always be kept.

As far as we can tell, babies don't emerge into the world as inveterate marshmallow scoffers or marshmallow savers. There might have been a propensity one way or another, but the marshmallow savers in the study are likely to have had an average of five years of experience of kept promises and consistent rewards. In contrast, marshmallow scoffers may have learned that life is full of disappointments, that rewards aren't always fair, and that a guaranteed marshmallow now is worth more than the hope that a total stranger will *maybe* give up the goods. Being able to delay gratification is a useful skill, but it's also likely to be a proxy for all kinds of things: trust, security, parental resources. Those factors will be more relevant in terms of helping kids to grow into successful adults than the ability to delay gratification. And it is by no means foredoomed that marshmallow grabbers *will* be unsuccessful. Is it likely that the future Elon Musks of the world are the kind of kids who are patiently waiting for a reward? Though the prospect of guiding an Elon Musk type through puberty is probably not that reassuring ...

This marshmallow test is just one example of a too-pat conclusion built on too-scant data from a too-limited data set. There's also one important variable in children's lives that is *consistently* neglected by the research. The biggest blind spot in child development studies of the last eighty years is the almost complete erasure of the role of dads in the development of their children.

If it's not one thing, it's your mother

So many of the hundreds of papers that I've read for this book have 'mother' in the title. 'Mothers' impact on sleeping' or 'Maternal attitudes influence diet' or 'Mothers' language changes emotional processing'. Very few include dads or other non-parturient parents. Almost none look at other caregivers exclusively.

So when you see a paper that says something like 'maternal attitudes to infant sleep may be causing sleep deficits', dig a little deeper. Quite often dads weren't included. If most science suffers from an 'invisible women' problem, developmental science struggles with disappearing dads. So much research completely erases the idea that dedicated fathers, mothers by marriage or adoption, or other members of an extended family have an influence. The spotlight is turned on women who have given birth. And it's not a particularly flattering spotlight at that.

In WEIRD settings, mothers are far more likely to be criticised for their parenting choices than men. For example, 60 per cent of women who responded to a survey at the C.S. Mott Children's Hospital in Michigan said that they'd been criticised for their parenting choices – most commonly by their parents, in-laws or partner. New mothers are more likely to be on the receiving end of critical behaviours than new fathers, particularly when it comes to sleeping habits, feeding, going back to work, how they dress their child, and that perennial favourite, breast vs bottle. Even the *manner* in which women give birth is regularly judged.

Humanity would not exist without the input of male caregivers. According to Dr Anna Machin, an evolutionary anthropologist who has spent a decade researching fathers at the University of Oxford, our ancestor *Homo heidelbergensis* certainly shared the childrearing. Until this point in our evolution, the amount of time a baby was nutritionally dependent on its mother was short enough that our earlier ancestors could have offspring at a rate that more than guaranteed a replacement of the population. But for *Homo heidelbergensis*, their upright gait – and the resulting narrowing of the birth canal – together with the eventual size of their mature brains, meant that juveniles were dependent on their parents for food for months and years, rather than mere weeks. If the women were left to do all the childrearing, the time lag between children would have become too great, and the population would have dwindled as the birth rate fell behind the death rate. It was in this ancestor that proto-human-building dads stepped up, using the knowledge of fire to make food that immature offspring could eat, then teaching the skills required to eventually become nutritionally independent, while mothers could breastfeed for longer.[2] The involvement of the male parent in childrearing meant that families could get bigger, faster. And that teamwork still helps today: feeding a toddler and caring for a newborn solo is no picnic. Though it shares with picnics the following similarities: it's messy, there's an elevated chance of spillage, and it's nowhere near as relaxing as a meal in a nice restaurant.

If I don't have the answers why the hell should you read this book?

Well, it does say 'Don't Panic' in large friendly letters. But I admit that I'm not going to give you the scientifically proven way to get your kid to sleep/to eat their vegetables/into a top university. That's because there isn't one. Science is about exploration. This book will tell you about the explorations that others have carried out, the variance that we find in all psychology and neuroscience, the range of things that have been tried, and the reasons why parenting books from Dr Spock to Nurse Gina Ford contradict each other.

It's because science isn't a product: a neat set of correlations and laws. Science is a process based on observation, curiosity and openness. It also involves a lot of hope and resilience that this experiment, this set-up, this attempt will finally be the one that demystifies things.

This is a book about science as a verb; about sciencing the shit out of your own relationships with the kids in your life. Of course, the first step in any study is to look at what the prior research shows, and I'll provide a review of plenty of literature, but science proceeds by observation. If the results you see don't look like the literature, then you don't deny the evidence of your own eyes. You figure out what's going on right in front of you.*

For example, as an infant, our daughter cried when she was hungry but she screamed when she was full. Nothing prepared me for this. The literature – the parenting books – all said that a baby's day should consist of multiple cycles of 'wake, feed, change, play, sleep'. Our routine was sleep, feed, cry, change, scream, repeat ad nauseam. It felt like unremitting hell. The studies weren't wrong per se, but the approach didn't apply to our daughter at all. So I turned to what I know: observe, record, infer, repeat (ad nauseam).

I think I've thrown away the spiral-bound notebooks that my

* I'm talking specifically about psychology and behaviour here. The physiology of measles is significantly simpler than the psychology of your child. Vaccines work.

husband and I recorded every feed, every sleep, every activity in. I reread them when our daughter was about eighteen months old and they were dismal. Her weight was dropping, she wasn't getting on with breastfeeding, and bottle feeding only seemed to work contingently. A pattern emerged – upright feeding or feeding on her right side: fine. Feeding on her left side: disaster. Lying down for a change after feeding: disaster. Lying down on the play mat after feeding: utter disaster. I have a video from when she was about ten days old, lying on her back, flailing her legs at the dangling toys hanging above the play mat for about forty-five seconds, then she hiccups, and just *screams*. I drop the phone but I can hear myself saying 'sorry, sorry, sorry' over and over again as she wails inconsolably.

It seemed like everyone else in the NCT group had 'wake, feed, change, play, sleep' sorted, and their babies were thriving, while the only thing our daughter excelled at was the volume and persistence of her cries. Between the sleep deprivation, her obvious distress and my fear for her well-being, I was a wreck. I wanted my daughter's first few weeks to look like the photos they'd shown us in the NCT class – her cosy in a sling while we went hiking through sun-dappled woods, me popping out a boob when she was hungry, her being soothed to contented sleep. I nearly lost my mind trying to get our reality to look like the theoretical version.

When I finally regained my sanity enough to trust my observations, I started to realise that everything we observed fitted with a pattern of acid reflux. Any time we let our daughter lie down after eating, she'd end up with a burning throat. We ditched the play mat in favour of a bouncing chair, took turns letting her sleep upright on us, finally wangled a prescription for infant Gaviscon and at last our life began to look – if not exactly like the parenting manual – more like a version of success in which our daughter was thriving.

I can't stress enough the effect of that first ten days or so of feeling like a total failure, mixed with sleep deprivation and hormones. I was very lucky to get the diagnosis and treatment for postnatal depression in pretty rapid order, but when it came to getting help to figure out what was wrong with my daughter I just ran into the same standardised advice again and again. I had to re-learn to be scientific.

As a caregiver, one of the most important things you can be is a scientist. I don't mean a passive consumer of other people's findings. Instead you have to be curious, you have to wade through confusion and self-doubt; you will feel desperately lonely sometimes. Most of all you have to follow where your observations lead. Studies report on aggregates – and sometimes not very representative ones at that – whereas this child in front of you is unique.

This book will tell you what we know about what is *probably* happening neurologically and physiologically in your child. It will talk about the order in which things *tend* to develop. It will review some of the more interesting findings and talk about what these *suggest*. But it won't tell you how to raise your child. That is entirely up to you. Sorry!

This book will reassure you that, like all good scientists, you're going to screw up along the way. Not everything you try will work. You'll reach dead ends, you'll wrack your brains for new approaches, but if you stay creative, and stay calm as you watch what's *really* happening with your children, and your family, you will figure this out. Just in time for everything to change once again.

This book will look at results from studies done on babies still *in utero* through to young people at the end of adolescence, as late as the early twenties. It will look at how kids are kinder than we think, why social risk drives teenagers to do the stupidest-seeming things, why being a parent changes your brain for ever, why sleeping and eating can be such battlegrounds, and much more.

But most of all it will look at the variety, the uncertainty and the possibilities that exist, given that each child is different, each family is different, and that nothing in a child's life stays the same from one month to the next. It'll remind you not to be swayed by the latest headline or fashionable parenting 'method' but instead to stay curious about the kids you love, and follow wherever that data might lead.

This is your brain on parenthood

It's not just your kids' brains that are changing. Becoming a caregiver changes you. Not just in the lifestyle-related 'I used to be able to stay up later than 10 p.m. and own dry-clean-only clothing' kind of way, but also right up there in the workings of your brain.

While 'mummy brain' might be nauseating shorthand for the sleep-deprivation-induced memory loss that many new parents experience, the brains of new caregivers are indeed distinct from the brains of other adults. Male or female, the neural structures and signalling chemicals that drive your behaviour change drastically in the first few days and weeks of becoming responsible for a child. This holds true even if you became the parent of your child by adoption – what changes your brain is not the act of giving birth, but your sense of responsibility.[3] The same circuits that are active during parenting also get to work whenever we care for others, be they children or adults.[4] It's just that parenting – especially for very small children – is high-intensity interval training for the caring parts of our brains.

Because of these intense workouts, the brains of all committed caregivers grow, adding more volume in the prefrontal cortex, parietal lobes, midbrain, hypothalamus, substantia nigra and amygdala. All of this points to a period of learning new, complex, emotionally driven behaviours when we become parents.[5]

Irritatingly, we run into the scientific blind spot about fathers here. In humans, the vast majority of participants in the experiments that look at the changes in the parental brain have been mothers. But wherever dads have been studied, similar changes in brain volume and structure are found. What's more, in studies of other mammals, where male test subjects are used more often, fathers in all biparental species show strong parenting-induced brain changes.

Take prolactin, the hormone that helps promote breast milk production in nursing mothers (hence the name). Like 'tumour necrosis factor', which we will encounter in the chapter on sleep, the name is an anachronism, because it's responsible for far more than lactation. For example, prolactin is also found in the vast majority of mammalian dads. Regardless of sex, prolactin drives some drastic changes in the brain. In particular, it prompts a huge growth of new, generalised neural structures, ready to be connected up and pruned into shape as you get to know your child. In all mammals, parents of both sexes grow lots of new neurons in the time around their offspring's birth. In the months afterwards they start trimming those connections in order to imprint the sight, smell or sound of their babies, as well as all the new behaviour that parenting demands. 'Bonding' with a child is a process of neural topiary that takes place as we learn the unique features of a child, and prolactin acts as the fertiliser that causes the branches to grow.

For example, when you block or damage the secretion of prolactin in male rats, these new dads never learn to recognise their own pups. Normally, rats are biparental, but prolactin-deprived dads neglect their litter.[6] Damage to the hippocampus – the part of the brain where these new prolactin-induced memories are processed – also makes female rats neglectful. If you can't learn what makes your offspring unique, it's hard to summon up the extra effort needed in parenting.

In fact, the way we respond to children's emotional cues changes when we become parents. Non-parents' brains are more motivated by the sound of a laughing child. In contrast, other parts of the brain become hugely active when someone who has parented hears a child in distress. What used to be a sound you'd go out of your way to avoid becomes a sound you just can't ignore once you've spent time as a committed caregiver.[7]

The process in the brain responsible for teaching us to get out of our nice warm bed in favour of comforting the noisy, tiny human is an interaction between the thalamus and the cingulate cortex. This circuit takes signals from the thalamus, which essentially acts as a junction box that jolts parents into alertness or action when we sense a problem, to the cingulate cortex, which promotes learning and memory. The currently available data suggests that a child in distress jolts us into action. A child who is no longer in distress makes us feel really good. The thalamus gathers the data on the emotional states of the child, and on what we did, and the cingulate cortex sifts out and allows us to store patterns like 'Lying her on her back makes the screaming worse!' or 'He likes the sound of the vacuum cleaner!' Over time the sound of a child's cry leads straight to the action that previously got the quickest results.

For several decades it's been known that new parents who are given extra testosterone respond much more intensely to the sound of their child crying and act faster and for longer in order to care for them. Professor Peter Bos of Leiden University recruited sixteen mothers who were willing to listen to recordings of their child crying while lying in an fMRI scanner and being injected with either testosterone or a placebo. The thalamocortical circuit of each mother was far more active when given the real hormone than when they were in the control condition.[8] Testosterone helps all caregivers learn to move heaven and earth to help their child.

And the motivations for caring for a child are strong. When a child that we care for rewards us with a smile, humans and other mammals alike get a huge hit in the opiate receptors.[9] Tiring as it is, successful caregiving is extremely rewarding. And it does get easier over time, partly as a baby's needs get less intense, and partly as you get used to what works and what doesn't – at least for the time being.

When you become a parent – no matter how it happens – you're embarking on an apprenticeship. You might give birth, adopt, foster, or blend your families, but the very act of caring for a child trains you to care for a child. Your brain is having to grow new connections, produce and process greater volumes of neurotransmitters, and respond to new sensory inputs while mastering new behaviours. Your child isn't the only one with growing to do. When it comes to building a human, you also need to spend some time upgrading yourself. It's tough work, so accept all the help that is offered. You've got this, but you don't have to do it alone.

Why this isn't a 'mummy book'

Here's a little aside to all my fellow female parents raising kids in a heterosexual couple. Yeah, I'm talking to you, fellow mummy.

It's heady, isn't it? After years of being patronised by plumbers and condescended to by colleagues, the power of the 'motherhood' is a potent drug. Suddenly we have our own websites. Things cost a premium because they're 'approved by mums'. We get invited to special 'mummy and me' sessions. 'Speaking as a mother' we somehow assume a respect we never commanded before. Not universally, of course. There's definitely a particular type of medical professional who pronounces 'mum' so that it rhymes with 'cretin'. Contrast the connotations of the verbs 'to mother' and 'to father' though. For the most part we get the credit (and the blame) for parenting, as if 'daddy' was just a bumbling figure who donated some genetic material then dropped out of the picture.

I'm not saying that there *aren't* 'fathers' who do just that but I know – and I hope you do too – lots of committed male parents who show love, respect, patience and ingenuity. So I'm arguing that it's time we went cold turkey on the power of the m-word. Ask your 'mummy and me' group to change its name to something more inclusive so that fathers know they're welcome too. Let the brands you use know that you *and* your partner get to approve what you feed your kid (and what products you use for the inevitable clean-up). In the UK, shared parental leave is still pretty new, and overwhelmingly taken by women, but if we want to truly share parenting, we have to *say* parenting and leave the baggage of 'mothering' and 'fathering' behind. And we need to lobby for jobs for all people that are flexible enough to allow for any kind of caregiving. That means more part-time work and more job-sharing, and more of the kind of flexibility that benefits employees rather than employers. And more efforts to welcome men into the role of active parenting.

Firefighters, postal delivery workers, police officers, and business people have all changed their titles in the last few decades. Mums, we can do it too. And here's the upside – maybe we'll stop being *blamed* for all our children's struggles too. While plenty of studies show that men in heterosexual couples do far less of the domestic work, and take home far more of the wages available, there's no reason why this should still be the case. Sharing the recognition and the responsibility is long overdue.

So now it's time to meet the subject of our book. The human child in all its glorious, frustrating complexity.

1

Little Aliens

After 280 of Earth's rotations safely travelling in their life support system, Nrobwen the Ybab left the mothership and took their first breath of Earth's atmosphere. Never before had they experienced something so alien. There were wavelengths in the electromagnetic spectrum that Nrobwen had never experienced, exciting receptors in their sight organs, causing a cascade of fizzing, aimless activity in their cortex. There were vibrations in the atmosphere – the strangely thin atmosphere – that reached Nrobwen's auditory sensor with more power and range than anything they'd ever felt before. And without the external support of their fluid-filled capsule, the air on this planet was viciously cold and Nrobwen's movements were weak and ineffective. Earth seemed hostile; Nrobwen's mothership had filtered the sights, sounds, and sensations of this entirely alien world. But now the mothership had closed behind them. The lone Ybab gulped in a lungful of the strange gas that surrounded them and started to wail.

Sorry. That all got a bit space operatic for a minute, didn't it? But it's the only way I can envisage just how fucking strange the world is for a newborn baby. According to UNICEF, around a third of a million Nrobwen Ybabs take their first breath of this planet's atmosphere every day. And somehow we only spend a relatively small fraction of our lives screaming in abject terror. While our kids are perfectly capable of *adapting* to this strange new planet, for the first few years they're incapable of surviving in it alone.

This is the trade-off: compared to frogs, chickens, turtles and sharks, mammals spend a long time growing *potential* members of our species. Vast amounts of energy go into the process of gestating our offspring: carrying them around internally, feeding them and processing their waste via the placenta. Even more energy goes into the milk-fed newborn stage, where our offspring, be they puppies or ponies, kids or cubs, are incapable of finding and digesting an adult diet. Typically, during this time, mammal infants are unable to sense or navigate the world in any meaningful way. In a period of time that lasts from a few hours to a few months, newborn mammals are utterly dependent on their caregivers. They need to learn to develop the ability to walk, to see, to hear. The longer it takes to learn to do these things, the more 'altricial' a species is. Turtles are 'precocial' – their offspring are *literally* born ready. Foals are fairly precocial: they can see, hear and move within minutes of their birth, though they're reliant on milk for some months. Members of the cat family are on the more altricial end of the spectrum: functionally blind and deaf, and hardly able to crawl for the first few days and weeks. Humans are, in the main, one of the most altricial species – although we're oddly precocious among the mammals when it comes to hearing. Wherever you are in that altricial–precocial spectrum, those first few months of life are spent trying to adapt to this entirely new environment.

Why do some species expend all this time and energy on altricial reproduction? Why do turtles and sharks get to lay-and-leave, while we humans have a couple of decades ahead of us, getting our kids ready to leave the nest?

There are two reasons for this. The first is adaptability. If your offspring enter the world with most of their behaviours fully developed, they're ideally placed to cope in an environment that you, their parent, managed to survive in. However, if your offspring are born with senses and behaviours that develop in response to their experiences, well, as long as you can keep them *alive* for the first few months or years, they'll develop in such a way that they can *thrive* in whatever environment you happen to have brought them into. Basically: the more developing your brain needs to do at the time you're born, the more likely it is that you can spread out and occupy new niches.

There's also a physical constraint on how much development human brains can undergo *in utero*. Among the mammalian order, we have freakishly narrow pelvises as a consequence of being able to walk on two legs. Babies' heads have to fit through those pelvises. Something had to give, and evolution settled on leaving baby brains plenty of scope for growth, rather than killing labouring mothers – although it's a pretty close-run race, which is why interventions like caesarean sections save thousands of maternal lives a year.

Evolution optimised thus: you want to walk on two legs so that you can see further? Better spend the first three months of your baby's life watching them try to figure out what the fuck their hands are. I don't know about you, but I'm happy with the trade-off, not least because tiny, flaily babies are *hilarious*.

This chapter is all about how children navigate a world through a mind that begins in a state of 'blooming, buzzing confusion'[1] but that becomes a well-knit set of senses by the end of their first year, and that continues to develop through adolescence and beyond.

Making sense of Planet Earth

Before our children can start to get a sense of who they are, they need to get a sense of the world in which they live. To adults this might seem counterintuitive: surely we judge the world based on our sense of self? This is bigger than me, that is smaller. This is near to me, that is far. This smells good to me, this smells bad.

But, even up to adolescence, our children don't experience the world in the way that we do. What might seem like cluelessness, clumsiness or confusion on their part is often simply down to the fact that children's perception of the world – and of themselves in it – is still developing. It takes two decades or so to become an adult earthling: yet that is who we design the world around. As a result, in the first two decades of life, our children have a lot of work to do to develop their eyesight, their hearing and their sense of their own bodies. They also have to work out what is important in the constant stream of sensory data, long before they can figure out what's going on and who they are.

That's because the senses that we take most for granted are those senses that are the least developed at birth. Perceiving depth, understanding sounds, knowing where our bodies are and what they're doing – these are all things that human infants need several months of experience in the world just to begin to learn. In contrast, the chemical senses of taste and smell have had a pretty thorough apprenticeship in the womb. We'll look at these chemical senses in depth in the chapter on food and eating. This first chapter is about Nrobwen the Ybab's most alien experiences: vision, hearing and the sense of self.

What are the senses? If you're my sort of age you were probably taught that there are five senses: vision, hearing, touch, taste and smell, and that these contribute to what we know about the world in roughly descending order. You might even have an idea of the sensors that each of our senses rely upon, like 'eyes are for seeing, ears are for hearing', and so on. If you were lucky enough to have had a slightly more modern education, then proprioception – the sense of your body in space – might also have made the list.

However, life (and biology) are seldom that simple. Sensors have multiple functions. Ears don't just contribute to hearing, they also tell us a great deal about posture and movement. Sight can overrule our sense of proprioception, making a rubber hand feel like it belongs to us, or making smaller objects feel heavier than larger ones of the same mass. Hearing contributes to vision: when presented with two flashes, but hearing three beeps, human volunteers will *swear* that they've seen three flashes.

That's because perception is as much about what's happening in our brains as it is about what reaches our eyeballs, earholes or skin. Perception relies on three things: sensors, salience and synthesis.

Sensors are the parts of our bodies that turn physical stimulus (vibration, electromagnetic excitation, movement) into the neural messages that our brains process. In hearing, for example, hairs in the inner ear vibrate, releasing ions that cause auditory nerves to fire. In our visual system, the rods and cones on the retina turn photons into neural messages. In addition, feedback from the muscles around our eyes contributes to depth perception: the extent to which your eyes start to cross when focusing on something gives you information about how close that object is.

Try it now if you can: switch between focusing on your finger in front of your face and looking at something far away. You'll feel tension in the muscles around your eyes as you look at your finger, which releases when you look further away. Your brain uses that muscle strain to determine how large, close or fast an object is. Proprioception's sensors are even more widespread and are found in the ears, the skin, our muscles and joints, and even in the early parts of the visual system.

But the sensors are only the first stage in processing data from the outside world. Our 'sense' of sight is a complex interplay between light falling on the retina, neural detectors for simple structures (lines, corners), important objects (faces, spiders), and important features (movement, contrast). We also confabulate – our brains make up missing data to fill in any gaps in the signal. For example, every time that your eyes make small jumps called saccades, which happen about three times a second, your brain discards the most recent information that it got from the retina, so that the world seems stable. We don't experience life with a 3Hz flicker because our brains fill in the gaps for us. It's this confabulation that also allows us to enjoy animated images from flipbooks to 3D films – we're *always* running static pictures together in order to give the impression of movement. Our vision is nothing like a camera; it's more like the cinematographer, director and editor of a feature film. In fact film editors exploit our saccadic filter; cuts in movies are made in such a way as to mimic the saccadic patterns of our eyes, which is why we're comfortable watching scenes with many switches of viewpoint and angle, treating them as if they were a continuous view of the world.[2]

Beyond these sensors and early processors, our brains then apply further filtering for salience. Just like my inbox, there's simply way too much data arriving from our sensors for our brains to process everything, so quite a lot of stuff gets filtered out. With our salience detectors, as with our spam filters, we're usually spared from interruptions that aren't helpful or relevant and can switch our focus to objects in the world that *matter*.

Our visual system decides whether the raw data looks like it might indicate a danger or a threat early on in the sequence of sensory processes: even before we can name the species we've been shown, pictures of snakes and spiders trigger human autonomic responses like faster heart rates and sweaty palms, while pictures of flowers or trees don't. But occasionally we still manage to miss something truly remarkable. For example, in the famous 'did you see the gorilla' experiment, you can be attentively counting the passes between two basketball teams and – as a result of your intense focus – completely miss the person in a large gorilla suit who strolls through the court, stops to beat their chest at the camera, and strolls off. It's not that your vision is *faulty* – this inattentional blindness filter keeps us focused on the task at hand while listening out for anything that might need our immediate attention.

The sense of hearing, too, has an internal mixing desk, deciding what signals are worthy of note. One of the most prevalent demonstrations of this is the so-called cocktail party effect where you suddenly hear your name mentioned by someone standing at the other side of the room during a noisy *soirée*.* The speaker

* 'The cocktail party effect' is a hell of a WEIRD name but it seems to be a universal phenomenon. Studies of frogs, bats and dogs also reveal a cocktail party effect. And if you're not imagining a cocktail party populated by

didn't say your name any louder than the rest of their chatter – in fact they probably said it even more quietly, given that they were talking about you behind your back – but your hearing flagged up that particular pattern of pressure waves for your attention because it matters to you; it's *salient.* For years after we're born, we continue to develop these salience filters until we make more sense of the world, doing so at the expense of noticing things that are unusual and unexpected. As the writer Will Storr puts it, 'we see with our pasts'.[3]

But what about our children, with their pretty limited experience of the world? Research demonstrates that they do indeed struggle to switch their attention to things that we as adults assume to be salient. Like a request to pause a tablet or pick up a discarded shoe. It's not that your kids are (necessarily) ignoring you on purpose: you're just not very salient compared to almost every other thing in their world.

The younger your child, the harder you need to work to get them to pay attention to you. In preschoolers, the voice of a parent or teacher has to be at least 10 dB louder than background noise for a child to be able to follow what you're saying, according to a study that is entitled, delightfully, 'The cocktail party effect in infants'.[4] Adult salience detectors are very narrowly tuned compared to those of our children, which allows us to hear things that are important but quiet. Children's salience filters are wide open, which makes them very distractible by things that are bright, noisy or unexpected. Sometimes this is frustrating, but occasionally it is beautiful, as on a supermarket trip with our daughter when she was about eighteen months old. From her vantage point in the trolley, she pointed out everything that interested her. Distracted by the task of getting through the shopping list (and oriented solely to the shelves-that-might-have-the-things-I-need-and-for-goodness'-sakes-Tesco-stop-moving-them-please!) I was doing

creatures drawn by Axel Scheffler at this point then you have no joy in your heart!

that kind of parental echoing that – as we'll see in the language chapter – is a really important part of teaching language. 'Storbees!' 'Yes, darling, yummy strawberries.' 'Oranges!' 'Yes, juicy oranges!' 'A elephant!' 'Yes, darling, a nice, big ... what? Where?' 'A elephant in the bananas!'

There was indeed an abandoned toy elephant in the bananas. Without the attentional shackles of a shopping list, my eighteen-month-old's attention could wander happily. I sometimes miss those days when everything from 'windmills' (wind turbines) to 'pijishins' (her first attempts at 'pigeon') and 'bishisicles' (bicycles) was worthy of note. As her spotlight of attention narrows she's more capable of navigating the adult world, of helping us find the coffee and cornflakes, but I wonder if we'll ever spot the rogue elephant in the bananas again.

Learning to see

Even at the tender age of three, our daughter's filters had started tuning into the things that we had suggested were important, either by paying attention to those things or by rewarding her for noticing them. This is one of the particular advantages of altricial development that I mentioned earlier: our children develop filters that fit their environments, no matter whether they grow up in a forest, on a farm or in a flat.

The process of development that children go through makes them incredibly adaptable, but it's surprising how much space in a newborn's skull is already devoted to vision. A newborn's eyeballs are already about two-thirds of the diameter they'll be at adulthood, and their visual cortex is largely in place: that's a large amount of precious skull real estate given over to vision. Don't forget that the functional limit of the size of a newborn's brain is the width of the human birth canal, so it's not like evolution can just keep adding more space. So why is so much of that space given over to vision?

It may be because of the extremely early (at least compared to most other mammals) ability to fixate on faces. Despite having very little fine-grained vision at birth, human babies can track high-contrast patterns, and are particularly adept at focusing on faces within hours. But they don't see the world in anything like the same way that we do. Human offspring are among the quickest to recognise our kin (within days if not hours of birth). Human infants may be so precocious when it comes to facial recognition *because* we're so altricial in other ways – our dependence on our kin means that we need to recognise them early. But for all that precocity with regard to faces, human babies take proportionally far longer than other primates to develop the rest of their visual systems.

Take visual acuity: that's the measure of how much fine-grained detail you can see. Your standard optician's chart (the Snellen chart) isn't testing your *literacy*. In fact there are several versions of the Snellen chart for non-readers that have pictures of boats, balls and bears. What the eye test is *really* measuring is how thick a set of lines must be before you can decipher what shapes they form. The higher your visual acuity, the more lines of the chart you can read, which equates to the thinner lines (also called a higher spatial frequency) that you can resolve.

Far from having a young-eyes advantage, the small letters on the optician's chart don't come fully into focus until at least the age at which children start school. In a review of over three decades' worth of research, Professor Susan Leat and her colleagues at the University of Waterloo found that visual acuity doesn't reach adult levels in humans until at least the age of five, and possibly as late as the early teens, depending on the methods used. For the first decade and a half of life, children need a lower spatial frequency (thicker lines) than do adults in their twenties and thirties. This isn't just an eyeball thing: cortical processing of thinner lines takes time to develop. Up until the mid-teens, brain activity is still weaker than that of adults at higher spatial frequencies.[5]

What's more, the world looks flat – or at least it doesn't appear to have depth in the way that we understand it – for at least ten weeks after birth. Three-dimensional vision doesn't emerge until around three months on average, and the variance in when it begins to develop is huge. In testing, babies showed no difference in brain activity when being shown the same picture to both eyes (a 2D image), or slightly different pictures to each eye (that would resolve to a 3D image in any organism that can perceive depth by using binocular cues). This indicates that, for the first three to four months of life, human babies simply don't perceive depth.

Those first three months of vision are totally alien to us as adults. Babies live in a world where it is impossible to determine whether things are small or far away.[6] They're going to need to knock over a whole lot of sippy cups before they can start to figure this out. The neural wiring for spatial awareness has to be developed through trial and error.

At around three months babies start to get other cues from the environment – they are usually strong enough to reach for things by that point. Knocking teddy on the floor is literally a data-gathering exercise on how three-dimensional space works.

Does it take three months for babies to start to use their eyes as a depth-perceiving team because the necessary neural structures don't develop until about twelve months after conception? Or is it the experience of spending three months in the world – and in particular, starting to move – that causes binocular vision to emerge? Babies born prematurely have given the world some fascinating data: brain scans of babies who were born three months early, taken three months after their birth, show just as strong neural signals in the three-dimensional processing parts of their brains as full-term babies who reach three months.[7] It turns out that experience matters more than chronological age since conception when it comes to figuring out that the world has three dimensions.

Even past the original trial-and-error stage, children's brains take time to fully integrate visual cues. The strength of the brain activity that is involved in computing depth from vision doesn't reach its full strength until well into the teenage years: our children, quite sensibly, don't fully rely on stereoscopic vision to figure out three-dimensional shapes until their heads have stopped growing and the signals have stabilised.[8] If you're a glasses wearer like me, you might say that each growth spurt for your gangly tween is like getting a new prescription: it takes a few days to stop missing the edge of the stairs.

There's another remarkable difference between the visual systems of young children and ours as adults. We develop an ability called lightness constancy: we know that the actual surface colours of objects don't alter, even though their appearance can change wildly under varying lighting conditions. A white mug might look more red under a warm light or more blue under a cool light but my brain *knows* it's a white mug. But we're not born with this knowledge. Just as it's hard to imagine seeing a flat world, it's hard to imagine seeing a world that appears chameleonic, but that's the confusing world that babies experience. For some time now we've known that experience is what trains our brains to see surfaces as constant even when light is changing. We can even teach computers to 'see' lightness constancy through experience, to the point where they start to fall for the same optical illusions that we do.[9]

Thanks to more recent research we now know roughly *when* babies tend to accumulate enough experience to figure out lightness constancy, and it seems to take about six months. Dr Jiale Yang and colleagues studied alternating pairs of images where either the lighting changed, or the colour of a surface changed. Babies at five months noticed the surface and lighting changes equally, but, at seven months, only the surface changes were noticed. Already, by seven months, our perceptual filters are kicking in.[10]

Even once they've figured out the position or colour of objects in the world, tracking and anticipating *movement* takes some time to develop. Active vision – the art of spotting things in a scene – doesn't reach adult-like levels until mid-adolescence. When Professor Heather Kirkorian of the University of Wisconsin-Madison and Professor Daniel Anderson of the University of

Massachusetts studied the way that babies, preschoolers and adults watched video clips they discovered that our patterns of watching moving scenes changes by age.[11] They edited together cartoons of characters playing catch or tag, or jumping on a trampoline. In each of these videos there were moments when the characters went off-screen and reappeared after a cut.

When the researchers tracked the eye movements of the adults, they found that these volunteers pre-emptively shifted their gaze to where the characters would reappear after the cut: these twenty-somethings were well versed enough in the physics of the world (and the ways these are represented on-screen) to be able to anticipate where they should look. In contrast, twelve-month-olds tend to lag behind the movement, with their gaze trailing after the characters in the videos. Four-year-olds adopt a different strategy again, keeping their vision fixed on the centre of the screen and making small movements to wherever the character reappears. According to the researchers, these four-year-olds were making a smart choice: unlike twelve-month-olds, they knew that a cut in the video meant that the positions of the characters was about to change but, unlike adults, they hadn't yet internalised the kinds of informal physics that allowed the adults to anticipate where the characters would re-emerge. By focusing on the centre of the screen these children were making sure that they had the shortest possible eye-movement trajectory on average. So when it seems like your child is staring off at something in the distance, or that they don't notice an important but subtle change, it's likely that their eyes just need a little while to catch up.

We don't just have to figure out how appearances might change when *objects* move – we have to account for our own movement as well. Intriguingly, children get very good at mental reconstruction if they themselves are moving, as opposed to figuring out a changing scene when they have stayed seated. It's easier to figure out the position of hidden objects when walking around a table than when sitting still and watching the table being turned. Rather than being a distraction, the extra cognitive load of processing their own movement in space helps them to mentally rotate the objects in the world. In contrast, when the objects are moved and the child sits still, it's harder for them to figure out where things have shifted to.[12]

Even in a static world, we struggle to spot things that we're looking for. That seems to happen to me more as I age, but this sort of recognition deficit is most common in children. That's because the brain activity that is linked to spotting particular (non-moving) objects in a scene also takes about fifteen years to reach near adult levels. If your tween can't see the glass of milk that's *right there in front of you – look, I just put it on the table – right there!* – then it's probably just that their brains can't pick it out of a cluttered scene.

To try to understand how little they notice compared to what you can perceive, think of the difference between a trained wine taster and a mere enthusiastic amateur. I can probably tell you if a wine is one that I like – or even what meal I might enjoy it with. But I can't *describe* the components to you. I'm not even necessarily conscious of what makes a wine appeal to me. But with a few years' training, people learn to notice things that I'm not conscious of, like the scent of red peppers or freshly mown grass. It takes time and experience to consciously filter out features of note from an undifferentiated whole. And what is your teenager's bedroom other than an undifferentiated hole?

If you want to speed up your child's ability to spot things in the world around them, may I suggest a rigorous programme of video gaming? In a study of 114 children and 47 young adults, researchers found that eighteen- to twenty-two-year-olds are much faster at spotting a target shape in a screen full of other, similar, distractor shapes than are seven- to seventeen-year-olds. Older adolescents can reorient themselves after a distraction faster than the younger adolescents, and the older adolescents can keep track of more moving targets than the younger ones. However, no matter what the age of the participants, kids who play video games turn out to be much faster target-spotters and attention-reorienters, and can track far more moving targets than non-gamers.[13]

Gamers or not, most children do eventually manage to integrate the three parts of vision: sense data, salience and synthesis. They may start as tiny aliens but they get over the initial culture shock pretty quickly. By the time they start school, children's senses of sight and hearing can *almost* pass in a world built for adults. But not quite. The changes through later childhood and early adolescence might be less dramatic but they're still building the structures that we adults take for granted. At any time between now and adolescence, your child may fail to notice the cup that needs washing, or the laundry that needs picking up. Or they may be lazy. Either way, be prepared to have to point things out for many, many years. They're not necessarily *ignoring* you. Even into adolescence, your children are still strangers in a strange land.

Do you hear what I hear?

While vision has a steep developmental trajectory, most humans are born with a highly selective sense of hearing. That makes us pretty special in the animal kingdom; most other mammals are born with their ears still closed to the outside world. Most humans leave the womb already knowing some things about their native language. That's probably because language is so important to humanity. Without its civilising influence we couldn't have hoped to form social groups as large and as (relatively) peaceful as we have. Having precocious hearing (particularly when it comes to language) is an advantage that is worth devoting some extra brain space to.

Unlike the rest of our bodies, human ears do most of their development before birth. From a small pit that first appears in the mass of barely differentiated cells at three weeks post conception, to the first connections between auditory nerves and the still-forming cochleae at the end of the first trimester, to the moment that the plug that protects the immature middle and inner ear dissolves around the twenty-first week of pregnancy, a human foetus has almost all of the auditory equipment it needs to begin hearing at around ten weeks before due date, although it is able to sense some vibrations through the skull before that.[14] In contrast, many animals (including mink, mice and cats) are born with the meatal plug – the layer of cells that blocks off the still-developing ear canal – still intact. What's more, this plug stays put while their auditory equipment continues developing for weeks or even months after birth. For example, the squeaky mink can't actually hear a thing until about four weeks after being born, whereas human babies just hours old are expert at picking out and noticing language above all other sounds.[15] Despite never having heard sound travelling through air until that day, newborn babies can pick out language, sucking more vigorously when they hear human voices rather than other, similarly rhythmic noises. This is unparalleled auditory genius; impressive in a creature that won't even be able to feed itself for another six months or so.

It's little wonder that many species delay the onset of hearing; this sense is a complex and metabolically expensive part of development. Humans are odd, in that we come into the world with our sound sensors intact and our salience detectors already partially tuned. Our incredibly sensitive auditory apparatus needs a lot of protection, so it's hidden deep inside the hardest bone in the body, the petrous bone of the skull. It is accessible via a series of bones – the ossicles – that transmit and amplify vibrations, and the ear canal, which channels and filters sound. We're born with all of these structures in place and at almost adult size.

In order to hear, land-based mammals need to develop a set of intricate structures including a fluid-filled chamber (the cochlea) that contains incredibly fine hairs that, in humans, can detect vibrations that are smaller than the diameter of a hydrogen atom.[16] To get an idea of how mind-buggeringly tiny that is, note that a human hair is roughly 80,000 nanometres in diameter, but the human ear can detect displacements that are just 0.06 of a nanometre in width. So if a human hair was scaled up to the size of an Olympic-size swimming pool, the ear could detect waves that are less than one hundredth of a millimetre high. That's because each tiny movement of these hairs opens minuscule gaps, which allow ions to flow into the receptors at the start of the auditory nerves. The wider the gap, the faster the ions flow, which we then experience as the pitch (and volume) of sounds.

But the uterine experience is anything but adult-like. For a start, it's soggy in the amniotic sac. Sound travels faster in liquids than in gases, obscuring the direction sound is coming from – ask any disoriented diver trying to work out where that boat engine noise is coming from.

In the uterine environment, high-frequency sounds are filtered out and what is transmitted is more of a bass rumble. What's more, the interior workings of your mother's body also make for a very particular soundscape. About two-thirds of the way through pregnancy your ears are mature enough to hear noise from the outside world. The sounds of a pregnant woman's heartbeat, her digestion, and the other assorted gurgles and rumbles of her body make up the majority of what a thirty-week-old foetus can hear, but the amniotic sac also transmits a highly filtered version of the mother's voice.

Parents searching SoundCloud or YouTube for 'womb noises' get a lot of bassy heartbeat noises and wooshy circulatory sounds but nowhere near enough gurgles and farts. According to Dr Joanna Parga-Belinkie of the Children's Hospital of Philadelphia, recordings of genuine uterine symphonies 'show a predominance of low frequency noise and bowel sounds which are distinct from popular commercial products'.[17] Weirdly, expectant parents don't seem to be in the market for the sounds of the typical gastric distress of a woman in the third trimester as white noise for the nursery. Go figure.

Farty or not, the particular features and frequencies that make up womb noises seem to play an essential role in training the foetal brain to focus on the human voice and their native language: premature babies who were played womb noises (including a filtered version of their mother's voice) showed much faster development in the hearing areas of the brain than those babies who were simply exposed to the ambient sounds of a NICU.[18]

Evolution has favoured humans that are born with a pre-existing soundscape. And a major component of that soundscape is language. That's because unborn babies are busy learning about prosody for the last three months *in utero*. Prosody is the particular set of rhythm and sounds that make up your native language. We know that babies are born with an ear for prosody thanks to a cunning experiment from the 1980s. Professors Anthony DeCasper and Melanie Spence asked expectant mothers to read one of three stories – *The Cat in the Hat* by Dr Seuss; *The Dog in the Fog*; or *The King, the Mice, and the Cheese. The Dog in the Fog* was created by DeCasper and Spence by changing some of the vocabulary of *The Cat in the Hat. The King, the Mice, and the Cheese* by Nancy Gurney had a very different rhythm to the other two tales. Each mother read one of these stories twice a day – an average of sixty-seven times, before the birth of their babies.

Three days after giving birth, these heroic new parents brought their babies back into the lab to listen to all three stories read by their mothers, while DeCasper and Spence measured how hard the babies sucked at an artificial nipple; faster rates of sucking signal higher rates of interest on the part of newborn babies so this is the closest we can get to asking them for a book review.

If the babies were interested in their mother's voice in general, then we wouldn't expect to see any difference in how salient they found each of the stories to be. If they had been paying attention to the *rhythms* of language while they were still *in utero* then we'd expect babies who heard *The Cat in the Hat* or *The Dog in the Fog* to be equally interested in either of the stories after being born. But if it was intonation – the rising and falling pitches in their mothers' voices – that made the story salient, then we'd expect the babies to be specifically interested in just the one story they had been read. And indeed it turns out that the babies would accept no canine (or feline) substitute: the specific story that they had heard before birth, with its particular changes in pitch and volume, was uniquely salient.[19]

This gives some clue as to why such a head start is so useful when it comes to developing language. By paying attention to intonation, human babies get a foundation in a process called 'chunking' – figuring out the boundaries between individual words in a continuous flow of speech. For example, ambiguous chunking can lead to some fun mishearing. For me, the phrase 'I'll have no ifs or buts' is a perfectly reasonable English idiom. To my daughter, aged three, this is just another set of words to try to parse. While listening to the *Highway Rat* CD one night (an attempt to lull her to sleep), she suddenly sat bolt upright and demanded to know why Imelda Staunton was talking about 'sore butts'.

Even at three days old, most newborns can work out where the words in their language begin and end. Contrast that with the difficulty you might have experienced as an adult in a country whose language you don't know: finding word boundaries in a string of continuous speech is a big challenge. Research shows that the filtering effect of hearing language while still in the womb makes it easier to find those boundaries in your mother tongue. All of this prenatal apprenticeship gives us an early advantage when it comes to communication, although there's still a long way to go, as we'll see in the chapter on language.

But our contextual processing of sounds isn't just about learning language. The non-verbal sounds of someone's voice also give us strong social cues, which babies start to figure out at around three months. The ability to process some emotions from sounds can be spotted on fMRI scans of sleeping infants. When played sad vocalisations (crying), as well as happy (laughing) and neutral (yawning, sneezing) noises, the emotion processing parts of the babies' brains responded to the sad sounds, but not to the other types of noise. Babies seem to recognise distress earlier than they recognise happiness, perhaps because they have connected the sound of their own crying to feelings of distress, but they haven't had much experience of laughing yet.[20]

As well as helping us relate to other humans, sound is important for navigating the world. Over time, children develop the ability to work out where sound is coming from. Babies can't learn this *in utero* as there aren't any spatial cues (like vision or touch) to tie sounds to places. As adults, we largely figure out where things are by comparing the minuscule differences in the time that sounds reach our left and right ears. The shape of our earlobes, the width of our heads, even the shape of facial features like the nose, all cast 'shadows' that filter and delay some frequencies. Over time we learn to integrate what we see with what we hear. As a result, we learn to figure out which sounds come from where, without ever truly being conscious of how we do it.

But kids are at a major disadvantage: while their ears are pretty much adult-sized, their heads are relatively tiny. For adults, the difference in the time it takes for sound to reach the nearest and furthest ear is a maximum of about 700 microseconds – an extremely short interval, about 1/1000th of a blink in length. But newborns have even less of a margin to compare, with only a 420-microsecond maximum delay between their ears, while a four-month-old has about a 520-microsecond delay.[21] It's not just a lack of experience that makes it harder for children to locate the source of a sound: in the nicest possible way, they just have less between their ears.

Smaller outer ears and earlobes also make it harder for children to figure out the elevation of the source of a sound – whether it's in front, above or even slightly behind. What's more, children's ears, and heads, and indeed their entire bodies, are growing – and changing in proportion – all the time. As with changes in vision and coordination, don't be surprised if your kid seems a little lost in space after a growth spurt: their brains are still desperately trying to reprogramme for the new hardware. And recalibrating their hearing is just part of the challenge.

In fact every growth spurt leads to a major rewiring: a little bit of klutziness is inevitable as your child's brain tries to get a sense of what just changed. Children's sense of their bodies –

their proprioception – is constantly playing catch-up. But there's a trade-off for all this flexibility. While we are pretty precocious when it comes to hearing, we're comparatively slow when it comes to understanding how our bodies work.

Proprioception

Any foal can walk within minutes of its birth but humans have a long way to go before we have a sense of balance, posture, movement and control. In order to learn to walk, babies first need to learn about their (rapidly changing) bodies.

As I write this, our three-year-old wants to help with everything. She likes tidying things away (score!) and would happily 'cook' for the whole family, left to her own devices. I've yet to sample the fish finger and marmalade sandwiches she wants to make for me but I'm worried that there are only so many more times I can politely demur. And while she is as well-intentioned as it is possible for a little human to be, her attempts are not always successful. Big things get put on little things, cups and bowls get overfilled, I even watched her trying to plug in the wrong end of a USB cable last night, waiting to see how long it would take her to realise that the mini end won't fit in the big end's socket.

I wasn't watching her struggle just for my own amusement (not *just* for my own amusement). I wanted to see whether she has achieved an important developmental milestone: figuring out the relative sizes of things. Kids are *awful* at judging scale, partly because they have no fixed notion of their own size. As adults we have a pretty stable body plan, so knowing that something is about a handful in volume for example, or is at arm's length, is a pretty good heuristic. Rapidly growing children have to rely on trying stuff out each and every time. That includes figuring out if *they* fit in or on something.

Professor Judy DeLoache, of the University of Virginia, and her colleagues devised an adorable experiment in which fifty-four toddlers were allowed to play with a slide that was big enough to slide down, a toy car they could drive in, and a chair they could sit on. The children were then taken out of the room for a moment while the experimenters replaced the objects with miniature replicas, each about 10 cm high.

The pictures in the paper are a little fuzzy, but you might enjoy these captions:

A) This 21-month-old child has committed a scale error by attempting to slide down a miniature slide; she has fallen off in this serious effort to carry out an impossible task. B) This 24-month-old child has opened the door to the miniature car and is repeatedly trying to force his foot inside the car. C) This 28-month-old child is looking between his legs to precisely locate the miniature chair he is in the process of sitting on.[22]

Around half of the children studied by Professor DeLoache tried seriously to use the miniature versions of the objects in the apparent expectation that they would be able to play with them in exactly the same way they had played with the full-sized versions. In fact they didn't even seem to notice the substitution. There were still plenty of scale errors from the two-and-a-half-year-olds despite their thirty months of experience.

When you consider how rapidly a toddler's body plan is changing, and how little experience they have had in piloting their bodies, it's not surprising that they make a few mistakes. The miniature car experiment really does bring home how utterly alien your toddler's sense of the world is, compared to yours. To you, the fact that the mini car is too small to get inside is axiomatic, but to them it's something that requires empirical testing, more often than not.

Even after a few years, when children have figured out an approximate scale for themselves in relation to objects in the world, it still takes several more years of experience to reliably know where their limbs and extremities are. As a species, our physical growth period is incredibly prolonged – it lasts for about a decade and a half. As a side effect of this, our proprioception stays fluid in order for it to adjust to this repeated growth. For children, getting feedback from their muscles, skin, even their joints, and integrating that with their visual system is an ongoing process, and it stays malleable even into adulthood – which is a good job given that our bodies change throughout adulthood too, as my ever-widening waistline, and my lengthening list of aches and pains, attests.

A phenomenon known as the rubber hand illusion dramatically illustrates the plasticity of our proprioception by moving someone's awareness of their arm into another, dummy limb. A fake arm and hand is placed next to a volunteer while their own arm and hand are covered up. Provided the hand is in a 'plausible' position – and experiments have painstakingly determined exactly which positions your mind rejects as too creepy to be true – it is possible to make the volunteer believe that the rubber hand is their real hand. To link the rubber hand to the person's proprioception, it's enough to stroke the back of their real (hidden) hand and the back of the visible (rubber) hand in synchrony for anything from a few seconds to a minute.[23]

People become so invested in the rubber hand that they will flinch or scream when they see the experimenter hit it with a hammer, which is another fun trick you can play at parties, provided you're prepared to show up with the severed limb of a mannequin and a blunt instrument. And to never be invited back.

As well as providing the mechanism for questionable practical jokes, the rubber hand illusion demonstrates how proprioception develops. The plasticity responsible for this illusion is the exact same plasticity that allows kids to adapt to rapidly lengthening limbs. You know: the ones that always seem to grow two weeks before the end of summer term so you're left with the dilemma of either buying a new uniform for the last fortnight of school or sending them in with draughty ankles. But it's summer. The fresh air is good for them, right?

How do children tie together what they see and how they feel in order to get a sense of self? Humans and other primates have a set of specialist neurons in their brains that keep track of where their bodies are by combining what is seen with the information from signals sent by muscles and joints.[24] Professor Michael Graziano and his colleagues at Princeton University recorded the activity for neurons in monkeys who were being subjected to the simian equivalent of the rubber hand illusion. The same neurons responded to both the sight of the fake arm being moved, and also to changes in the position of their hidden, real arm. These neurons, found in both human and monkey brains, give us a sense of self by 'matching up' what we see and what we feel. These neurons learn quickly (and are willing to quickly forget) that seeing your arm in *this* position corresponds to feeling it in *that* position. The plasticity of our proprioception is largely due to these flighty, promiscuous neurons that are willing to hook up at a moment's notice.

But teenagers are at a major disadvantage: these neurons are having to integrate some very noisy signals indeed. Professor Catherine Quatman-Yates and her colleagues at the Cincinnati Children's Hospital Medical Center Research Foundation reviewed all of the available research on why adolescents suffer proportionally more injuries than their older and younger peers. It's not just that teens play more sports, or play them more competitively. There are multiple neural systems that aren't quite mature, which makes them more accident-prone.[25]

For example, as we saw earlier, the visual systems of fifteen- and sixteen-year-olds are still developing, and adolescents can't process visual movement information as well as adults do. What's more, eleven- to fourteen-year-olds take longer to process movement data from their joints, muscles and skin. Yet more data shows that the inner ear of young adolescents is still maturing, and that their brains take time to adapt to the new data that the vestibular system contributes to their sense of where they are in space. The nerves in the bodies of teens, and in their brains, are still maturing up to the age of twenty-two. Your spacey teen is probably feeling a little disorientated right now: laying down that final signalling in a fully-grown body takes time.

At all ages, we're constantly integrating clues from vision and proprioception based on the feeling of muscles in tension, and our inner ears and their orientation, in order to update our sense of self. But children give very different weights to cues from their joints, muscles, inner ear and eyes than we do as adults: children rely on vision first and foremost. Joint information takes much longer to mature.

In a simple and elegant experiment from the 1970s, a team of psychologists got people to sit or stand on a fixed platform on a stable floor in what looked like a normal room. But here's the fun bit – the walls and ceiling were actually suspended, disconnected from the floor, and could be swung in any direction. As a wall swings towards you, your eyes insist that you are actually falling forwards towards it and, to humour your vision, you tend to rock backwards. Likewise, when the walls tilt away, adults lean forward to compensate – even though their muscles and inner ears are getting absolutely no motion data. Vision has a pretty loud voice on the proprioceptive committee, but muscle, joint and vestibular data usually manage to override this noisy voice and stop you from staggering, stumbling or suddenly sitting down.

But when the team repeated the swinging room experiment with small children, their responses seemed to be driven almost entirely by their visual systems.[26] For babies who are crawling, or young toddlers, the visual impact of the room moving is significant: 26 per cent of the babies swayed to compensate for the apparent movement, 23 per cent staggered – moving their feet (or hands, in the case of the crawling infants) to compensate. And in a glorious 33 per cent of the trials the small children simply fell over.

Professor Daniela Godoi of the Universidade Federal de São Carlos has painstakingly studied children from the ages of four to fourteen years and has plotted the way that the size of their visually induced sway decreases by age. The size of the wobble decreases over time, which suggests that throughout childhood we start to rely less and less on our eyes and more and more on our ears and muscles to tell us where we are in space.[27]

By the time children are in their fourth year of life, they still respond more dramatically than adults to the swaying room, but at least they don't tend to fall over. It seems that their inner ears start to weigh in on the 'are we moving right now?' debate, which could explain why so many children experience their first bout of car sickness around this time. I know ours did. We still keep Febreze, sick bags and a full change of clothes in the car, just in case.

Car sickness grabs you in its queasy grasp whenever your brain is trying to figure out conflicting signals from the inner ears ('we're swaying, we're swaying') and the eyes ('I'm too busy reading this fascinating book to notice that I'm moving'). Signals from the inner ear are in conflict with signals from elsewhere in the body. Your brain makes the Very Wise Decision that you must have been poisoned to cause such an appalling neurological disturbance. The next thing you know, you're pale, clammy and – in the worst cases – profoundly apologetic to fellow passengers. If you *are* travelling and I just induced motion sickness a) I'm sorry, and b) look out of the window right now! Suffice to say that the integration of visual and vestibular systems is an important part of your proprioception, but it's also the reason why long car journeys can suck. And why kids – who are still trying to balance the vestibular and visual systems' voices on their committee – are particularly susceptible to sickness.

The reason that vision dominates for children for so long is that their joint and muscle signals are constantly changing as they grow, so their brains don't give them much weight. It may be obvious to you where your feet are without looking, but children need some other form of feedback – either from sight or touch – to tell them where their hands and feet are. As a result, kids experience a lot of trips and falls.[28] But each tumble helps them learn how to *not* fall in future. We can even plot the relationship between the number of falls a child has had, and how confidently and competently they can navigate obstacles.

A study from the early 2000s looked at the size of gaps that toddlers could cross without falling down. All the children in the study began by stepping from one 14 cm high block to another that was 6 cm away. If they managed to cross the gap, the experimenters moved the block, making the gap bigger by 6 cm every time. If a child fell down they were given another chance to cross the gap but after two tumbles they were eliminated from the experiment. The maximum gap they could cross would be measured as the last one they successfully navigated.

In this set of toddlers, the maximum jumpable gap varied between 24 cm and 38 cm. You might expect that lankier or older toddlers would be at an advantage, but the team looked for relationships between children's leg lengths, overall height, flexibility and age, but didn't find any significant predictive relationships. What *did* predict better gap-clearing skills was how long each child had been walking (and falling over). The smallest gaps were cleared by infants with ten months of walking experience. Each extra six months of face-planting resulted in about another eight centimetres of reach.[29] Experience matters, and small children and adolescents are learning all the time. So what can we do to make this experience as helpful as possible?

Making your alien feel at home

When your Ybab first arrives on Planet Earth it's pretty obvious that they're a stranger in a strange land. But once they become bipedal language users there's a tendency to assume that children are perceptually fully baked. That's not true: your kid's brain is incredibly different to your own all the way up to and including adolescence. Children spend nearly two decades as little aliens, surrounded by a world built mainly for adult sensors, salience and synthesis. It takes until at least mid-adolescence to fully perceive the world the way that we do. Give your kids a little more time (and a little more help) to notice things. Make important information louder, brighter and clearer. Accept that you'd be clumsy too if your body changed as rapidly as theirs does. Once you understand the differences between you and your little alien, you can start to see the world – at least figuratively – through their eyes.

In the meantime, don't panic when they fall, engage in lots of physical play with them, and let them really experience the world. It's the only way they can make it their home. It's up to us to play with them in ways that make the most of babies' and children's innate curiosity. Is the Duplo block heavier than the toy train? How tall is the tower before it falls? Can you jump over these cushions? Join in with their experiments. They're important – and they're fun.

2

Learning to Eat: From Bump to Broccoli

Choosing to eat healthily isn't just a matter of knowing which foods are good for you. The $240 billion global diet and weight management market would vanish overnight if it was that easy. So what gives us our appetite? And how does it start?

For the last couple of months before full-term gestation, an unborn mammal has no choice but to share whatever their birth mother is eating. Research shows that this pattern of flavours has a long-standing influence on our preferred tastes for the rest of our lives. But there are multiple ways that kids' appetites (and our own) change over time – from the differing proportions of taste buds in infant and adult mouths to the influence of peer pressure and advertising.

But what makes us enjoy some foods more than others? One of the important sets of sensors are our taste buds. Those little bumps on our tongue play host to millions of cells that have specially shaped receptors on their surface. Taste buds that respond to salt have sodium channels on the surface so when a sodium ion binds to the receptor, a neural signal is released, which results in the salty taste that we experience. But the same receptors also trigger a whole cascade of digestive behaviour, prepping your gut to process something savoury. We experience sour tastes when taste buds with hydrogen ion receptors find something to bind with. Acids have free hydrogen ions – citrusy tastes can be pleasantly sour. But in greater concentrations the presence of hydrogen ions signals the fact that some bacteria have been enjoying your lunch before you got to it, and unexpected sourness triggers an automatic disgust response.

Some taste buds respond to particular proteins found in foods and drinks. There are thought to be at least forty and perhaps as many as eighty different bitter receptors that identify proteins in quinine, caffeine, green leafy vegetables, and even in saccharine. Sweet receptors bind to proteins found in sucrose, fructose and glucose, and also in saccharine. Umami receptors bind to glutamate, inosinate and guanylate, compounds that are found in tomato, onion, seaweed, mushrooms, meat and fish.

But these chemical switches aren't just found on your tongue. Dr Akihiko Kitamura of the Ajinomoto Company Institute of Life Sciences* gave rats monosodium glutamate (MSG) – a compound that triggers the umami receptors on our tongues. He found that the rats' stomachs reacted in response, sending signals to begin the digestive process. This cascade happened whether or not the rats drank the MSG in solution, had it infused directly into their stomachs, had it infused into their duodenums, or had it introduced via the main nerve that feeds the liver. From this he and his team deduced that the whole length of the digestive tract has receptors that respond to the exact same compounds that our tongues do. These proteins that we perceive as taste compounds also act as identity badges throughout our gastro-intestinal tract. Our taste buds are great receptionists, helping us to reject the undesirables and announcing welcome visitors, but along the length of our digestive system these same identifying compounds are telling our bodies what kinds of nutrients to expect, and priming our metabolism appropriately.[1]

* Ajinomoto ('essence of taste') is best known as a manufacturer of Japanese foodstuffs in general, and of MSG in cute panda bottles in particular. It was founded by one of Japan's pioneering food scientists, Professor Kikunae Ikeda, who was the first person to identify glutamates as taste compounds.

Smell is the other major component of flavour.* The olfactory receptors make up your sense of smell. These receptors are chemical gates, much like the taste receptors, but they are responsive to volatile compounds – chemicals that are released into the air. According to research carried out in 2014, humans can distinguish between at least 1 trillion different compounds.[2] And as with taste, smell is just a receptionist to your digestive complex. In 2018 a review was published that showed that humans have receptors for 'smells' far beyond the nose: these chemical sensors are spread through the respiratory tract and as far afield as the liver, the gut and the pancreas.[3]

In short, your nose and your tongue are only a small part of what tells us what is safe and good to eat. Your gut and respiratory tract also play a role in processing – and rejecting – food. And long before a baby's hearing and vision really get to work, the chemical senses of a foetus are starting to take shape: the amniotic fluid of all expectant mums is a buffet of smells and tastes.

The amniotic menu

You're probably familiar with the phenomenon of not being able to face something that you used to enjoy because you were sick the last time you went near it. For us mammals, these sorts of associations begin in the womb. Thanks to the amniotic environment, all mammals get the opportunity to learn which compounds are associated with feeling good and which are associated with bad things. From the last third of pregnancy, a baby's belief about nice and nasty tastes and smells starts to develop.

One piece of evidence that supports this picture comes from experiments on foetal rats. Professor William Smotherman of Oregon State University injected apple flavouring into the amniotic

---

* Flavour is usually defined as the combination of taste, smell and texture. However, we now know that things like sight and even sound play a huge part in the way we respond to food (see Vickers 1991).

sacs of pregnant rats, just before the birth of their pups. Half of the foetal pups were also injected with lithium chloride at the same time, inducing what Professor Smotherman calls 'visceral malaise', less technically known as feeling a bit pukey. Two months after they were born, Professor Smotherman tested the pups in the lab by offering them apple-flavoured water to drink. Those who had only the apple flavour injected into their amniotic sac happily drank the water but those poor pups who'd been given the lithium chloride at the same time wouldn't go anywhere near it.[4]

It's not just sickness that has this effect. Any painful or frightening stimulus seems to put someone off a flavour. By the same token, a flavour linked to something pleasant (or the end of something awful) becomes more appetising. For example, Professor Peter Hepper from Queen's University Belfast clamped the umbilical cords of foetal rats, briefly starving them of oxygen and, in lay terms, massively stressing them out. Then, just after releasing the clamp and ending the stress, he injected either an unscented saline solution or an orange-scented solution into their amniotic sacs. Three months later, those rats that had received the orange flavour as they were reoxygenated made a beeline for orange-flavoured water hidden in a maze, while the other rats made no extra effort to find the citrusy treat.[5] The terpenes – the volatile chemicals that make for the orange's citrusy smell – seem to have been associated with the feeling of relief that the pups experienced *in utero* as they reoxygenated.

So far so rodential. We've also known that human foetuses are able to experience second-hand savours since the 1970s, when research at the University of Western Ontario showed that, at thirty-one weeks of gestation, foetuses pseudo-breathe.[6] Their abdominal walls and diaphragms move and, while they're not getting any air, amniotic fluid is sloshing through their developing mouths, noses and upper respiratory tracts – all places where we have chemical sensors that pick up flavour compounds. By thirty to forty weeks of gestation, a healthy foetus spends about 30 to 40 per cent of the time 'breathing'.

As well as giving the developing lungs and respiratory tract a workout, this breathing action also seems to peak at the times during which amniotic fluid is most likely to contain the tastes and smells of the mother's meals. In 1979, Dr John Patrick and his colleagues managed to persuade twenty women in the last ten weeks of pregnancy to stay still for a twenty-four-hour period while they monitored their foetuses with ultrasound. Not only did the team record fifty-eight episodes of foetal hiccups (a bizarre sensation I remember all too well from my own pregnancy – like having a jumping bean on board), they also noted distinct patterns of pseudo-breathing. At thirty to thirty-one weeks of development, each foetus 'breathed' in short bursts throughout the day. But pseudo-breathing was more common and went on for longer just after their mothers had something to eat. The team discovered that the peak of maternal blood glucose coincides with the peak of pseudo-breathing duration, increasing the likelihood that the foetus picks up smells and tastes from their mother's diet.[7]

We also have evidence that whatever a pregnant person eats does actually make it into the amnion. The smell of garlic, for example, is such a distinctive chemical compound that it can be detected in amniotic fluid an hour later. Professor Julie Mennella of the Monell Chemical Senses Center in Philadelphia recruited ten pregnant volunteers who were about to undergo routine amniocentesis. Forty-five minutes before the procedure, she gave half of the women a capsule of garlic oil and the other half a placebo. During the amniocentesis, her team took an extra five millilitres of amniotic fluid, which was then frozen. Shortly afterwards, a team of strangers was given pairs of samples to smell. This sensory panel was consistently capable of identifying which samples were garlicky and which weren't. Sometimes science needs fMRI scanners or large hadron colliders. Sometimes it just needs people who are willing to sniff the amniotic fluid of ten strangers.[8]

At least newborns are pretty used to the smell of amniotic fluid. They, too, have had samples wafted at them in the name of science.

Four-day-olds consistently turn their heads towards a sample of amniotic fluid from their own mothers rather than samples taken from strangers.[9] Individual diets and metabolisms create a unique chemical profile and babies know these smells long before they take their first breath of air.

As a result, whatever a mother's diet in pregnancy, it is likely to have persuaded their future offspring that certain smells and tastes are great while others are terrible. This is the first opportunity to lead by parental example. I suspect I influenced my daughter's tastes. Children tend to reject bitter flavours, which is one of the reasons why dark green vegetables are often rejected by toddlers starting to wean. But I drank a *lot* of tonic water during pregnancy: it was the only thing that seemed to help with my morning sickness. The active ingredient in tonic water is quinine, which contains a compound so bitter that it's used in the lab whenever experiments with bitterness take place. This *may* be why my daughter doesn't seem to have a problem with broccoli or sprouts, while meat – which I found revolting during pregnancy – is something she tends to reject more often than not.

That example is purely anecdotal of course, but there is one natural experiment that suggests a definite link between tastes experienced *in utero* and preferences later in life. Pregnant women who suffered from extreme sickness – and, as a result, who were more dehydrated – tended to have children who preferred salty flavours. Mothers who hadn't experienced dehydration had children who rejected salty flavours.[10] That inadvertent increase in the briny-ness of your bodily fluid is enough to set up a liking for salty snacks.

Milk, marvellous milk

Those initial flavour preferences, learned *in utero*, last well into later life. After that, the milk-only diet of a newborn also influences lifelong taste preferences, whether you breastfeed, formula feed or do both.

Newborn mammals – humans included – start life drinking milk. Most often, that milk comes from their birth mother, but throughout history, there have always been babies who got their milk another way. As far back as the written word goes, there are guides for how to pick out a wet nurse.[11] In fact the availability of wet nurses seems to have led to the prolonged breastfeeding of infants in the Roman empire, while in the absence of a lactation gig economy in Iron Age Britain, parents found other ways to feed their babies.

Some of the evidence for this comes from the relative levels of different types of nitrogen found in 3,000-year-old remains. The chemical signature of your diet lives on long after your death in the form of different isotopes of calcium and nitrogen. Archaeologists have studied the remains of mothers and infants who died just before or during childbirth, and – unsurprisingly – the mothers and infants have the same ratio of nitrogen isotopes: the foetus is made from the same foodstuffs as the mother.

But something interesting happens during breastfeeding. The relative amount of the isotope ^{15}N compared to the isotope ^{13}N is higher in milk than that found in meat: more animal protein is passed on to babies in the form of milk than is retained by mothers in their diets. So you can tell which babies were being breastfed (and for how long) by looking at the ratio of these isotopes in different bony structures in the body, like the ribs, that are known to develop at different rates in the early years of life.

While a child is exclusively breastfed, the calcium and nitrogen in their bones has a distinct isotopic signature, containing a higher ratio of ^{15}N to ^{13}N than in the adult population. But as soon as complementary food is introduced, that ratio drops back to the same level as the adults in the group. Professor Mandy Jay and Professor Michael Richards of the University of Durham found a very clear pattern among the remains of children who were buried in a large Iron Age cemetery in Wetwang,* Yorkshire. For

* No sniggering at the back. Wetwang is a fine Yorkshire place name. As is Penistone.

most of the child remains, there was no sign of an increase in the proportion of ^{15}N in their bones, even in the first few weeks after their birth. Instead, the ratios stayed the same as, or even dropped lower than, that of the adult population. This indicates that the babies in this community were fed a complementary diet of cereal or vegetable gruel from the earliest weeks or months of life.[12]

And we now know how those babies were getting their prehistoric formula. Bronze Age gravesites in what is now modern Germany yielded clay 'sippy cups' – small pottery vessels, sometimes shaped like animals, with tiny spouts on the side. These were buried with babies, and researchers speculated that they might have been early baby bottles. In a fun feat of practical archaeology, Professor Julie Dunne and her team at the University of Bristol made reproductions of the cups, and found that even very small babies were happy to drink from these proto Tommee Tippee cups.[13] So a technology existed far back enough in history that might explain how some of those Iron Age babies were getting their cereal or vegetables.

But the clincher came when Dunne took very small samples – weighing just a few milligrams – from some of these precious artefacts. She analysed them to find out what chemical residues could be found inside. Fatty molecules get soaked up into the pottery and locked away for millennia. These molecules yielded their secrets when Dunne put them through a gas chromatograph. She found that milk from ruminants – cows, goats or sheep – was definitely part of these babies' diets, showing that they weren't exclusively breastfed.

However, as Dunne points out, milk from other animals doesn't have all the nutrition that a growing baby needs. Carbohydrates aren't preserved in the way that fats are, so it's impossible to know exactly what went into these formulas, but we do know that these Bronze Age babies, like their Iron Age counterparts, would have needed some sort of cereal or starchy vegetable to increase the amount of carbohydrate in their diet.

To Professor Dunne's surprise, one of the vessels also seemed to have residues of non-ruminant milk – possibly from the baby's mother or another breastfeeding woman – although she does point out that the chemical signature is also consistent with it being pig milk. The challenges of pig-milking aside, it seems that combination feeding is nothing new.

Combination feeding sparked something of a panic a few decades ago, after the more widespread recognition of the benefits of breastfeeding. 'Nipple confusion' is a term that caught on in the 1990s as a result of a paper that was as long on dire prognostications as it was short on data. In the pushback against bottle feeding, some practitioners gave ominous warnings that babies were incapable of adapting between bottle and breast. Once given the easy option of bottle feeding, so the argument went, babies would never return to the breast, so confused would they be at the different ways that human and artificial nipples work.[14]

But babies need to be nipple-adaptable because any individual human breast is *super* variable depending on the level of engorgement, the current state of health and hydration of the tit-haver, and the side being used. Babies are delightfully unconfused by this: looks like a boob? – let's have a go. In fact anyone who has had their finger (or nose – always hilarious) latched onto and vigorously suckled by a small baby can testify: if they can latch on, then babies will try anything!

In an extremely salty letter to the *Journal of Pediatrics*, Chloe Fisher and Sally Inch, two research midwives at Oxford's John Radcliffe Hospital, responded to the paper that 'defined' the phenomenon of nipple confusion. They pointed out that some babies are genuinely distressed when faced with the breast – that doesn't make them *confused*. Quite often there is a physiological condition – like a tongue tie, reflux, or difficulty with getting a good attachment. Their practice over several decades had been to bottle-feed (with expressed milk) so that the baby could get stronger, while sorting out any breast aversion rather than worrying about nipple confusion.

'This gives us and the mother time, and the baby can be offered the breast, with help, at each available opportunity, until he can do it himself. In no instance, in these circumstances, has a baby ever refused the breast, even when breast-feedings have been separated by several days of exclusive bottle feeding,' they wrote. 'We wonder if it is the grown-ups, rather than the babies, who are confused,' they signed off.[15]

But nipple confusion has been taught as an unquestioned phenomenon for about two decades now, despite the fact that Fisher and Inch seem to have been vindicated, and that the research doesn't back it up *at all*. While there's a slight inverse correlation between bottle use and *number* of breastfeeds – which arises from the fact that babies do have finite appetites – combination feeding is widespread and successful.[16]

Using a dummy (pacifier) from birth doesn't seem to cause any confusion either: babies given dummies were just as likely to be breastfed at four months as those who were not.[17] And dummy use seems to reduce the risk of sudden infant death syndrome (SIDS), so don't feel bad about using one if it helps soothe your baby.[18]

If you're super keen on exclusively (or predominantly) breastfeeding, it's worth noting that babies who co-sleep (we'll look at what that actually means in the sleep chapter) at least some of the night with their mothers tend to be breastfed for longer (on average just over sixteen months) than those who sleep in their own rooms (six months on average).[19] Partly that's just because you don't have to traipse downstairs or to the baby's room, and everyone gets better sleep – and the trade-off between cracked nipples and an extra hour in bed can be so worth it in those sleep-deprived months of a newborn's life. For those who have or are expecting a baby, see the sleep chapter for more data on what constitutes safe co-sleeping.

Breast milk can be very convenient, *if* you've been able to overcome any difficulties with latching or lactating. Not having to sterilise or prep your boobs, or even remember to pack them, is great. Breast milk also carries useful antibodies, for sure. And, by passing on flavour molecules, it continues to educate our offspring about what we as parents think is an appropriate diet: breast milk that is expressed about two hours after taking a garlic oil capsule is sufficiently garlicky that volunteers can differentiate between milk that smells like Pizza Express and milk that doesn't, even from only a half-teaspoon's worth.[20]

But much of the evidence of the need to *exclusively* breastfeed is overblown. The impact of breastfeeding on long-term weight, intelligence or mental health can't be easily dissociated from the impact of having the time, resources and support required to exclusively breastfeed. Guilt-free combination feeding, on the other hand, has many potential benefits. Other caregivers get to experience the sheer joy of getting a baby milk-drunk. New mothers get more chance to rest and recover. The crippling guilt of 'failing' to exclusively breastfeed can get in the bin: we've been supplementary feeding since prehistory, and in the absence of networks of wet nurses and other milk donors, sterilely prepared, well-balanced formula isn't going to poison your baby.

It's worth noting that formula milk can also play a role in shaping children's future tastes. Formula milk comes in various types: cow's milk-based, soy-based, and something called hydrolysate formulas, where the larger proteins found in soy or cow's milk are broken down into smaller, more easily digested proteins. Hydrolysed formulas have a distinct smell and flavour: the hydrolysing process creates a bunch of free hydrogen ions, which are exactly what makes things taste sour. Many parents are put off by the smell of this kind of formula, associating that sourness with being spoiled, but babies who are fed on it from an early age happily get the taste for it. Soy formula on the other hand has phenols from the original plant which make it taste relatively bitter compared to cow's milk.

Professor Julie Mennella recruited 104 children aged four or five. About half of these had been fed on hydrolysed formula, one-quarter on soy-based formula, and the rest on cow's milk-based formula. When she offered the children apple juice that was plain, spiked with a bitter taste or spiked with a sour taste, the children who had been fed cow's milk formula as infants pulled seriously disgruntled faces and rejected the two doctored juices. Those who had had a soy-based diet liked the bitter-flavoured juice, and the hydrolysate crew liked the sour juice. Keep in mind that it would have been three or four years since they'd last tasted formula. The parents of the hydrolysate group were also much more likely to report that their children liked broccoli.[21]

Because parents don't like the smell of hydrolysed formula, there is currently a huge research effort towards trying to mask or eliminate the bitter flavours by adding sweeteners, by further altering the protein structures, or by adding compounds that change the way that taste buds respond in order to block that sour taste. But if it helps children enjoy their greens, maybe a little sour milk isn't the worst thing in the world.

Those children fed on hydrolysed formula, the ones with a taste for broccoli, were further studied by Dr Mennella and her colleague Professor Djin Gie Liem. They found that formula choice was a strong predictor for whether or not children liked bitter foods, with soy and hydrolysed formula both instilling a taste for them. But the choice of formula had no impact on preference for sweet foods – relatively sweet cow's milk formula doesn't nurture a sweet tooth. What *does* make a difference is the amount of sugar added to a child's breakfast cereal. Those with the most sugary breakfast routine also had the greatest tolerance for sweetness. Sweet teeth are something we acquire through habit once we're on solids, it seems.[22]

Neonatal taste tests

Humans aren't especially precocious when it comes to the sense of taste. Studies on a whole range of mammals suggest that smell and taste help them to navigate their brave new postnatal world from the get-go, while sight and (in some cases) hearing are generally a bit slower off the blocks for most species. From birth, human infants turn and make sucking and lip-smacking movements towards things that smell of glucose, sucrose or monosodium glutamate (the compound responsible for the flavour known as umami). When offered smells that are bitter or sour, most infants who are just hours or days old will turn their heads away, grimace, and even gag.

Professor Diana Rosenstein of the University of Pennsylvania and Professor Harriet Oster of Adelphi University made videos of a dozen two-hour-old infants as they wafted sweet, sour, salty and bitter smells over them. There were distinct differences in the ways that the infants reacted to the different aromas, although none of the babies responded particularly to the smell of salt – possibly because the compounds that we respond to in salt aren't especially volatile: they're harder to waft.[23]

Human babies' rejection of the bitter smell may be a safety measure that keeps small humans from being poisoned. In our species, bitterness is often an acquired taste, and we usually seek it out only in things that have an added benefit, such as coffee, tea and alcohol. But in nature most bitter things are also highly toxic to mammals – those proteins that are responsible for bitter flavours are also those that play havoc with our ability to digest the beneficial proteins in our food. Carnivores and omnivores like us can afford to be fussy – there are plenty of non-bitter things we can eat. Herbivores, by contrast, have to be much more tolerant of bitter flavours. In an epic study, Professor John Glendinning of the University of Arizona, Tucson, compared thirty different mammal species and how likely they were to reject bitter flavours, as demonstrated by how much they shook their head, spat or otherwise rejected them.[24] Meat eaters like cats and dogs are extremely sensitive to bitter flavours, while omnivores like the cactus mouse are a bit less picky. Grazers, animals that eat low-growing plants like weeds and grasses, don't mind a bit of bitterness, but the bitter-tolerating champions are the browsers – animals that eat the leaves and shoots off trees and bushes.*

* Sheep graze and goats browse, if you need a way to remember the difference.

Browsers have also evolved to produce special proteins in their saliva that allow them to neutralise the toxicity of the bitter tannins that are regularly found in these plants.[25] This reduces the flavour of tannins and also their toxic effects. When bitterness is unavoidable you have to learn to tolerate it. Humans can hold off enjoying bitterness, at least until the need for coffee kicks in.

Because of the potential toxicity of bitter compounds, babies and small children are more sensitive to bitter flavours than we are. Maybe our acceptance of bitter flavours is something that naturally happens as we age, as we're less likely to be damaged by the toxin; our ratio of bitter to other taste buds changes as we age, for sure. And maybe we teach ourselves tolerance of bitterness by seeking out those bitter compounds that have fringe benefits. Either way, it's important to remember that vegetables, particularly the mustard descendants like kale, cabbage, sprouts and broccoli, are likely to taste much more bitter to your children than they do to you. The chemical called glucosinolate, found in all mustard descendants, makes that distinctive boiled cabbage/soggy sprout smell, and it's also this protein that binds to the bitter receptors. Sautéing sprouts and blanching broccoli with salt (if your child is over one year old) can help reduce the bitterness, as can eating it as fresh as you can get it. But basically, if a vegetable smells of wet farts, consider serving it with cheese sauce, herbs or even a pinch of brown sugar to mask the bitter taste. Or try anything that doesn't have mustard in its family tree: peas, carrots, sweetcorn, beans. Broccoli is not the only green.

As children get older, their senses of smell and taste start to combine with the other senses to determine whether they like things. Humans start to judge food by how it looks and feels, and even how it sounds, as they grow up. Welcome to the world of solids.

Baby-led weaning

When I was a child, Heinz baby purees were what every busy

mother reached for when they weaned their child. To this day, the sound of a teaspoon in a 100 ml jar takes me back to feeding my baby brother in the early 1980s. And sales of baby purees continue to rise, especially in newly emerged middle classes where women are going out to work in increasing numbers. But in WEIRD societies, our love of strained vegetables for weaning is waning.

Jarred baby foods first caught on not because of their convenience but because of their cleanliness. Victorian babies weren't given vegetables until two years of age; before then, they subsisted mainly on cereals, fruits and milks of various kinds. That was because vegetables were often fertilised using 'night soil' – the contents of bedpans and chamber pots. And that is a recipe for E. coli, dysentery, cholera, salmonella and all sorts of other fun pathogens. Boiled to a mush and sealed in sterile jars, 'invalid foods' made by companies like Gerber and Heinz really took off when they started being marketed as a supplementary food for babies as young as six weeks.[26] For just over 100 years, baby's first adventures in (semi-)solids involved puree on a spoon.

But more recently, research into baby-led weaning – where you just put out food and let them help themselves rather than messing around with purees – shows that, far from being a recipe for choking, it actually helps with hand–eye coordination, a more varied diet, and a decreased likelihood of your toddler putting non-food things in their mouths.[27] Babies that are allowed to choose their own foods are much less likely to develop a sweet tooth, preferring unsweetened carbs and other savoury food, compared to spoon-weaned children who tend to prefer sweet foods to any other food group. This might be to do with the overall sweetness of commercially prepared food, which is deliberately designed to taste good to parents.[28]

The guidelines for baby-led weaning from the World Health Organization say that children should be offered 'family food' in graspable pieces from six months and up.[29] That's all well and good, but our daughter baby-led her own way into baby-led weaning. We used to have her in a sling at the dinner table and she became a carb-kleptomaniac at about four months, literally pinching pasta from our forks as it passed by. Her ability to chew, to hold her head up and – let's face it – her hand–eye coordination had all advanced to the point where it would have been counterproductive, if not impossible, to try to constrain Fingers Farfalle the Baby Bandit. Had I realised that she'd still be predominantly living on broccoli, butterfly pasta and cheese three years later, I might have let her snag a greater variety of what I was eating.

Baby-led weaning isn't new. That's what cultures around the world do, sharing family food with anyone who is old enough to chew. Baby-led weaning can be an exercise in holding your nerve: your baby *will* gag at some point. Coughing and gagging aren't the same as choking: gagging is the reflex that *prevents* choking. When babies are very small, their gag reflex is triggered at the front of their mouths, but it slowly moves back up the tongue during the first twelve months, until it resembles the adult gag reflex, triggered when something solid hits the base of the tongue, tonsils or uvula. Rather neatly, the larger the pieces of food you can safely chew, the further back your gag reflex moves.

One downside is that baby-led weaning is a bit of an exercise in buffet preparation. It can take multiple presentations to get your weanling to try something new. Dr Catherine Forestell and Professor Julie Mennella gave forty-five babies (aged between four and eight months) green beans and peaches once a day for eight consecutive days. While the babies all grimaced at the start, the amount of that food that they were prepared to eat rose over the week, and they ate an average of 94 grams of green beans apiece by the end of the week.[30] It didn't matter if the babies were breast- or formula-fed – beans went from yuck to yay in a pattern over the week. Forestell and Mennella advise keeping on giving the same things over and over again, rather than being disheartened by the first revolted facial expression. You might have to have slightly repetitive meals yourself for a week or so, though persistence usually pays off.

So in those early months of experimenting with food that can be chewed, have fun. Offer as many different things as possible. It's time for you and your baby to treat food like an adventure. *Do* play with your food. Join your baby in playing with the texture and colour of food. Try to be patient with the mess. It won't last long: mealtime's worst enemy, neophobia, is probably not far behind ...

3

Food Fights

The other night, I found myself plaintively asking my family 'What if she's not getting enough to eat?', as our tall-for-her-age, exuberant* child climbed down from the table and ran to throw herself on the sofa for approximately the seventeenth time in three minutes, leaving her staple meal of broccoli-pasta-and-cheese untouched. Then I realised how much energy she was using while turning the sofa into soft-play equipment and decided I might as well focus on my own food, because I sure as hell don't have that much stamina.

Family mealtimes can all too easily turn into battlegrounds. When the kids won't eat your lovingly prepared dishes from the River Cottage cookbook. When you can feel Jamie Oliver glowering disapprovingly as you serve yet *another* variant of breaded-protein-with-extra-carbs. When fellow restaurant patrons are tutting. When the dinner table turns into a game of musical chairs without the music. It can all feel like mealtimes are just 'going wrong' somehow. But it's simply the act of eating together that helps – there's no need to try to teach your child decorum at this point.

* I feel better referring to my daughter as 'exuberant' rather than 'a fucking nutball' – but if you're ever reading this, my love, you are totally – and delightfully – bonkers.

And if you want to be a little bit more of a hard-ass if you're in a restaurant, the best way to do this is brief your kids *beforehand* about what it means to eat with other people outside your immediate family. Things that might need mentioning are: 'Other people don't like to see your half-chewed pasta – it makes them feel a bit sick,' or 'Not everyone loves songs with "bum" in the chorus.' From the age where they can understand some simple facts ('germs are bad, sharing is good, loud noises stress people out') come up with sets of 'restaurant rules' and 'home rules' together with your child. Home rules can usually be a bit more relaxed, without the fear of a sniffy mâitre'd, or tutting fellow diners.

Research shows that it's worth persevering in the attempt to have family dinners together, even if they're anarchic. In a recent review of the last two decades of research, Professor Barbara Fiese of the University of Illinois and Professor Marlene Schwartz of Yale University concluded that the twenty minutes (on average) that families spend together at the table are a powerful, positive influence on a child's language and social development, that family meals lower their risk of obesity or disordered eating, and reduce the likelihood of substance abuse and risky social behaviour.[1] No pressure!

From birth to adolescence, there are multiple, different challenges to sitting down together to eat. How do you meet those challenges? Research shows that doubling down on mealtime mandates doesn't work: it just entrenches the idea of dinner-as-discord. As with baby-led weaning, an experimental approach to mealtimes means that things might get messy but you'll learn something as a result. Table manners will just have to wait.

Who is it you're sitting down to eat with? If your kid seems fussy, it's worth remembering that they have three times as many taste buds as you do. As an over-forty I'm faced with the sobering fact that I'll probably lose about half of my remaining taste buds between now and my seventies, consigning me to a future of blandness. Not only that, the distribution of those taste buds changes throughout our lives. As we've already seen, the bitter notes in green vegetables literally taste stronger to children than they do to adults.

Kids are also far more sensitive to the *texture* of food than we are as adults. If you're preparing food for children, forget visual interest: just make sure that the texture is as uniform as possible. Exciting stews, lumpy mash, meatballs with herby flecks in: for younger kids at least, any food that has 'bits' in it is likely to lead to rejection before a bite has even been tried. For example, Professor Jessica Werthmann and colleagues offered yoghurt to thirty-two preschoolers who were aged between two and a half and four years old. Changing the colour of the yoghurt from pink to green or blue, or from strawberry and raspberry to apple or lemon flavour, had no effect on how much yoghurt the kids wolfed down. However, adding texture in the form of mashed or halved raspberries led to significant numbers of rejections – presumably with a few 'yeuchs' along the way.[2] Disgust-at-first-sight is a real phenomenon and pleading for your children to 'just try a bit' is about as reasonable as someone asking the average adult Brit to 'just try a bit' of the Swedish delicacy surströmming. Surströmming is a type of canned fermented fish that is so smelly it's usually eaten outdoors and is opened with care, far from the dining table, lest the gas produced by the fish's fermentation blast pungent brine all over the assembled diners. German food critic Wolfgang Fassbender dramatically wrote of his first experience of trying this delicacy thus: 'The biggest challenge when eating Surströmming is to throw up *after* the first bite and not before.'[3]

Go on, just a mouthful, you might like it …

As adults, we're far more likely to use touch rather than sight to determine if the texture of something is appetising or disgusting – with a marked preference among WEIRD populations for things that are *not* slimy.[4] Children, on the other hand, use vision as their main appetite-generating sense. Sometimes, presenting new food in a way that makes it look like other, trusted food is enough for it to be accepted. My daughter has no idea that she's eaten scallops because I told her that they were fish fingers with the breadcrumbs knocked off.*

Also, the gambit of insisting that the main course be finished before pudding is served can actually backfire, leading to your child eating *less*. Mixing up the courses leads to more adventurous eating – and it's been common practice in many societies over the centuries. If your child wants bananas with her fish fingers or cucumbers in her custard, let her.

A little experimentation is important, because – for adults and children alike – the brain structures that are responsible for signalling our appetite become sated by the sight and smell of a particular food after a while. That plate full of pasta and cheese that your child demanded is delicious for the first few mouthfuls, okay for the next, and then boring for the rest of the meal. The same thing happens to us, just more slowly. A repetitive diet makes most of us lose our appetite.

And I hate to break it to you but the argument 'if you're hungry enough for ice cream then you're hungry enough to finish your main course' is completely, neuroscientifically, untrue. Brain scans on adults have shown that our brains literally get tired of eating the same thing for too long. This is a very useful mechanism for controlling appetite and ensuring that we get enough variety in our diets. Kids have shorter attention spans than adults, and are less able to overcome their boredom so they probably need to change foods more quickly or they'll mistake being bored for being full.

But ice cream isn't a vegetable, and most of us try to limit the amount of sugary treats in our children's diets, while increasing their intake of fruit and veg. It's a noble fight: we know that WEIRD diets aren't the best. According to the World Health Organization, to avoid diet-related illnesses we should be eating at least 400 g

* Which rebounded on me horribly because I consistently lost half my scallops to a hungry toddler for the following year.

of non-starchy vegetables a day, less than 50 g of free sugars,* less than 5 g of salt, less than 10 g of saturated fat, and no manufactured trans-fats. It's distressingly easy to blow through the salt, fat and sugar limits in a single sitting because we've evolved to find those things just *so damned delicious*. That was fine when calorie-dense foods were scarce, but we've changed our dietary environment so much in the last couple of generations that the behaviour that used to keep us alive in times of shortages is now shortening our lives in times of excess.

So helping kids to appreciate fruit and vegetables as part of a balanced diet is really important, and no mean feat. We have to overcome millennia of evolutionary selection in order to do so but it's worth the effort: the average WEIRD kid doesn't eat enough fruit and vegetables to prevent cardiovascular problems later in life.[5] There has been a steep downward trend in the quantity of fruit and vegetables that we eat in industrialised nations over recent history,[6] and what's more, the amount of these foodstuffs that any individual eats tends to decrease rather than increase as they get older.[7] It's a tough job, but it really is important that your kids eat their greens, and, as we'll see later, your kids will copy your diet so you'd better start loading your own plate with spinach too.

Picky, fussy or eating-disordered?

Most caregivers stress about what their kids are eating. Has it been on the floor? Will it choke them? Is it healthy? Is there enough? In a child's early years at least, parents are extremely likely to worry about their children's refusal to eat enough: whether that's enough calories or enough variety. While it's important for children to get a range of nutrients, it's worth remembering that for most of human history we have survived on relatively limited diets,

* Free sugars are all sugars added to foods or drink as a flavour or texture enhancer, whether by the manufacturer or at home. It also includes the natural sugars in honey, syrups, fruit juices and fruit juice concentrates.

eating the same few locally and seasonally available items year in, year out. Those of us in an industrialised, urbanised setting – the WEIRD population again – are likely to have seen a far greater variety of foods by the time we go to school than our grandparents saw in a lifetime.

There are two types of food refusal among toddlers and preschoolers. The first, neophobia – the reflex greeting of any unfamiliar food with a 'yuck' – is as much a part of normal childhood development as sitting up or crawling. If anything, a child who gleefully eats every new thing you put in front of them is an aberration. Neophobia is a great survival instinct in a setting where a hungry child picking unfamiliar berries was unlikely to grow up to have offspring of their own. Most children have to see their parents or older siblings eat something dozens of times before they internalise that they're not going to be poisoned.[8] Neophobia isn't a huge risk factor when it comes to eating a balanced diet. When compared with children who would eat a wider variety of foods, neophobic children were found to be slightly more deficient in vitamin E, but there was no significant difference between all other nutrients, nor the number of calories consumed, between neophobic and non-neophobic children.[9]

Contrast this with pickiness: as well as refusing unfamiliar food, some children can insist on eating the same few foods, prepared in exactly the same way, over and over again. This can easily become a source of family tension, as well as leading to the child missing out on some nutrients. There is some evidence from questionnaires sent to parents that picky children eat less meat or fish, and fewer servings of fruit and vegetables, than their non-picky peers.[10] But there is no evidence of long-term harm from picky habits as long as there is at least some variety in a person's diet.

Pickiness is as much to do with a child's wiring as it is to do with their personality. Picky eaters – children and adults alike – also report higher sensory sensitivity. Several studies suggest that the more a child reports that certain textures are unpleasant or annoying – not just food textures but bedding and clothing too –

the more likely it is that they will also be picky eaters.[11] And the more sensitive your taste buds are as an adult, the more likely you are to be picky.[12] Being a supertaster is no recipe for a lifetime of foodie enjoyment – on the contrary, it seems to lead to unpleasant sensory overload.

Pickiness doesn't seem to be something that people naturally grow out of. We worry about kids but plenty of adults are picky too. In a US study of almost 500 randomly selected adults, about 35 per cent reported being fussy or picky eaters, and about 15 per cent said that they restrict themselves to ten or fewer foods.[13] But having a choice of ten or more foods is a pretty WEIRD phenomenon, so maybe it's the rest of us promiscuous eaters who are the odd ones. A little monotony isn't the end of the world, as long as your diet is balanced.

So what *does* constitute a problem? Most research suggests that children's picky or fussy eating is much more likely to lead to parental stress than it is to lead to any lasting problems for the child. But when you're the one *responsible* for a child, of course there's a tendency to agonise over whether or not they're all right. Be reassured that, as with so many other parts of development, what might seem worrying behaviour on the part of your kid probably falls well within the normal bounds of variability.

Doctors and psychiatrists have very strict definitions of what does and does not count as a disorder, largely so that they can base their diagnosis on each child's behaviour rather than parents' understandable but often misplaced anxieties. The very latest Diagnostic and Statistical Manual of Mental Disorders, the set of definitions drawn up by the American Psychological Association, defines unhealthy pickiness as avoidant-restrictive food intake disorder (Arfid). To be classified as suffering with Arfid, rather than simply being fussy, a child must meet the following criteria.

- An eating or feeding disturbance (e.g. apparent lack of interest in eating or food; avoidance based on the sensory characteristics of food; concern about aversive consequences

of eating) as manifested by persistent failure to meet appropriate nutritional and/or energy needs associated with one (or more) of the following:
 - Significant weight loss (or failure to achieve expected weight gain or faltering growth in children).
 - Significant nutritional deficiency.
 - Dependence on enteral feeding or oral nutritional supplements.
 - Marked interference with psychosocial functioning.

- The disturbance is not better explained by lack of available food or by an associated culturally sanctioned practice.
- The eating disturbance does not occur exclusively during the course of anorexia nervosa or bulimia nervosa, and there is no evidence of a disturbance in the way in which body weight or shape is experienced.
- The eating disturbance is not attributable to a concurrent medical condition or not better explained by another mental disorder. When the eating disturbance occurs in the context of another condition or disorder, the severity of the eating disturbance exceeds that routinely associated with the condition or disorder and warrants additional clinical attention.[14]

If that describes your kid, then it's time to find yourself a sympathetic GP. Don't try to fix it alone: research shows that the most counterproductive thing caregivers can do is to force children to eat something that they either dislike or are suspicious of. And when children don't like mealtimes, they will say that they're full sooner, and will more eat slowly and more pickily.[15] Turning mealtimes into a battleground increases stress, which reduces appetite. It also means that children learn that broccoli isn't just bitter-tasting, but that it is directly responsible for conflict and upset. Left to their own devices, kids are more likely to learn to like green veg in time. If you pressure them you'll probably put them off for life.[16]

Professor Amy Galloway of Appalachian State University measured the extent to which American parents use pressure to try to encourage children to eat, and looked at the impact of this pressure on children's behaviour. She asked parents how much (or little) the following statements described their outlook: 'My child should always eat all of the food on her plate'; 'I have to be especially careful to make sure my child eats enough'; 'If my child says, "I'm not hungry," I try to get her to eat anyway'; 'If I did not guide or regulate my child's eating, she would eat much less than she should.'[17] Parents who scored highly on the 'pressure' scale were also more likely to have children who were worryingly underweight than those parents who didn't pressure their kids to eat. But perhaps that's because pickier children *need* more pressure and encouragement.

Over eleven weeks, the children in Professor Galloway's study were given soup as a starter for their lunch. In the experimental condition, one member of the research team sat with the children at the table and said, 'Finish your soup, please,' once per minute during a five-minute session. During the control condition the children were given a different flavour of soup and the research assistant made no comment.

During the pressure condition, the children didn't eat any more soup. But they were much more likely to strop about it, with 157 negative comments in the pressure condition to just thirty in the no-pressure trials. Negative comments included the classics: 'Yuck, it's yellow soup again,' 'I never will eat my soup,' and 'You always say that to us and I don't want it. It's so annoying.' In the pressure condition, the researchers were doing what so many of us inadvertently do at home. By pressuring the kids to eat the soup, we're sending the message that it's not something they could ever want in and of itself. Instead it's a chore to be completed.

That pressure can have long-lasting effects. In a study of over 400 college-age students, 69 per cent of respondents said that they recalled at least one occasion when someone had insisted that they eat something they didn't want.[18] In the evocatively titled paper

'"You Will Eat All of That!": A retrospective analysis of forced consumption episodes', Dr Robert Batsell, Jr, of the department of psychology at Kalamazoo College and his colleagues report that 72 per cent of those people who were forced to eat something were still avoiding that food years later. The emotional impact of feeling out of control and helpless persists, causing a long-lasting aversion to eating. If you're trapped in this pattern, it may be time to ask for help.

Because of the pitfalls of pressure, most doctors will focus on the physical side of picky eating, prescribing supplements or meal replacements. But the emotional aspects of food aversion can be addressed too, though this might require a radically different approach to the one we often use as parents.

Novelist Tahmima Anam wrote a moving piece in the *Guardian* about her five-year struggle to get her son to eat.[19] After his premature birth he struggled with eating from the very start. The time he spent in intensive care, and those missing weeks of gestation, slowed down the physical developments required to chew, swallow and digest. Anam writes about how the family dreaded every meal. For a long time they struggled to find help: her son was surviving physically on a diet of baby porridge and so wasn't seen as being high risk. But so much of our lives and our well-being revolves around not just the basics of getting enough calories to survive, but the social nourishment of eating together.

The family managed to get a place at St Mary's Hospital for Children in New York. Rather than focusing on nutrition, the team there pays attention to treating children's anxiety about food. Each meal lasts only twenty minutes, regardless of how much or how little has been eaten. They focus on ensuring that the spoons used are soft, and as unlikely to cause a gag reflex as possible. They use endless patience, positive reinforcement, and a dogged persistence to help overcome the deep-seated aversion to eating that these children have developed.

'What I didn't realise was that he was afraid the whole time. Every time the spoon zoomed towards his little mouth, a flare of panic went up inside him and the fear built up until food was a terrifying, gag-inducing instrument of torture,' writes Tahmima. 'I did it because I had to, because I didn't know any better, and because as his mother it was my duty to ensure that my child did not go hungry.' I think that most of us have felt a similar pressure at one time or another.

It's also frightening and frustrating to face the opposite issue: if a child seems to be overeating (or overindulging in unhealthy foods) then parental fears for their long-term health can be overwhelming. And once again there's a fine balance to strike between encouraging your child to eat healthily and turning food into an obsession. As anyone who has ever tried to diet can testify, thinking about what you're *not* allowed to eat is a sure-fire way of making you crave it. Kids are no more immune to this effect than we are.

One experiment from the late 1990s makes this point very clearly: banning a food makes it more desirable. When given a free choice between cheesy, fish-shaped crackers and plain wheat crackers, the children in the study said they liked the cheesy fish slightly more. But when they were told that they couldn't have the cheesy fish crackers, their rating of them skyrocketed. The amount of time children spend pestering for, asking for, or just outright demanding the saltier snack was much higher when they were forbidden from having them. They also ate far more of the fish crackers once the restriction was lifted, compared to how much they'd eaten before the restriction was put in place.[20] Banning snacks for kids can backfire as badly as diets do for adults.

So how are we meant to navigate the responsibility of making sure that our kids are well-nourished while not making mealtime into an ordeal? To begin with, ask yourself if your child really is struggling with nutrition – is there an obvious health problem such as their being seriously overweight, underweight or showing signs of vitamin deficiency? If you're worried, check with a doctor. If there's nothing physically to be concerned about, try to relax. It's probably time to put the fun back into food.

Fun with food: a recipe for enjoyment

Demonstrating your own enjoyment of varied and healthy food is far more effective than all the pressure, bribery, punishment or wrangling in the world. Parental pressure and control – exhortations to clean your plate, or insisting that there will be no ice cream until you eat your spinach – makes kids hate mealtimes.

If neatly presented food on a plate prompts an instant rejection, then surely muddy carrots or knobbly pears should get even more of a thumbs-down. It turns out that kids can sometimes be a bit counterintuitive.* Pristine presentation isn't a prerequisite for palatability. Sometimes it's more important for kids to get their hands dirty in order to demystify their diet.

In 2011, Stephanie Heim and her colleagues from the University of Minnesota recruited eighty-three children who were attending a twelve-week YMCA summer programme. The children, aged between eight and eleven, were given the chance to set up and maintain a 'delicious and nutritious' garden, for twenty to thirty minutes, twice a week. At the end of the summer scheme, the children were a bit more likely to ask for fruit and vegetables at home, and the families made on average an extra serving of those foods available at the end of the study compared to the baseline.[21] But is it just talking about fruit and veg that helps? An Australian study compared children given nutrition lessons with those given nutrition and gardening lessons. While nutrition education made the children more likely to *say* that they liked vegetables, only the gardening project made the kids more likely to *try* the vegetables.[22] What's more, there is also some evidence that working on a garden project like this helps children's well-being in general. They learn to work with others, and to better understand their own strengths and abilities, both of which are valuable life skills.[23]

And if your kids aren't loving the dinner table but you're not in a position to dig for victory, then getting them into the kitchen first

* Litotes: figure of speech in which understatement is used to reinforce a point.

might be the answer. Professor Klazine van der Horst of the Swiss Federal Institute of Technology in Zurich (ETH Zurich) collected data from over 300 families in the German-speaking part of Switzerland. To determine whether any of the kids were budding chefs, the researchers asked the parents whether they agreed or disagreed with the following five statements: 1) My child loves to cook; 2) My child has an interest in cooking; 3) Cooking enriches the life of my child; 4) My child likes to try new recipes; and 5) My child likes to try [to help] while I am cooking. Among these families, those parents who involved their children with cooking were much more likely to report that their kids enjoyed their food, and were also significantly less likely than the population as a whole to complain that their kids were picky eaters.[24] It turns out that home economics lessons are about so much more than taking home a slightly soggy apple crumble.

But again, this correlation doesn't necessarily mean that cooking together reduces pickiness. It may well be that parents of picky kids don't want to risk extending their rows about food from mealtimes into prep time. To dig further into this, Professor van der Horst invited forty-seven children between the ages of six and ten to come in to their research kitchen-diner. Twenty-five of the children cooked their own lunch – pasta, chicken goujons, cauliflower and salad – with some parental help where necessary. The other twenty-two children had the same meal, but entirely prepared by their parents. The kids who prepared their own meals ate about a quarter more calories – and three-quarters more salad – than kids who were catered for.[25]

But how about children whose parents don't have the time – or the confidence – to play *Ratatouille* with their kids every mealtime? Kathryn Dougherty, a public health specialist at the University of North Carolina, decided to try an intervention study with children aged between eight and twelve, who were taking part in a local summer programme for disadvantaged families. Over five days, these children were given daily, two-hour cooking classes, with a chef and a nutritionist. The aim was to help the children understand the nutritional content of different foods, but the after-course feedback suggested that the children still felt pretty confused as to what constitutes a healthy meal. But they did have a new enthusiasm for cooking. Before the programme, almost none of them had prepared a meal from basic ingredients before – many of their parents were also avowed non-cooks. A few weeks after the five-day course, most of the parents said that their children had become much more interested in food, helping to prepare meals, and even suggesting healthy things to buy when out shopping.[26]

Here in the UK, after-school 'food clubs' have been trialled by researchers at the University of Newcastle.[27] The after-school clubs let the children try new flavours as well as learn practical cooking skills, and the food they made could be taken home to share with their families, at the cost of just £1.40 per child per session. The children also built up a book of their own cheap, simple but varied recipes.

The parents of the children were surprised at how well their children could cook. 'Some of the dishes she was coming back with were quite tasty. I was surprised that she'd actually knocked it up!' said the father of one of the girls. The mother of one of the boys said, 'Actually, I didn't think it would be that good, the cooking itself. I didn't think he could be that good at making things.'

Some parents, however, complained that the kids had too much homework for them to have time to try the recipes at home. And while the children were said by their families to be more confident, and while they had indeed picked up new skills, the habits of the food club rarely translated into daily life. It turns out that, unless such classes are backed up by parents showing an interest, and unless children have time in their already overscheduled lives, the effect wears off pretty fast. *Our* time and our motivation as parents are so often the make-or-break factor when it comes to our kids' enjoyment of food: yet another reason to rail against long and irregular working hours and the inadequate wages that so many are stuck with. Creating better working conditions for adults may be the one really meaningful government intervention when it comes to preventing unhealthy diets in children and in improving family well-being.

Come and get it! Eating together

Perhaps the most consistently effective way of getting children to eat is to sit down together as a family at mealtimes. A multitude of studies – albeit largely done on families in WEIRD settings – shows that families who eat together tend to have healthier and more varied diets, and have children with healthier BMIs, far fewer incidences of eating disorders, and are generally happier. As well as being less likely to have to struggle with picky eating, families who cook together are, unsurprisingly, more likely to eat together.[28]

The delightfully titled paper 'Come and get it!', authored by Professor Jennifer Martin-Biggers of the State University of New Jersey and her colleagues, reviews multiple studies of family mealtimes and their impact on family health. Children and adolescents who ate with their family regularly were more likely to eat healthy, balanced diets, and less likely to eat takeaways, fast food, and other unhealthy meals and snacks. Regardless of other demographic factors like race, class or income, kids who ate with their parents were more likely to have better levels of vitamins and minerals in their diets than those who did not. They were also much less likely to develop eating disorders, or to become obese. The only danger comes from using devices at the table: whether it's you or your kids doing so, checking social media, watching shows or reading at the table will all undermine these benefits.[29]

Of course, families who have time to teach their kids to cook are also likelier to have more overall quality family time – whether that's in the kitchen, the dining room or the park. Once again, the most tired and stressed families are at a disadvantage.

Professor Dianne Neumark-Sztainer of the University of Minnesota collected data from 1,923 families with adolescents in Minneapolis-St Paul in the US. In this comprehensive survey, she looked at the eating behaviours and health outcomes for families, as well as, crucially, why some families find it so much easier to have regular, healthy, sit-down family meals.[30] When taken as a whole, the respondents did pretty well. While only 28 per cent of parents reported serving a green salad at family dinner on a regular basis,* 70 per cent said that they regularly serve vegetables (not including potatoes). In the meantime, 21 per cent of families said that they had fast food or takeaways at least twice a week.

To try to bring those unhealthier families into line, policy-makers have suggested everything from advertising campaigns for fruit and veg to a tax on takeaways. But when you start to break down the data, it turns out that bashing the 21 per cent with some kind of 'fat tax' is not the answer. Families are much less likely to include vegetables in their family meals, and much more likely to serve takeaway, if they answer 'strongly agree' to some key statements in the questionnaire about work–life balance. These statements include things like: 'Because of the requirements of my job, I miss out on home or family activities that I would prefer to participate in'; 'Because of the requirements of my job, my family time is less enjoyable or more pressured'; and 'Working leaves me with too little time or energy to be the kind of parent I want to be.' The more extreme a parent's level of work and life stress, the more likely it is that they'd be calling on Deliveroo. Parents who reported depressive symptoms, or said that their family didn't have time to communicate effectively, were also far less likely to be able to set aside the time to cook a varied, healthy meal every night.†

---

* The irresponsible monsters! Per calorie, lettuce has a higher carbon footprint than bacon (Tom et al. 2016). That said, Brussels sprouts have a far lower carbon footprint. Data on their contribution to local methane levels is, sadly, not forthcoming.

† While this finding belongs in the 'No Shit, Sherlock' files, not a single policy currently under consideration suggests that the long hours, uncertain wages, and lack of support that many families experience should be addressed. Punishing purchasing decisions is *so* much easier than fixing the state of the workplace. The fact that these punishments won't work is, politically, neither here nor there.

What about at least throwing in some carrot sticks with those takeaways? It turns out that McDonald's may be doing more for fruit and vegetable consumption than we realised. That's not saying much: adding a fruit pouch, a vegetable pouch and a bottle of fresh juice still only gets you to three of your five a day.* But in some places, McDonalds is the *only* place stocking fresh fruit or vegetables locally. In a 2018 survey by the Institute for Local Self-Reliance in the US, dollar stores – which don't tend to stock fresh foods of any kind, limiting their lines to tinned and packet foods – are the only outlet for grocery shopping for many low-income and black communities.[31] In the UK, too, there is a trend in which supermarkets are leaving deprived communities, and leaving behind smaller convenience outlets that, while they do at least carry some fresh fruit and vegetables, tend to charge a premium. With 44 per cent of the lowest-income families saying that healthy food has become unaffordable where they live, it's little wonder that fast food makes up a higher proportion of meals in those areas.[32]

The increase in food deserts isn't inevitable, though. In the US, cities have started to limit the number of dollar stores, while offering lower taxes, loans and subsidies to stores offering affordable, healthier options. But above all, ensuring that families have higher – and more reliable – incomes consistently leads to them making healthier choices including spending mealtimes together.

Eating together is an important part of teaching your kids how to appreciate food: not just as a healthy diet but as an emotional and social thing. Studies have shown that parents who eat (and offer) a wide variety of foods, who eat with their kids, and who make mealtimes emotionally conducive to spending time together tend to have children who have healthier diets. Parents who resort to banning certain foods, or demanding to see a clean plate, tend to have less success.[33] A study of 182,836 children and adolescents

* Ketchup doesn't count, I'm afraid.

showed that those who had three or more family meals a week were more likely to be in a normal weight range and have healthier diets than those who had fewer than three family meals together.[34]

A recent policy review from the US, 'Reclaiming the family table: mealtimes and child health and well-being' says that: 'While lasting only twenty minutes, on average, family mealtimes are embedded in a social, cultural, and economic context that is associated with a variety of indicators of children's health and well-being.'[35] Put simply, you have about two hours a week in which to check in with your kids, have meaningful conversations, and build up feelings of trust and well-being. At the risk of becoming tedious, don't underestimate the importance of breaking bread with your kids, and of making sure that the experience is as relaxed as possible. It's in that twenty minutes or so a day that you can be at your most scientific, collecting data on your child's well-being, personality, likes and dislikes. It's also when you can experiment with new foods, new routines and new ideas. Let your kids see you try something new for the first time. Model healthy habits. Talk about your day. Leave the pressure behind.

So if, like me, you *are* worried that family mealtimes are impossible in the face of the kind of high-stress, low-return responsibilities that we have as adults, get together with your fellow parents and, armed with the data in this book, write to your MP to demand that things change. Not through 'fat taxes' but through stable jobs with reasonable hours and a living wage. In the long run, society as a whole will benefit from everyone sharing mealtimes with their kids.

4

From 'Go the F*ck to Sleep' to 'Why Are You Still in Bed?': Why Sleep Is Never Simple

Ask any new parent whether they're getting enough sleep and you're likely to get either hysterical laughter or bitter weeping in response. It seems terribly unfair that babies get, on average, thirteen hours' sleep, and toddlers get around eleven hours, while their caregivers are chronically sleep-deprived. That's why in this chapter I'll spend as much time (if not more) talking about *your* sleep as your child's: you're better able to parent – you're better able to do *everything* – when you're well rested.

Part of this is to do with the physical size and metabolic requirements of newborns. Put simply, those little buggers have to eat. Given that a newborn's stomach starts out about the size of a walnut, and yet they need to grow as rapidly as possible, frequent waking is the norm. The goal of babies sleeping through the night only arose in the 1950s and 1960s when bottle feeding was at its peak. As formula is more slowly digested than breast milk, waking for a midnight snack (or several) became, during this period, less common.

So it's a cultural hangover, the idea that sleeping through the night should be the norm, and it ignores the fact that it is incompatible both with breastfeeding and with the actual neurobiology of sleep. Add to this the reality that we're still miles away from having a standard eight-hour working day that would leave enough time for most of us to get adequate rest: clearly, most adults' sleep is already horribly compressed.

A wakeful child just adds to the sense of desperation, especially when accompanied by lurid headlines about the impact of chronic sleep deprivation. Bedtime conflicts have become stressful business for kids and parents alike. If you feel like there is not enough coffee in the world, I promise you're not alone. Read on, if you can stay awake.

We don't fall asleep, we cascade

The neurological mechanisms that underlie the way in which we fall asleep are still not fully understood. Of the fifty or so peer-reviewed papers I have sitting on my desk, about forty-five conclude that sleep is complicated. The other five conclude that it's *really* complicated. That's because we can only look at the activity of the human brain through snapshots of its metabolism (fMRI) or its electrical charge at the surface (EEG).

Functional magnetic resonance imaging (fMRI) measures the relative levels of O_2 saturation of the blood supply to different parts of the brain at a resolution of about 3 mm by 3 mm by 3 mm, and at roughly one-tenth of a second intervals. Trying to 'read thoughts' using fMRI is like using a flipbook animation drawn in crayon to determine if the offside rule was broken.

Electroencephalography (EEG) measures the way that current is changing in different areas of the brain by measuring voltage at several locations on the scalp. To continue the previous analogy, trying to 'read thoughts' using EEG is like trying to determine if the offside rule was broken by listening to the noises from the crowd in the stadium.

Genetics, too, is what we non-geneticists like to call 'fucking loopy'. For example, among those papers I mentioned, there are several that look at a crucial gene that helps to determine whether or not it's time to go to sleep. That gene, and the protein that it makes, is called TNFα. So far so acronym-y.* But TNFα is short for

* Initialism-y, if you're pedantic.

tumour necrosis factor alpha – causing necrosis in tumours. That's what it was first spotted doing somewhere else in the body, so the name stuck. But now we know that it also suppresses appetite, increases insulin resistance, and regulates how bitter things taste. But we're stuck with the name, because history. It's like calling a device you use to browse the internet, play games, send messages, navigate, take photographs and issue reminders a 'telephone'.

Because I care for you, dear reader, more than I care for my sanity, I've autopsied this mangled body of research, and here's what I've found.

We now know that TNFα expresses a protein inside star-shaped cells in the brain called astrocytes. These cells support neurons both physically and metabolically – they're both a scaffold and a glycogen supply mechanism. But it was recently discovered that these cells don't just support and supply neurons, they also have signalling duties of their own. Astrocytes accumulate TNFα throughout the day, and then release it into the adjacent neurons, where it binds with receptors, which then contributes to the drive to go to sleep.[1]

That's still not the whole story. There are at least two processes going on in the brain: Process C (our circadian rhythm) and Process S (sleep pressure).[2] Our circadian rhythm gets reset every day by *zeitgebers* (literally 'time givers') that include light levels, temperature, exercise levels, and even social interactions, which could explain that weird jet-lag feeling so many of us experienced during lockdown.

One of the strongest *zeitgebers* is the level (and the colour) of light. Bright, bluish light seems to reset your body clock, starting the twenty-four-hour cycle of appetite, energy levels and even body temperature, which all show predictable changes relative to the brightest time of day. You can test this by putting people in a lab and artificially simulating days of slightly shorter or longer lengths and seeing what happens to their circadian rhythms.

Your level of TNFα is just one of the things that varies through the day in line with your circadian rhythm. Another substance that helps to govern the circadian rhythm is the hormone melatonin. Almost absent during the day, melatonin is secreted by the pineal gland as evening draws on and then throughout the night, dissipating just before you wake up, suggesting that it has a role in keeping you asleep. Light levels over 300 lux inhibit the production of melatonin, which is bad news if you're reading yourself to sleep right now: 500 lux is for most people the minimum light level needed to read without eye strain.

Process S, or 'sleep pressure', is even less well understood than Process C. Sleep pressure is an ill-defined concept. It's like describing 'eat pressure' as 'the longer it is since humans have eaten, the more likely they are to eat': we know that there is more to feeling hungry than this. But while we can't report back on how it feels to really pig out on short-wave sleep, unconscious as we are at the time, experiments show that depriving people of sleep – inducing more sleep pressure – seriously alters not just how quickly they fall asleep, but how deeply too.

Processes C and S *usually* coincide – sleep pressure peaks around the time melatonin starts being produced – but for insomniacs, night workers, the jet-lagged and adolescents, the two signals often don't synch up. This can lead to us napping outside of the usual melatonin peak at night, because sleep pressure has built up. Or it can lead to lying awake at night when melatonin has risen but sleep pressure is still low.

Sleep appetite and circadian rhythm vary wildly between people and this variance is partly genetic. There are some extraordinary people who can thrive on about three-quarters of the amount of sleep that the rest of us need. One particular family has a mutation that allows them to function normally on just six-and-a-quarter hours of sleep per twenty-four-hour period. That might be how much sleep you're *getting*, but for this particular family, 375 minutes of sleep is all they *need*.

A single letter change from C to T on a single gene, present in only four in 100,000 people, is responsible for this change. According to Professor Ying-Hui Fu of the UCSF Weill Institute for Neurosciences, who led the study, the people with the mutation tend to be more optimistic, more energetic and better multi-taskers, are more tolerant of pain, and don't get jet lag. I had no idea it was possible to feel this much envy.

According to Professor Fu: 'Natural short sleepers experience better sleep quality and sleep efficiency ... By studying them, we hope to learn what makes for a good night's sleep, so that all of us can be better sleepers leading happier, healthier lives.' Forget trying to colonise Mars. *This* is the research that billionaires should be funding.

Perhaps the most studied, certainly the most intriguing, phase of sleep is paradoxical sleep, or rapid eye movement (REM) sleep. We know that the REM phase is important: as well as giving us trippy dreams, it makes up about 50 per cent of infant sleep, and 20 per cent of adult sleep. We also know that if we're sleep-deprived, the period that we spend in non-REM sleep (NREM) falls, while REM is preserved.[3] We favour REM over NREM despite the fact that NREM is necessary to keep us physically healthy, so whatever the benefits of REM sleep are, they have to outweigh the damage done by the loss of NREM sleep.

When human babies are born, they're unusual in that they fall straight into REM sleep while older children and adults generally go through a period of slow-wave sleep before these bursts of activity. At the beginning of sleep, it takes about ninety minutes for most adults to go from NREM sleep to REM sleep. So as adults we need a minimum of about two hours of sleep to get to the first of our REM phases, and we need multiple REM phases in a twenty-four-hour period in order to be able to cope with the stress of being new parents.

But the circadian rhythm doesn't properly start to emerge in *babies* until about three to six months, when the *zeitgeber*-responsive structures like the suprachiasmatic nucleus start to mature. Children's REM sleep patterns develop slowly, only beginning to take on adult-like patterns towards the end of the first year.[4] So how are we meant to cope with infants who fall straight into REM sleep and sleep for about two hours at a time, without turning into matted-haired, junk-food-gobbling, irritable sods?

You may not like the answer, but it seems to be a combination of:

- Accepting that kids, like adults, have different sleep appetites and patterns, and that some sleep loss is inevitable.
- Tag-teaming with another caregiver if you can, so you can get at least a solid four to five hours in a stretch.
- Giving yourself permission to nap whenever you can.

Because otherwise you'll feel wretched.

Parental Inhibition of Sleep Satiety Often Forces Failures

Hi, fellow sleep-deprived parent. If someone asks you why you're so grumpy/clumsy/distracted, I suggest you use the handy acronym for Parental Inhibition of Sleep Satiety Often Forces Failures.

In the 1880s, pioneering sleep researcher Dr Maria Manaseina systematically kept dogs awake in her laboratory and discovered that two weeks of sleep deprivation is enough to be fatal.[5] This could explain the sudden moral panic about children's bedtimes and sleep routines that appeared in the first two decades of the twentieth century, and that hasn't left us since.[6] The worry persists even though we've since learned that, unlike dogs, rats and rabbits, humans can't die from a lack of sleep: the human brain experiences a phenomenon called microsleep if kept awake too long.*

* At least it won't kill you *directly*. It might kill you indirectly. As of 1999 there were 1,500 annual fatalities in the US from drowsy driving and 40,000 nonfatal injuries (NCSDR/NHTSA Expert Panel on Driver Fatigue and Sleepiness 1999). In 1995 there were at least 679 sleep-related accidents, accounting for around 16 per cent of the accidents on major roads in South West England, and over 20 per cent on motorways in the Midlands. Most of the drivers were men, about half were under thirty, and commercial drivers made up a disproportionate number of those involved in the crashes. The worst times are 2 a.m., 6 a.m. and 4 p.m.[7]

But there are some lousy consequences of a lack of sleep. They collectively form a constellation of symptoms that is collectively known as 'being fucking knackered'. Sleep researchers who want to study the impact of chronic sleep restriction love to take advantage of what is sometimes called a natural experiment: a cohort of the population that is already fucking knackered. New parents provide fantastic data for studies of long-term sleep disturbances, which means that some of the best data about the effect of tiredness on mental performance comes from parent volunteers.

For example, Professor Franziska Plessow and her colleagues at universities in Dresden and Wurzburg compared parents who said they were getting less than seven hours of sleep a night with those who said that they were getting more than seven hours of sleep.* Astoundingly, both groups gave similar answers on surveys about how tired they felt, how happy they felt, and how stressed they felt. Both groups also said that they felt a similar degree of cognitive impairment. However, when they were confronted with a test of executive function, parents who had less sleep did slightly worse.[8]

In the test, the participants were prompted to either say whether a number was odd or even *or* to say whether the number was less or greater than five. The experimenters wanted to see how much longer it took each group to answer whenever the task switched between the 'odd or even' and the 'greater or less' versions. The better-rested parents took only an extra 0.2 seconds to answer when the tasks switched, while the tired parents took 0.3 seconds. That might not seem like much, but the difference is significant. No matter their sex, new parents struggle to shift their attention, and the less sleep they'd had the harder it was for them to switch. Professor Plessow and her colleagues stress that the more sleep-deprived parents don't *rate* themselves as any slower than the other cohort. 'Chronically sleep-curtailed new parents are not aware of their cognitive impairments,' they

---

* Who the hell *are* they?

warned. So if you're not *sure* if you're suffering from brain fog, you probably are.

Parental sleep is one of the few areas where fathers are *almost* as comprehensively studied as mothers. Don't get me wrong, when it comes to seeing why *babies* don't sleep, mothers are still the focus: more on that later. But recent studies acknowledge that dads and mums alike lose sleep in the first months and years of their baby's life. A groundbreaking paper in 2004 pointed out that 'new fathers are subject to the random sleep-wake cycles of newborns and often participate in their night-time care'.[9] I'm so glad we finally found that out!

How much of a burden is this? In the long term, you might be relieved to hear, it isn't likely to do you lasting harm. While chronic sleep deprivation, such as that experienced by shift workers, is known to lead to long-term health impacts like cardiovascular disease and some cancers, the effects of parental sleep loss are usually more irregular – at least after the first year to eighteen months – and lead to serious but short-lived problems.

Mental health is the most obvious casualty of sleep deprivation. Recent studies show that sleep deprivation leads to higher levels of depression and anxiety, and also leaves us struggling to recognise our emotional states – or the states of others.[10] For kids, this leads to meltdowns, tantrums and withdrawal. For parents, it leads to all of the above, plus frustration, narkiness and a lack of patience – or worse. Mothers who get less than four hours' sleep between midnight and 6 a.m., and who nap for less than sixty minutes in the day, are at much higher risk of depression than mothers who get more sleep, no matter whether their baby is a Zen master or a screaming rage-ball.[11] I'm certain that sleep deprivation was part of what tipped me headlong into depression during the first few weeks of our daughter's life.

Regardless of gender, people who suffer from disturbed sleep tend to have more difficulties with both long-term and short-term memory-making.[12] I had a point I was going to make here but I've forgotten what it was.

What's more, lack of sleep really does make you feel shittier. After a night of poor sleep, volunteers reported that they felt far more pain and, when observed in an fMRI scanner, showed more activation in the somatosensory cortex.* Just one night of interrupted sleep is enough to make *everything* feel worse.[13]

Lack of sleep can also damage your physical health. The *nemuri* gene creates a protein, NUR, that both kills microbes and induces sleep. Overriding the need to sleep when we're sick may also rob our bodies of these disease-bashing proteins, by slowing down the expression of this gene. Lack of sleep also buggers up the action of T-cells, the white blood cells that capture viruses in a sticky protein called integrin.[14] No amount of over-the-counter cold and flu remedy is going to get rid of your cold. Hopping yourself up on 'non-drowsy' (caffeine-laden) capsules might get you into the office, but they're also hobbling your immune response, allowing you to shed more rhinovirus around the place, infecting more people, creating more demand for cold and flu remedies.† Sniffly children and sniffly adults alike should go the hell to sleep.

But again, for kids and adults alike, getting enough sleep can be easier said than done. For new parents in particular, it can be tricky. I know that my telling you to get an early night is about as welcome as you telling your kid it's time for bed, but looking after your own sleep is an essential part of coping with the sleep turmoil that adding a child to the family can cause.

It's a good idea to spend at least as much time focusing on your own sleep needs, and sleep habits, as you do on your child's. Research shows that parents often neglect their own sleep hygiene in all the stress of raising a child. Even simple sleep hygiene practices can be some help. Dr Robyn Stremler and her colleagues

---

* The area of the brain that receives, and sends on, the signals from sensory receptors around the body, including the nociceptors – receptors that signal different types of harm.

† I'm no conspiracy nut, but it really does seem that there's much more profit to be made out of sending us out to sneeze on each other than there is from letting us just go to bed.

at the University of Toronto found, at a six-week follow-up appointment, that mothers who were given *personalised* sleep advice got almost an hour's more sleep a night than those mothers who were simply called to see how they were doing.[15] Interestingly, this is one of the few studies where the research team spent time finding out about the needs, wants and habits of the mothers and babies before offering guidance. The team's advice included things like progressive muscle relaxation for mothers who were finding it hard to get to sleep; reassuring concerned mothers that through-the-night sleeping *isn't* the norm in the first few months, especially when babies are breastfed; advising exhausted mothers to nap and let someone else put the laundry on; and basically just confirming that everyone finds this stuff *hard*. By the end of this study, the mothers who received personalised advice were better rested, felt more positive, and were simply better able to cope with whatever life threw at them. So tonight, turn the lights low, switch off your phone before bedtime, try some deep breathing or muscle relaxation, and get *yourself* as good a night's sleep as you can.

And if your kid does wake you up, maybe just let them fall asleep next to you.

To co-sleep or not?

Humans are the only primate that doesn't consistently co-sleep with their offspring, even though our babies are the least mature at birth, with only 25 per cent of their adult brain volume. Non-primate infants whose parents leave them in a nest while they go hunting go into a sort of stasis in case they become something else's lunch: they don't exactly sleep, but they become very still, and neither cry nor crap while their parents are away. Little humans definitely cry (and crap) when we leave them alone.[16]

In WEIRD cultures, we're overwhelmingly advised not to co-sleep. Putting your infant to sleep on their back, foot-to-foot in their own crib so they can sleep throughout the night, is the normally accepted gold standard. But it's worth examining where those norms come from. Advice to put the baby in another room came about because of the twin beliefs that babies who co-slept would fail to be independent,* and that co-sleeping interrupted the husband's 'access' to his wife.[17] As a result, mothers were (and still are) sternly advised that solo, consolidated sleep is what they should be training their baby for. But looking at evidence from around the world, WEIRD sleep training practices are, well, weird.

In Japan, for example, there is the concept of 'amae', which is extremely difficult to translate, but is roughly the overlap between a child's dependence on their parents and a parent's indulgence of their child. This emphasis on interdependence means that co-sleeping is much more prevalent in Japan than in similarly industrialised Western societies, which prize the fostering of independence instead of the cultivation of closeness.[18] This difference in parenting philosophy may be why Japanese families report far less night waking and bedtime disagreements between the ages of six months and four years than do families in the US.[19]

In northern Europe, particularly in Iceland and Sweden, co-sleeping is still practised with no sign of ill effects. In the West, children in Sweden regularly share their parents' bed, with about a third of boys and half of all girls sleeping there for at least some of the night up to the age of eight. It's not that there's no space for these children to sleep alone; rather, it's a voluntary practice that parents appreciate as much as children. Anthropologist Dr Barbara Welles-Nystrom of the Karolinska Institutet said that parents weren't worried about the effects of co-sleeping at all, saying that children grow out of it at their own pace, that it's a good way of providing for their child's emotional needs without getting out of bed, and that actually it's quite cosy to be together. 'We see so little of the children during the day that we all want to fill up our tanks with love at night,' explained one parent of school-aged children.[20]

This might be cosy in colder climes, but surely sleeping next to

* We now know that the data does not support this at all. Quite the reverse.

the baby or toddler who is keeping you awake is just going to keep you more awake? Except that co-sleeping seems to cut down on sleep problems. In parts of the world where babies and toddlers share a room with their parents at least, even if they don't sleep on the same surface, reports of sleep problems are nearly non-existent.[21] It may seem counterintuitive that spending the night in the same room as the person who keeps waking you up would lead to a better night's sleep, but co-sleeping that involves being within arm's length (and close enough to hear small noises of distress before they turn into loud yells) seems to make sleep easier all round.

It's also likely to make breastfeeding easier. Professors McKenna and McDade reviewed international studies on the prevalence of co-sleeping, and found a clear link between breastfeeding and co-sleeping in Western societies. And in other societies, breastfeeding and co-sleeping were so prevalent that there was little to compare it to. The studies suggest that – as breastfeeding a baby in another room through the night is so challenging – the link between breast and bed is reciprocal. More breastfeeding leads to more co-sleeping and more co-sleeping leads to more breastfeeding.[22]

But is bed sharing dangerous? According to the 'sleep through, sleep alone' advocates, co-sleeping is incredibly dangerous. But looking into the cases of deaths that have been reported while co-sleeping, it is apparent that the causes aren't co-sleeping per se. Almost all recorded cases have other factors that include drug or alcohol use by the parent, co-sleeping with a sibling rather than a parent, or sleeping on a couch or waterbed.[23] Tragically, the injunction not to bed share may even have contributed to some of these deaths: at least two families in a UK study that interviewed recently bereaved parents said that they'd been on the sofa with their babies *because* they'd been advised against taking the baby to bed, and had fallen asleep accidentally.[24]

Professors James McKenna and Thomas McDade of the University of Notre Dame in Indiana have comprehensively studied the risks and benefits of co-sleeping in a WEIRD context. Their conclusion: babies should never sleep alone.[25] They don't mince their words about it either. In the abstract of their 2005 review paper that drew on all the research to date, they conclude that: 'Co-sleeping at least in the form of room sharing especially with an actively breastfeeding mother saves lives [and] is a powerful reason why the simplistic, scientifically inaccurate and misleading statement "never sleep with your baby" needs to be rescinded, wherever and whenever it is published.' Mothers who shared their beds were significantly more likely to continue breastfeeding for three months than those who didn't. Because 'night feeds' can be done with both mother and baby in bed, breastfeeding can actually buy you an extra thirty minutes or so of sleep a night compared to bottle feeding.[26]

Not all co-sleeping is the same, though. Researchers in the field are increasingly careful to differentiate between room sharing and bed sharing. What complicates the picture still further is that some researchers describe the use of side-car cribs as room sharing, others as bed sharing. There seems to be little difference in outcomes, however, as long as a 'trusted and committed caregiver' is within easy reach.[27] But when it comes to safety there are some important findings. You should never bed share with any baby, or small child who isn't yet old enough to crawl, 1) on a sofa, waterbed or other unstable surface; 2) if you've been drinking or taken any drugs that might make it harder for you to wake up; 3) with loose bedding or pillows that could completely cover your child; and 4) anywhere where there is a gap down which your child could roll, between the wall and the bed, for example.[28]

Large-scale studies suggest that at least 50 per cent of children in Western cultures do bed share at some point – and the prevalence rises to 70 per cent for breastfeeding mothers and their babies.[29] But most of us are doing this on the sly, feeling that we're going against the best medical advice, and that we might be putting our babies in danger. Professors McKenna and McDade exaggerate only slightly when they say that 'mothers' bodies, whether offering breast milk or not and independent of sobriety, continue to be regarded as potentially lethal weapons – wooden rolling pins, if you will, over which neither mothers nor their infants have control during sleep'. In reality, breastfeeding mothers who are observed sleeping with their babies will rouse more often, and more frequently, in response to changes in their baby's breathing or position, than parents who don't bed share. Safe bed sharing has a 50 per cent lower incidence of SIDS than sleeping in separate rooms: the 'proximity of a committed caregiver' is, say McKenna and McDade, powerfully protective of infants.[30]

Some parents are nevertheless concerned about the levels of CO_2 that they might exhale while sharing a bed with their baby. Dr Sarah Mosko of the University of California Irvine Medical Center and her colleagues investigated this by videotaping twelve pairs of three-month-old babies and their mothers who regularly co-slept to see what positions they usually adopted.[31] The team found that mothers and babies automatically tended to spend about two-thirds of the night sleeping face to face within 20 cm of one another, with mothers sleeping on their sides facing their babies, and babies either on their sides or on their backs. With this in mind, Dr Mosko's team recruited women to lie on their sides and breathe while they measured CO_2 concentrations at distances between 3 cm and 21 cm from their nostrils. The mothers lay on their sides next to a doll with a sampling tube attached, and CO_2 concentrations were measured both with and without a blanket over the mother and doll's face.

Even with the blanket and at the closest distances, peak levels of CO_2 never reached concentrations high enough to cause an injury. But they did reach levels high enough to prompt infants to take a breath. That's because the impulse to take a breath is driven not by the absence of oxygen but by the *presence* of carbon dioxide. This is why freedivers are strongly advised not to hyperventilate to try to prolong their dives. Sure, by expelling lots of CO_2 you reduce the desire to breathe in, but your brain has absolutely no way of telling whether or not you're running out of O_2. Blackouts among freedivers, and prolonged fatal apnoea in newborns, are both caused by the *absence* of CO_2, not its presence. Dr Mosko and her team suggest that the slightly CO_2-enriched atmosphere is likely to promote more regular breathing in babies.

Another way that co-sleeping might actually prevent rather than increase the risk of SIDS comes from the indirect effect of prolonged breastfeeding. Breastfeeding is thought to have a slight protective effect against the occurrence of SIDS.* Co-sleeping mothers also tend to wake more easily, and their waking follows the pattern of their baby's awakenings, which *might* mean that co-sleeping allows parents to respond more rapidly to infants in trouble.

So co-sleeping is safe in the short term. But what about long-term impacts? Some parenting thought leaders insist that co-sleeping is crippling your child's independence: you're raising a needy milquetoast who will never cut the apron strings. But the data says otherwise. Children whose parents opted to have them co-sleep for at least part of the night from a few weeks old until the end of their first year are faster to learn practical independence skills, such as how to dress themselves. They are also more socially independent, making friends and initiating conversation earlier and more often.[32] Professors Meret Keller and Wendy Goldberg hypothesised that co-sleeping parents might also be the kind of parents who give their children a lot of autonomy, and while this was somewhat true – there *was* a mild preference for co-sleeping among parents who gave their children more freedom – this wasn't enough to explain the difference in the social and practical independence scores of early co-sleepers and early solo sleepers.

Co-sleepers seem to have a sweeter temperament too. Co-sleeping children living on military bases were found to have

* Which is not to say that bottle feeding is a contributor to SIDS. The phenomenon is complex and there are only a few things we know that help: not smoking, not leaving loose bedding in the cot, and putting your baby down on their back to sleep. If you're doing those then you're doing everything right.

better comportment scores from their teachers, and were more sociable than those who slept alone.[33] Male college students who had co-slept as children had lower scores for guilt and anxiety, and higher self-esteem, than those who were never allowed to share their parents' bed. Women who co-slept as girls were much more relaxed about giving and receiving affection than those who didn't;[34] and they also had higher self-esteem.[35] Far from damaging confidence, independence and self-esteem, co-sleeping seems to promote them.

One famous sleep-training book insists that any parent wanting to sleep with their baby should 'examine their feelings very carefully'.[36] But if you look at the *data* carefully, strict injunctions against co-sleeping are counterproductive in terms of both child development and safety, reduce breastfeeding duration, pathologise perfectly normal sleep patterns, and rob parents and children of what can actually be a really lovely experience. If it's the best way for your family to get a good night's sleep, pile in!

Some waking is normal

But what if you really do want your child to sleep independently? Gradual withdrawal can work, but many parents have unrealistic expectations about how quickly or how completely it can work.

All children will go through periods of insomnia, waking, bed-wetting or resisting bedtime – a set of behaviours that are collectively called 'sleep disturbances'. It *may* be reassuring to know that sleep disturbances are incredibly prevalent, self-limiting and seem to do no lasting damage.[37] Basically, if you can survive with most of your patience intact, and your child isn't noticeably falling behind socially, developmentally or educationally, sleep 'problems' in the early years could probably be more accurately termed 'frustrations'. Babies (and children) around the world wake up, cry, request cuddles, say they're thirsty, insist that there are monsters under the bed, sing, ask for just one more story, or wail, 'I'm *hungry*.' It's definitely not just WEIRD behaviour. The differences in how these behaviours are classified seem to arise from the differences between us as parents and how our dominant culture suggests that we should feel about all this.

Though as someone on their third caffeinated beverage of the morning I have to say that the argument, 'Have you tried being more relaxed about sleep interruptions?' is far from compelling. Unless you count feeling compelled to hurl my collection of empty coffee mugs at the wall.

Research now recognises that what constitutes a 'sleep problem' is largely culturally dependent.[38] In the 1990s, research that compared the sleep of Italian and American toddlers found that Italian children had no clear bedtimes, and went to sleep later and awoke earlier than their American counterparts with no obvious ill effects. Italian children were also far more likely to participate in their families' social lives, going out with parents and falling asleep long before being put to bed.[39] In Japan, school-aged children regularly 'nap' in the early evening before being reawakened by their parents, who bring them tea and snacks; and this fuels their studies long after their parents have gone to bed.[40]

There are even several societies where there is no such thing as bedtime. In Balinese society, anthropologists report that babies are held continuously, day and night, and the extended family all take turns in helping to care for the child. Because society is organised around religious observances that often take place at night and that last until dawn, it's not uncommon for adults and children alike to slip in and out of sleep during social events. Even during performances that include music, singing and chanting, even when standing up, the ability to fall asleep wherever and whenever is preserved until adulthood. Pioneering anthropologist Professor Margaret Mead noted that spontaneous naps happened not only among members of the audience but sometimes among the performers too.[41]

Similarly, in Mayan families in the highlands of Guatemala, children tend to fall asleep whenever they are sleepy, often in someone's arms, or when taken to bed with a parent. Children sleep in their mother's bed until they are about two or three years old, when they typically 'move in' to the bed of their father or an older sibling. All the family members share the same bedroom, and often mothers and fathers will sleep in separate beds so that each child can have a parent to sleep next to.[42] Having to sleep alone is considered a sad thing indeed, and when the anthropologists told them that Western parents put their babies to sleep in rooms by themselves they were horrified at the idea of such neglect.

No particular culture is 'right' or 'wrong' – they just embody different values. The Mayan approach values closeness and mutual support, the WEIRD approach aims for independence. 'Mayan parents clearly ... draw the connection between child sleeping patterns and promotion of desirable socialisation goals, just as American parents do,' write Professor Oskar Jenni and Professor Bonnie O'Connor, authors of a review of cultural and biological influences on sleep.[43]

So why do so many WEIRD cultures stress the idea of independent, whole-night sleep, if it's such an elusive goal? That might be to do with the way our working lives are organised. There is another natural experiment that lets us watch as a society transitions from largely subsistence farming to wage-based employment. This is happening in Cameroon, and in particular among the Nso people.[44] Among subsistence farmers, everyone falls asleep together at the same time and in the same bed, while among the families where at least one parent works outside the home, separate bedtimes in separate beds become the norm, at least for children over the age of four.

In WEIRD societies, sleeping through the night, or at least trying to, and sleeping in a single block from night until morning is seen as the 'right' way to sleep. It's what we condition our kids to do. But this single block of sleep – a monophasic sleep pattern – is a relatively recent invention.[45] From at least the thirteenth century to the nineteenth century, there are records that talk about 'first sleep' and 'second sleep'. First sleep was a deep and restful sleep, followed by a period of calm wakefulness in which people would pray and meditate.

The phenomenon is even documented in medical texts from the fifteenth to the eighteenth century that advised people to sleep on their right side for the first sleep and the left side for the second sleep in order to promote good digestion and better sleep. According to historians, sleeping through the night is a trend that post-dates the invention of 'modern lighting technology'.[46]

In the WEIRD world, we aspire to have our kids become independent, monophasic sleepers. But that independence, as we've seen, is not the norm around the world. According to research by Professor Jodi Mindell, vice chairman of the board of directors of the National Sleep Foundation and a professor of psychology at St Joseph's University, 25 per cent of parents – in Western, urban populations at least – will complain about some sort of sleep disturbance while their child is between the ages of one and five. These disturbances can include night terrors, wetting the bed, grinding their teeth, sleep talking or walking, not wanting to go to sleep, or being unable to sleep without a special object like a teddy or blanket. Another survey from the early 1980s found that parents were most likely to seek expert help for their school-age children for sleep talking, sleep refusal, and 'refusal to go to bed without a nightlight'. I'm not sure whether I'm overly permissive, or whether I've lived so close to street lights for so long that I can't remember what it was like to actually achieve full darkness, but 'wanting a night light' seems like quite a stretch as far as the definition of 'disorder' is concerned. Other physicians class wanting a drink or a snack in the middle of the night as a disorder: according to some doctors my occasional midnight snack of pickled onion Monster Munch in bed is harmful to more than just my marriage.[47]

Many of the difficulties that delay or disrupt sleep can be extremely frustrating, but they usually sort themselves out as your child matures. However, they can go on for a surprisingly long time. It's rarely talked about, but night-time incontinence is thought to affect about three per cent of fifteen-year-olds. Even after three to six months of dryness, bed-wetting can begin again as a result of tiredness, stress or illness.

As many as 50 per cent of children will be woken at some point by nightmares* and they tend to learn to deal with them rather than growing out of them, comforting themselves back to sleep. But in the meantime, a reassuring hug isn't going to do them any harm.

Kids do eventually grow out of sleep terrors. The difference between a nightmare and a sleep terror is that nightmares tend to wake your child up. Sleep terrors tend to happen while your child is sleeping so deeply that nothing you do will wake them. Their heart may pound, they may breathe heavily, they may sweat profusely. They'll likely thrash and cry. For most children they last less than five minutes but they can go on for about thirty minutes. And they tend to happen about ninety minutes to two hours after falling asleep.

Sleep terrors are utterly terrifying and if your child has roused you from your slumber with screaming and crying that is *completely* impervious to comforting, stays resolutely asleep while appearing to fight a horde of wingéd dæmons† and wakes in the morning with no recollection of the event then congratulations, you have survived a sleep terror. I can vouch for the fact that seeing your child in this state is heart-wrenchingly, soul-searingly awful. But the best thing you can do is to let your child ride it out, being sure that there's no way for them to injure themselves.

Thankfully, most children only experience sleep terrors between the ages of three and twelve when they tend to resolve of their own accord. Because, as we'll see later, teenage sleep is a whole other basket of snakes.

---

* I was surprised to read that 50 per cent is also the estimated prevalence of nightmares in adults. Who are these people who *haven't* been waking up in a cold sweat for the last few years? Are they just not reading the news?
† So much more terrifying than mere winged demons.

The truth is that all kids wake up a few times a night. Research from Israel suggests that children under three years old all tend to wake up at similar rates but that the ones who end up referred to a sleep clinic are often those whose parents are awakened every time.[48] The problem that sleep training addresses is frequently not that of the child's disturbed sleep but that of their parents. But it's important to realise that getting a child to sleep all night is an uphill battle: not because of their brains, but because of their stomachs.

Rock-a-bye baby: sleep in the first year

Sometimes you read a scholarly paper and think, 'Yeah, I kind of suspected as much but I'm glad to see the data.' At other times you just think, 'Are you *shitting* me?'

I just had one of those moments, dear reader. I'm more or less typing this by smashing my head against my keyboard. Are you ready for this:

'Norms of infant sleep in the United Kingdom and the United States were established when breastfeeding rates were at their lowest, leading medical personnel to expect young infants to sleep through the night, *but this is only characteristic of formula-fed infants.*' Emphasis, and piss-boiling outrage, mine. These words, simultaneously reassuring and infuriating to anyone who thought their breastfed child had sleep problems, come from Professor Helen Ball at Durham University – and should be taught at every prenatal class.[49] Breastfed babies tend to wake often in the night, while bottle-fed babies fall into REM sleep faster, and drop the need for night feeds sooner.[50] What is sometimes touted as a 'disorder' is actually the natural consequence of being breastfed.

But the outdated research on 'sleeping through' is still informing clinical practice long after its usefulness has run out. At the turn of the millennium, the UK NHS was spending about £750,000 annually giving advice to parents of infants under twelve weeks who were worried that their babies were 'still' waking up at night.[51] Given what we now know about the need for 'night feeds' among breastfeeding babies, advocating that parents should be aiming to get their babies to sleep through while also promoting breastfeeding is contradictory as well as counterproductive, dooming parents as it does to feelings of frustration and failure.

The truth is that breastfed babies tend *not* to sleep through, not because of any parental failings but because breast milk is just not as calorie dense as bottle milk. Professor Ball discovered that breastfed babies were feeding as often in the night at three months as they had been at one month (an average of two to three feeds a night). Formula-fed babies had, on average, less than one bottle-feed a night.[52]

But here's what infuriates me the most. Because the outdated studies on bottle-fed babies were setting sleep norms, night-feeding was seen as disordered for the second half of the twentieth century and, so far, some of the twenty-first. Rather than looking at how baby feeding practices had changed, researchers tried to determine what *mums* were doing to ruin their children's sleep. For about twenty years the gold standard for collecting data on sleep relationships was the Maternal Cognitions about Infant Sleep Questionnaire. Two decades of sleep research consistently blamed insecure, disorganised or unwilling mothers for sleep problems. Dads were advised that mums would be unable to resist the 'signalling' given by babies (otherwise known as 'crying') because their maternal emotions were too high: a mother's distress at not being able to comfort her crying baby was deemed pathological rather than an entirely sane response. Cooler, more rational dads could be advised to lead the efforts to leave their babies to cry it out, so the conclusion went.[53]

It was only in 2007 that the 'what's wrong with mummy's brain' questionnaire was finally extended (in Hebrew at least) to become the *Parental* Cognitions about Infant Sleep Questionnaire.[54] Lo and behold, it turns out that dads get just as stressed by their babies and children and their inability to fall asleep. Now researchers are *finally* noticing that feeding, working, and parenting practices have all changed since the 1950s. And yet, expecting babies to 'sleep through' is still maddeningly prevalent with many parenting 'experts' uncritically claiming that this should be the goal of all new parents.

One of the more popular methods in the last couple of decades has been what is sometimes called 'Ferberising' or the 'cry it out' method. In the research this is often referred to as the 'extinction' method – the name is taken from its behaviourist origins. In the 1930s and 1940s, the behavioural psychologist B. F. Skinner noticed that rats who had been trained to receive a food pellet on pressing a lever will go on pressing that lever after the pellets stop being delivered. However, the presses get further and further apart until the rat eventually stops pushing the lever altogether. This is what Skinner called extinction.

But here's where 'extinction training' is wrong-headed when it comes to babies waking up to feed, be changed or be comforted. Extinction in behaviourism was observed when a *learned* response stops being rewarded. Extinction was never about stopping behaviours that are innate. A baby crying in hunger, discomfort or fear isn't a learned response: nothing could *be* more innate.

But the idea of extinction training caught on, becoming popularised in the early 2000s by Dr Richard Ferber, a paediatrician at the Children's Hospital in Boston. His book *Solve Your Child's Sleep Problems* is a perennial bestseller and is on its third edition. He commands parents not to intervene during strictly timed intervals, no matter how much their children cry. The intervals start short and get longer. Over time a baby is meant to learn how to get themselves to sleep. This approach was first documented in 1999, as physicians were getting frustrated with parents (mothers in particular) who 'resisted' total extinction – that is, who wouldn't leave their hungry or uncomfortable babies to cry.[55]

If you're one of those parents who has tried graduated extinction (or cry it out, or the Ferber Method) and has 'failed', don't berate yourself. There is absolutely no evidence that it's the best method for all families, or that it will confer any eventual benefit on your child. It's effective at reducing parental waking, but graduated extinction has benefits for parents and parents alone. It doesn't harm your child, but it doesn't do them any particular favours either.

If you are a keen monophasic sleeper who isn't in the market to change your own sleep patterns, and if your baby is no longer reliant on breastfeeding, then there are options that combine a gentle form of retreat over days or even weeks. But rather than simply withdrawing, you emphasise positive things that help your child get to sleep – such as relaxation, soft music, or a cuddly toy or other 'transitional object', a concept introduced by psychoanalyst and paediatrician Donald Winnicott in the 1950s. Something like a beloved teddy or Linus's safety blanket, the transitional object helps a child get back to sleep in the absence of their parents. But outside western Europe and the US, in countries where co-sleeping is more common, transitional objects are much rarer.

Dr Wendy Hall of the University of British Columbia recruited the families of thirty-nine infants, aged between six and twelve months old. All these families had called a Newborn Hotline for advice with sleep. Dr Hall and her team suggested a four-pronged approach. First, parents were asked to maintain a strictly limited nap schedule during the day, rather than letting their child sleep whenever they were drowsy. Second, they asked parents to try to wean children off hand-holding, being held, having a bottle, or other forms of external comfort.* They also encouraged the parents to draw up a bedtime routine and make sure that they stuck to it. Finally, they suggested a programme of graduated extinction.[56]

The children did manage a significant increase in the period of

* These are sometimes known as negative sleep associations. The 'negative' in that phrase is doing a lot of heavy lifting. Falling asleep in proximity to someone you love and trust is not in and of itself negative. Other cultures, like the Mayans, would be baffled by the classification of physical contact as negative.

longest uninterrupted night-time sleep but there was no control group for this study, so it's tricky to see what gains were made due to the programme and what were simply to do with the children growing up. What's more, there was no increase in total sleep overall, suggesting that curtailing naps might have made the largest contribution.

Trying to move towards behaviour that fosters independence, like providing a transitional object, talking to but not holding a child, or slowly increasing the time it takes to respond to crying, can help a child to self settle, and encourage them to bank more hours of sleep through the night.[57] But there's no evidence that this leads to more sleep for families overall.

Perhaps the most useful finding in Dr Hall's study was the fact that many parents, once they started logging the times that their babies ate, played and slept, found that they had no routine at all. Other than co-sleeping and breastfeeding, one strategy that *has* been demonstrated to improve sleep (for children and adults alike) is setting a bedtime routine and sticking to it. A survey of the behaviour of over 1,000 families determined that a regular routine (and keeping screens out of the bedroom) had the most significant impact, making it far more likely that children got a good night's sleep. At three and four years of age, night-time routines lead to more sleep and better learning.[58]

Professor Jodi Mindell of the US National Sleep Foundation divided families into groups who committed to bedtime routines with their infants and toddlers every night, five or six nights a week, three or four nights a week, one or two nights a week, or never. They found a 'dose dependent' effect of routines: even having a routine that is occasionally missed is better than having no routine at all. And the more consistent a bedtime routine, the more sleep the children got: they went to bed earlier, fell asleep faster, and also didn't wake as much in the night.[59] That might be because regular routines lead to less stress, or it might be that parents who have the motivation and resources to set down routines are also likely to be those that encourage independent sleeping early on.

We know, for example, that in households where there is stress over food and housing, night-time routines are much more likely to be disrupted.[60]

The advantage of setting a routine and sticking to it is that bedtime behaviour quickly becomes natural law rather than a nightly litigation: habit is a wonderful thing. With slightly older children, you can even have a discussion about setting good bedtime habits. A one-off negotiation is much easier than an argument every evening.

So when should bedtime be and what should it consist of? That doesn't just depend on your child's age, it also depends on where you live. We know this thanks to Professor Jodi Mindell, who studied nearly 30,000 three-year-olds in seventeen different countries and found that bedtimes vary from between 7.30 to 8 p.m. (UK, New Zealand and Australia) to after 10 p.m. (South Korea, Taiwan, India and Hong Kong). Although there seems to be some relationship between early bedtimes and predominantly Caucasian cultures, the relationship is not entirely clear-cut. For example, Professor Sara Harkness, director of the Center for the Study of Culture, Health, and Human Development at the University of Connecticut, recalls seeing a preschool pageant at a local festival in Spain that started at about 11 p.m.[61] Forget the kids, *I'm* not awake at that hour these days.

Children's bedtime routines vary around the world. In the US, 60 per cent of families have a bath as part of their bedtime routine. In the UK, 81 per cent of families do bath then bed. In Indonesia, families are much more likely to save bathing for another time of the day, with only 6 per cent of families making it part of the bedtime routine of their three-year-olds. There's no set of components that make up a neurologically ideal routine – it's simply the repetitive, predictable nature of the steps that works. As with dieting, the best bedtime routines are the ones that work for your family so that you can stick to them.

So the evidence suggests that you shouldn't stress about following a particular sleep training 'regime'. The skills needed to go to sleep alone don't translate to any other form of independence in childhood or adulthood. In fact, over 60 per cent of we adults whose parents followed the independent, sleeping-through-the-night-in-the-first-six-months advice when we were children now have difficulty either falling or staying asleep. Sleep 'training' doesn't result in a lifetime of sleep skill. Experiment with what works for *your* family. Whether that's co-sleeping, polyphasic sleep, or 'early to bed, early to rise'. As long as you're getting enough sleep, it doesn't matter how you get it. But don't get too comfy: come adolescence, the body clock of your child is likely to go haywire once again.

Sleepy teens? It's more than screens

I remember in my early adolescence thinking, 'When I'm an adult, I'll go to bed when I damn well want.' I didn't expect that would be 8.30 p.m. most nights.

Puberty changes processes C and S (see p. 83), and turns most adolescents into night owls. The phenomenon of the layabout adolescent has been documented since at least the time of Plato. As children hit (or are hit by) puberty there are some physiological changes that predispose them to a permanent state of jet lag. Around mid-adolescence, a child's circadian period starts to lengthen. Across the population, our 'free running' circadian rhythms vary, with some of us having periods slightly shorter than twenty-four hours from peak body temperature to peak body temperature, while most of us have a natural rhythm that is slightly longer. Whatever a child's circadian rhythm had been previously, as an adolescent they will end up with a period between peaks that gets progressively longer – Process C slows down.

On top of that, the 'appetite' for sleep – Process S – seems to wane in adolescence. Remember that, while we can't measure sleep pressure directly, the amount of slow-wave activity in the first few sleep cycles of someone who is sleep-deprived tends to be much higher than on non-sleep-deprived nights. But for adolescents, it takes much more sleep deprivation for this effect to show up, and when it does show up, the amount of extra slow-wave activity isn't as pronounced as it is for children or adults; their sleep appetite gets suppressed. Adolescents are neurologically nobbled by changes in both of the sleep-stimulating processes that we go through. Late nights and missing sleep aren't simply a matter of willpower or routine.

A recent longitudinal study of 1,351 schoolchildren in the same cohort looked at sleep patterns at the age of ten and again at twelve and fifteen years old. Some 71 per cent of the children were getting enough sleep at ten years old. By fifteen, that had dropped to just 19 per cent. Almost a quarter of fifteen-year-olds said they were sleepy in the day, while 13 per cent of them had said as much when they were ten. And girls lose sleep earlier and more drastically than boys, with a bigger drop in sleep overall, and a more noticeable drop at age twelve.[62]

Many parents, policy-makers and teachers blame social media for this lack of sleep, and there are indeed three ways in which social media use can mess up the sleep patterns of adults as well as adolescents. The first and most clear-cut link is that if you're checking your phone, you're not sleeping. 'Time displacement' – the idea that checking on messages and content takes up time that would be used doing other things – is a well-studied effect.[63]

Screen use – especially social media screen use – can also delay sleep by simply getting us worked up. The 'psychological stimulation' effect describes the impact of reading or viewing things that are contentious, upsetting or alarming right before trying to sleep.[64] Facebook, Twitter and YouTube are advertising platforms first and foremost, and they all make more money the longer you spend on their sites and apps. Greater 'dwell time' leads to more opportunities to advertise to you. As a result, these organisations have repurposed ideas from gambling or gaming, finding ways to keep you chasing the rewards that come with 'engagement'. They push the most provocative content, hijacking your amygdala, leaving you angry and afraid and desperate to see more.[65] Nothing makes you lose sleep quite like trying to correct everyone who is wrong on the internet.

Nearly 10,000 children in over 800 schools were followed for two years by researchers from UCL and Imperial College. The researchers collected data about the teenagers' mental health and well-being, as well as how often they checked social media, how much sleep they got, whether or not they were being bullied online, and whether they got outside to exercise regularly. At thirteen years old, just over half of the girls and a third of the boys tended to access social media 'very frequently' (three or more times daily). By the time they reached sixteen, three-quarters of girls and nearly two-thirds of boys were accessing social media multiple times a day.[66]

The researchers did find a correlation between high social media use and high reports of feeling anxious, unhappy or dissatisfied with life. But when they unpicked the data, it seemed that social media itself was unlikely to be the cause. Lack of sleep, as well as exposure to bullying and lack of exercise, swamped the significance of social media. You don't need to pester your child to get off TikTok, but do talk to them about whether or not they feel happy about what they see there, and whether it's taking up some of the time that could be spent doing other, more rewarding things.

These findings could form the basis of your family's own social experiment. Talk to your children about setting device-free times, or using the phone's usage-limiting features in order to reduce the amount of social media you consume. See what feels better, and what things feel worse. Experiment with your device usage *as a family* rather than making it just your children's problem.

Professor Russell Viner, from University College London, who led the research, explained: 'Our results suggest that social media itself doesn't cause harm, but that frequent use may disrupt activities that have a positive impact on mental health such as sleeping and exercising, while increasing exposure of young people to harmful content, particularly the negative experience of cyber-bullying.'

Finally, there is a direct physiological link between screen use and insomnia. Teens are no different from the rest of us – in fact they may even be more savvy than us – when it comes to the pernicious effects of social media.[67] But they, like us, are still prone to using a screen late at night. In a 2019 survey of 6,616 adolescents in London, the researchers found that 71 per cent of them used at least one screen at night-time.[68]

Regardless of content, screen use is a problem because there are specialist connections from your retinal cells to different areas of the brain that regulate sleep, alertness and mood.[69] Triggered by strong light in the blue part of the spectrum, these act as the *zeitgebers* we met earlier, which then buggers up your circadian rhythm, fooling your body that it's early morning. We know that these specific connections are responsible: when Professor Alan Rupp and his team at Johns Hopkins and Northwestern universities genetically modified a population of mice they found that exposure to light in the middle of the night disrupts the sleep patterns of unmodified mice, while those mice whose connections between the retina and the brain had been knocked out were largely immune to the stimulating effect of light at night.[70] Unless you're fortunate enough to be mutated in a similar way to Professor Rupp's mice, I'm afraid that night-time screen use may indeed be keeping you awake.

Because of this effect, neither we nor our kids should be checking our phones in the hour or so before bed. In a survey of over 6,000 London teens, about a third were using their phones in darkness, about a third in the light, and about a third weren't using their phones at all.[71] This rather nicely sets up a natural experiment that allowed Professor Michael Mireku and his colleagues from universities around the UK to contrast the effects of using no screen, using a screen in a lit room, and using a screen in darkness.

All adolescents using screens at bedtime were more likely to get to sleep later, to not get enough sleep, and to say that they felt less good overall, than those teenagers who were not using their phones in bed. But those adolescents who used their phones in the dark were *particularly* at risk of missing sleep and feeling bad. Mireku and his team hypothesise that low levels of ambient lighting lead to wider pupils, letting more of the screen's blue light through. So far there is no research on the impact of using your screen in 'night mode', which cuts down the amount of blue light coming from your screen. But if you do need to use your phone at night, maybe even to read this book, it's better to do so in a room that is gently lit than it is to read in the dark. Having no ambient light seems to lead to greater sensitivity to the light coming directly from your screen. Watch this space (from a dimly lit room).

While this lack of sleep isn't likely to cause long-term damage, it does functionally change the brain in the short term. It's been known for some time that adolescents who are sleep-deprived are more likely to do things that are risky. Professor Eva Telzer, director of the developmental social neuroscience lab at the University of North Carolina, examined what was happening in the brains of sleepy teens when they played games that involved some level of risk.

The balloon analogue risk task, or Bart, is simple enough to play while lying down inside an fMRI scanner. Players are shown a balloon on-screen and can press a button to pump it up. In the control condition the balloon is white and simply floats away after a random number of pumps. But if the balloon is red, you're rewarded with 25 cents per press. The catch is that the bigger the balloon gets, the more likely it is that it will pop, at which point you lose all the money. To avoid this, you can press another button at any time to bank your balloon and the resulting cash.[72] Volunteers were told in advance that they would get to keep the money they had won at the end of the experiment.

Professor Telzer and her team wanted to know whether sleep deprivation is correlated with how many times the volunteers pressed the pump button. Those volunteers who reported worse sleep quality and shorter sleep durations did indeed press their buttons more often, and suffered more burst-balloon-based losses as a result.

But to understand why, Professor Telzer and her team also

examined the activation of the volunteers' brains while playing the game. The patterns of activity shown on the control task – the white balloon trials – could be safely discounted: these are just the neural correlates of pretending to blow up a balloon while in an fMRI tube.* What they wanted to see was what happened in the red balloon trials that was different. Activity was higher in a part of the brain called the dorsolateral prefrontal cortex (DLPFC) for those adolescents who didn't take as many risks, and lower in those who took more. From other studies we know that the DLPFC helps to coordinate our executive function; it helps with inhibiting unhelpful behaviours, with assessing risk, and with longer-term planning, and is one of the areas that continues to mature until the mid-twenties, as we'll see later.

Those volunteers who took more risks had higher activity in the insula, an area thought to be active when we're experiencing strong emotions, or when we're focused more on the present than on the past or future.

Professor Telzer's study doesn't answer whether tiredness makes it harder to use the DLFPC (or easier to use the insula), or whether adolescents who happen to have a more developed DLFPC also experience better sleep regulation. It's worth noting that sleep loss in adults makes them act more like teenagers when it comes to risk. Sleep-deprived adults are more impulsive, less inhibited and more likely to choose a quick, small reward over a delayed, larger one. Cortisol rises as a result of sleep deprivation, and a lack of melatonin keeps dopamine levels high, and high levels of both hormones seem to drive more impulsive and aggressive behaviour in adults and adolescents.[73]

---

* This is worth bearing in mind the next time you see a headline saying 'Scientists find area of the brain involved in X'. The brain is never *only* doing X. At the very least it's handling the sensations of a body in an fMRI tube. And in the studies I've volunteered in, it's also usually thinking, 'I should have gone to the toilet *before* I got in here.' We've no idea how much of the 'neural correlates of X' for any given person are actually 'the neural correlates of X while trying not to wet yourself/sneeze/fart ...'

According to professors Stacey Rucas and Alissa Miller, we can't differentiate between two things: a lack of sleep making teenagers more impulsive, or stress leading to teenagers getting less sleep *and* taking more risks. These features may come as part and parcel of the pubertal package. Teenagers may be hormonally, emotionally or socially more prone to live fast/die young than we conservative adults.* This has led some researchers to speculate that adolescents may historically have had an essential 'night watch' role, being more willing to put themselves in situations where there is physical risk, and staying awake while the rest of us got our deepest sleep. These almost-adults with no offspring are in some ways the most ideal members of a society to watch over the rest in the dead of night. But like all things in evolutionary psychology, that's not something that we can test: all we can say is that it's consistent with observations that we can make today. Spare a thought for your restless teen – they may just have evolved to be on the prowl.

* The technical term for this in neuroscience and psychology is a 'fast life history strategy'. But we know what we mean.

5

Listening Ears On, Please! How to Communicate with Babies

Language typically emerges over the first three years of life and continues to develop all the way through adolescence. But well before they start *using* language, babies are born communicators.

In the first twelve months, babies master a surprisingly eloquent range of cries, gestures and facial expressions. Babies engage in sound play from a very early age: as soon as they discover that a burp, a raspberry or a giggle gets a positive reaction from a caregiver. The very first sounds and movements that a baby makes are all powerful forms of communication and we soon come to understand the moods and meanings of babies that we care for. For example, even after a few days, parents are capable of recognising their own baby from a recording when the sound is compared to the cries of four other random babies.[1]

I still sometimes hear people say that babies aren't interesting until they can talk. But this is nonsense. While language is undoubtedly impressive, it is only one form of communication. Babies use cries, facial expressions and basic gestures like grasping and reaching (or pushing away) to communicate their wants and needs, but even among older humans, the way we sit, walk, dress, look at one another (or not) also speak volumes about our mood, intimacy, health and personality. Most members of the animal kingdom also communicate in one way or another: bees dance, ants leave pheromone trails, and dogs smell each other's arses (when it comes to communicating details about diet, health, sex and mood, an anal gland can be surprisingly eloquent).

Non-verbal communication is both powerful and prevalent. And communicating with pre-verbal babies and toddlers is essential. Children won't start using language until several months after they've learned to understand it. That's partly because the coordination of lips, teeth, tongue, vocal chords, lungs and diaphragm is *fiendishly* complex to master – not least because most of that physical apparatus is hidden, so straightforward mimicry is right out. It's not surprising that babies who are taught to sign – to use overt physical symbols that are easy to mimic – start producing signed words before they can manage their verbal equivalents.[2]

Spend any time with a toddler and you'll quickly realise that their ability to suss out what you're telling them wildly outpaces the things *they* can tell *you*. Even very small kids can understand simple instructions like, 'Please get your coat,' 'Time to tidy up the blocks' and, 'Please make mummy a cuppa.' That last one never actually worked but it was worth a try: for adults and children alike, understanding instructions is not the same as following them.

Long before a baby's first word, most adults and older children talk to infants in the expectation that the words will mean something to them. All the evidence shows that having those somewhat one-sided conversations is essential when it comes to laying the foundations of communication and language. Playing together is great for this. Simple questions like, 'Please can you pass me the red block?' or, 'Would teddy like this cup of tea?' lead to brilliant, non-verbal responses. Cooperation and play-acting start very early, and prove that communication can begin long before speech.

This ability to understand and (non-verbally) respond shows some serious brainpower on the part of your child. Imagine having a similar conversation with a colleague who speaks Samoan or Xhosa. (If you speak both Samoan and Xhosa, first of all, congratulations. Secondly, please pick another language for the purpose of this thought experiment.) If your colleague said, 'Faamolemole pasi mai a'u le piliki mumu,' or, 'Ndicela undigqithisele isitena esibomvu,' the chances that you would know to pass them the red block are *pretty* slim.

Even working out where the words for 'pass', 'red' and 'block' begin and end is tricky. This is one of the first challenges in picking up a language. As adult English speakers we can distinguish between the phrase, 'I wrapped the parcel with the grey tape,' and the entertaining but less likely sentence, 'I wrapped the parcel with the great ape.' But how does that journey into 'chunking' happen – how does a continuous stream of noises or gestures become a discrete set of words? First we need to look at where and how the brain receives sounds or signs and turns them into meaning. The language preference that develops before birth sets up a child's brain for years of learning.

Language in the brain

One of the bits of neuroscience that has made it into the mainstream is the notion that language is (usually) dealt with in the left hemisphere of the brain. The first known data to suggest that this *might* be the case was recorded in the 1860s when the French physician Paul Broca published a post-mortem study of his patient 'Tan'. Tan wasn't the man's real name – 'tan' was the only syllable he could say. For more than twenty years Tan was almost completely mute and he eventually developed paralysis on the right side of his body.

After Tan's death, Broca carried out an autopsy in which he noticed a fluid-filled cyst on the left side of Tan's brain. After reporting on Tan's condition, Broca became the go-to guy when other physicians' patients lost their language. Broca would study them until (and after) their deaths, autopsy being the only method of observing the human brain in the 1860s. He noticed a pattern emerging: people with language loss had also usually suffered some sort of injury to the left hemisphere of the brain.

From this pattern, Broca concluded that 'we speak with the left hemisphere'. That's somewhat true, but it's far from the whole story. First, it's not just speech that is affected by damage to this part of the brain. *All* expressive language – signed, written or spoken – is affected by damage to a particular area, usually found in the left hemisphere, now known as Broca's area. The same pattern of damage results in aphasia for speakers of sign language too.[3]

Second, the right hemisphere isn't a complete slacker when it comes to language. Studies using fMRI have shown that we use the right hemisphere to determine vocal characteristics such as the sex of a speaker.[4] Also, if the left brain handles the 'core' of language, such as sound, semantics and syntax, then the right seems to be in charge of *pragmatics*: the important job of figuring out what people *really* mean.[5] Patients with right hemisphere damage struggle to understand jokes, sarcasm, figurative language and indirect requests. These same patients tend to speak with unusual intonation and often have difficulty recognising the emotions that underlie someone else's speech.[6] They also seem to stop swearing altogether, suggesting that swearing is an extremely pragmatic form of language.[7]

But this left–right pattern only holds true for about 95 per cent of right-handers and 70 per cent of left-handers – about one in twenty of us have a mirror image of this set-up.[8] Despite the variation and the distribution of language abilities in the brain, we've developed some pretty odd ideas about the 'specialities' of the hemispheres. Most of these owe more to speculation than data. Throughout human history, left-handed people have been thought to be *sinister* – literally 'lefties'. In the Victorian era, observations like those made by Paul Broca seemed to show that the left side of the brain was responsible for the right side of the body – the non-sinister side – and also solely responsible for speech. These observations, melded with post-Darwinian insecurity and a desire to 'prove' that humans, while evolved, had evolved into something *special*, led to the conclusion that the left hemisphere was what had made man (*sic*) civilised.

The argument runs thus: as humans are the only animal with speech, and speech is the 'product' of the left hemisphere of the brain, then a) humans were unique in dividing the brains into the civilised and uncivilised parts; and b) the left hemisphere is cultured, civilised and male. Women, children and 'savages' (defined here as anyone not wearing a three-piece suit and a top hat) were cursed to be slaves to the right brain. Men – or well-educated gentlemen, at least – had cultivated their refined left hemisphere and were indeed superior to the animals (and women, children, and non-suit-wearing peoples ...).

These ideas even made it into the popular fiction of the day. Robert Louis Stevenson's *The Strange Case of Dr Jekyll and Mr Hyde*, published in 1886, drew on this new theory of left-brain civilisation and right-brain beastliness. Dr Jekyll ('M.D., D.C.L., L.L.D., F.R.S., etc.') personifies the qualities that the Victorians believed were 'left-brained' – male, white, rational, educated, civilised. Mr Hyde on the other hand is described as 'dusky' and prone to 'hysteria' and effeminacy. Stevenson's novel gives form to the notion of the 'divided ecstasy of mind', an idea that has influenced popular (mis)understandings of neuroscience for more than a century.[9] Even in the last decade, several researchers have proceeded with the view that lateralisation is distinctively human,[10] and popular books consistently make bestseller lists by promising to make lateralisation work for you.*

But we've known for several decades that lateralisation is *not* uniquely human – we share this feature with animals ranging from aardvarks to zebrafish. Since the 1980s, multiple researchers have recorded left-hemisphere activation during squeaks and croaks in mice and frogs.[11] Our closest cousins, chimpanzees, tend to have enlarged sections of the left hemisphere that respond to gesture and that are found in places very similar to the two areas most closely related to speech and language in humans. Communication

* Like *The Master and His Emissary* or the evergreen *Drawing on the Right Side of the Brain*, now in its fifth edition.

has a clear evolutionary pedigree: while speech may be human, communication is widespread.

Noam Chomsky's argument that language appeared 'spontaneously' in humans is as Victorian as the idea that 'right-brained people' are sinister, degenerate, foreign or female.[12] Decades of research support the hypothesis that language has a traceable lineage in the evolutionary record, with gestures and action recognition forming a linguistic launch pad.[13] For a really accessible (and free-to-access) review, look for *Left Brain, Right Brain: Facts and Fantasies* by Professor Michael Corballis of the University of Auckland.[14]

Chomsky's arguments in favour of a special language module seriously undervalues both our evolutionary inheritance and our long apprenticeship into human culture. This inheritance gives us multiple specialised areas for communication – both verbal and non-verbal. To make use of these structures, which make sense of communication, babies have a lot to learn.

'Baby talk': the language apprenticeship

The notion of a universal grammar, some kind of language-producing circuitry just waiting to be deployed whichever of the world's languages you happen to need, has been asserted for decades. But it is based on some very questionable assumptions. Noam Chomsky, Steven Pinker and their adherents started with the observation that 'the way that adults speak is messy and irregular' – which is true, in general. But from this they have concluded that babies couldn't *possibly* learn the rules of language from the terrible ways that adults speak to each other.

Their argument runs as follows. Either the language that children hear is a close approximation of 'correct' language (in which case the child doesn't need to have an innate language module since the environment does all the work of shaping vocabulary and syntax), OR what children hear is messy, inconsistent, noisy and often incorrect or informal, in which case there is no way that they can learn from this 'faulty' data and an intrinsic structure must be required for them to acquire language.[15] Chomsky maintained that adult language *is* too messy and incomplete to be a good guide for children and therefore the 'innate structure' must be doing all the heavy lifting.

When Chomsky was writing in the 1970s, and asserting that the conversation that children learned from was 'degraded' or 'degenerate', he set up what seemed to be an unsolvable conundrum, one that only a special 'black box' in the brains of human babies could possibly resolve.[16] But as early as 1971, Professor Susan Ervin-Tripp, a pioneer in the field of psycholinguistics, countered that just because Chomsky couldn't figure out *how* something is learned, that doesn't make it unlearnable. There is no need for Chomsky's special mechanism, she argued, just a better understanding of the linguistic environment of children.[17]

The thing is, that understanding was there for the having. The linguistic environment of children *had* been widely studied. What Chomsky and his adherents could (and indeed should) have known is that people (largely women) had been studying how parents (largely mothers) spoke to their children for about a decade before Chomsky first published his theory.

And rather than showing a linguistic culture that was 'degenerate and degraded', those studies showed that people speak to children in a type of language that used to be called motherese. This type of language has since been observed being used by fathers, grandparents, siblings and professional carers in societies worldwide, and so it is now more correctly called infant-directed speech (IDS) and child-directed speech (CDS).[18]

This distinction is important. Even in societies where 'motherese' is absent, there is always someone providing the infant- and child-directed speech. In Western Samoa, for example, 'motherese' is not common among mothers. Instead, older siblings of the child – or younger siblings of the parent – are much more likely to be the ones doing most of the 'minding'. Recording how these children speak to their younger siblings or close-in-age nieces and nephews reveals plenty of this type of speech.[19]

For all that it is sometimes derided as 'baby talk', the structure of the language that caregivers use with children is incredibly sophisticated. It provides a scaffold that grows with the child in order to give them exactly the support they need to manage the next stage of language development. At every phase, adults (and older children) are helping the infant understanding and the toddler conversation to unfurl.

For example, when you measure the length of the sentences that people use when talking to babies and toddlers, and the variation and size of their vocabulary, it's clear that caregivers tend to stay just a step or two ahead when talking to their little ones – enough to stretch them without breaking them.[20] While barely even conscious of what they're doing, adults begin using lots of very short phrases (often just one or two words with lots of repetition: 'Doggy. Yes doggy. Look: doggy!') until the child figures out those individual words.

The next stage follows when a caregiver starts taking the child's single words (usually nouns) and adding new words in their replies. So now your kid says, 'Doggy' and you respond, 'Yes, *big* doggy.' And then, as soon as a child starts providing their own two-word phrases, we switch to adding more words ('that *is* a big doggy over there') or initiating conversational turns ('do *you* like the doggy?') or helping with pronunciation ('yes, doggy' in response to 'goggy' – an example of something called recasting, which has been observed in every culture that has been studied).* Rates of repetition are extremely high in infant-directed speech too. I'm writing this in a library where a baby song-and-story session is

* A 'recast' is a repetition where the parent says what the child has just said, but correctly: 'Daddy goed to work?' 'Yes, darling, Daddy went to work.' Caregivers use recasts to tacitly teach pronunciation, grammar and morphology. Cast your mind back to second-language lessons at school and how hard your teacher worked to teach you grammar, not to mention the textbooks and worksheets involved. Meanwhile, we teach our children these features of our own language while hardly being aware of it, just by patiently providing counterexamples.

taking place. 'Five Little Ducks' is currently being performed by a massed choir of caregivers (and an occasional enthusiastic 'quack, quack, quack, quack!' from some of the more precocious infants). A quick tally reveals that there are twenty-five distinct words in the song (counting 'duck' and 'ducks' as two different words) but 135 words in the song as a whole. The word 'quack' appears twenty times, which explains why even some of the babies can join in.* The song 'A Big Red Bus' has an even more repetitive structure, with just seven words of vocabulary for a fifty-two-word song, which probably explains why it is still such a persistent earworm, three years after my last visit to a story-and-song session with my daughter.

Eventually, caregivers get to move on to more abstract concepts than mummy ducks and big red buses. In many cultures, the next tranche of vocabulary tends to relate to bodily sensations ('are you hungry?' 'is that warm?'), then emotions ('you seem sad'), and finally beliefs and desires. Caregivers worldwide alter their speech patterns so that the language they use is *just complicated enough* for their children to learn from.[21] Despite the fact that most of us have absolutely no linguistics training we still manage a complex adaptation to our children's needs when we let ourselves talk using 'baby talk'.

Professor Toni Cross of the University of Melbourne was one of the early experimenters in this field and, in one of her most comprehensive studies, she collected a set of 20 one-hour-long conversations between mothers and their toddlers. She laboriously coded every part of speech. In a feat of intense labour, Professor Cross did this in the 1970s when all this coding had to be done by hand, or possibly on punch cards if you were very lucky. She looked at the relationships between mothers' speech patterns, and the level of language ability that their children

* My daughter used to pronounce all her 'k'/hard 'c' sounds as 't' so the mummy duck used to say 'twat, twat, twat, twat' when the little ducks came back. I miss those days sometimes.

showed in a test. She looked at how often mothers expanded on, repeated, or recast what their child had said. She looked at the length and complexity of words and sentences. She looked at whether mothers predominantly spoke about things that their child could see or that they were doing, and at how fast and how clearly the mothers spoke. She even coded every single time mothers explicitly corrected or coached their children. Of the sixty-two different data items she collected, forty-five features of maternal speech were strongly correlated with each child's ability to understand, to speak, and to make themselves understood. And each and every mother was observed making complex adaptations to help their children develop new skills. For example, as children became more fluent, the mothers in the study stopped repeating and recasting their children's sentences and began to use more sophisticated language, regardless of age.[22]

Although Professor Cross only studied mothers, we know now that all caregivers follow similar patterns.[23] So how do parents, siblings and other caregivers know what to do? It's not entirely clear, but being able to see a child and gauge how receptive they are seems to help. In a 1972 study, mothers who were asked to tape-record instructions for their child made far fewer adjustments in speed, pitch, tone or vocabulary than they did while giving similar instructions to the same child face to face.[24] Far from being 'degenerate', infant- and child-directed speech is an extremely carefully curated diet of input that is tailored to our children right here and right now. It's not noise- or error-free but it is exquisitely structured to be as useful as possible.

But linguists like Steven Pinker still assert that only WEIRDMOMs do this. 'The belief that Motherese is essential to language development is part of the same mentality that sends yuppies to "learning centers" to buy little mittens with bull's-eyes to help their babies find their hands sooner.'[25] So far so delightfully scathing: particularly in his insistence on using the term 'motherese', which, even in the early 1990s had fallen out of mainstream academic use in favour of the more accurate 'infant- or child-directed speech'. But he does a huge disservice to caregivers by making people feel silly or self-conscious for doing something that is both necessary and extremely sophisticated.

Pinker clings to one particular citation in support of his belief that such speech is a 'yuppie' phenomenon: the testimony of a person he calls 'Aunt Mae' that was originally given to anthropologist Professor Shirley Brice Heath.

> Now just how crazy is dat? White folks uh hear dey kids say sump'n, dey say it back to 'em, dey aks 'em 'gain 'n 'gain 'bout things, like they 'posed to be born knowin' ... Ain't no use me tellin' 'im: 'Learn dis, learn dat. What dis? What dat?' He just gotta learn, gotta know.[26]

But Pinker allows himself to be misled in several ways. For a start the woman is named in Professor Heath's original study as *Annie* May not *Aunt* May as he has it. She is not the child in question's aunt or main caregiver. But this study, indeed this single quote, by one person, has been widely used to assert that African American parents don't converse with their children.

But this assertion *really* needs unpacking.* In the first place, Professor Heath herself reports instances that she observed of parents recasting and repeating what children say: a key component of infant- and child-directed speech. Annie Mae may have strong opinions on how people *should* talk to children, but this isn't what Professor Heath noticed them doing in practice.

We also know that parents regularly underestimate how *much* infant- and child-directed speech they use. This underestimation is a widespread, cross-cultural phenomenon. Professor Madeline Haggan of the University of Kuwait asked eighty-two parents whether or not they believed that they modified their speech when they spoke to their small children.[27] Eighteen of the parents *swore* they didn't change how they spoke at all, but when Professor Haggan examined recordings of these same parents interacting

* 'Needs unpacking' is a formal way to say 'is bollocks'.

with their children, she discovered that they certainly did modify their speech, unless this forty-six-year-old PhD-educated chemist usually speaks like this:

Who is this in the picture? Huh? Who is this? ... And who is that? ... What's Jassim doing? What's he doing? ... (The child responds: Car.) Yes, he's sitting in the car. And who is sitting there? Who is that? ... You don't know who this is? This is Abdullah. What's your name? ... And mummy? What's her name? ... Go get ball so we can play outside. Ball. Ball. Go bring it. ... Yes, the red ball.

Every single one of the eighteen parents in the group who *swore* they didn't use infant-directed speech spoke like this in their interactions with their children. This happens throughout the world. The stereotypical higher-pitch, slower-paced, exaggerated speech sounds of infant-directed speech have been observed in German, Spanish, Italian, Hebrew, Japanese and Luo (a language spoken in East Africa) among others.[28]

But you have to be a bit sneaky to catch parents in the act. Perhaps unsurprisingly, adults *don't* express themselves in infant- or child-directed speech when a researcher shows up to ask them questions. But each study that relied on unobtrusive recordings found that child-directed speech is used all the time when there were no strangers around to interfere.

So Pinker's straw woman – the hothousing yuppie mommy with her career on hold, ambitiously project managing her child's infancy – is fantasy. Evidence suggests that every single culture has some form of infant- and child-directed speech. The few existing, utterly tragic, case studies of those children who have suffered isolation and neglect show that every child needs this specialised input from a caring adult or older sibling in order to learn language.

Playing together

Caregivers tend to use infant-directed speech as soon as their babies arrive, but the amount of time spent doing so really explodes when babies are capable of a phenomenon known as joint attention. Simply put, joint attention is two or more people paying attention to the same thing. It seems to be crucial that caregivers are willing to follow their baby's attention, as well as trying to lead it. In studies from the 1990s, those parent–child pairs where the parent followed the child's gaze or pointing most often had the earliest and most fluent talkers at follow-up some months later. Kids whose caregivers spend more time looking at or interacting with whatever their child is looking at have an advantage over those whose caregivers ignore what the child is paying attention to, or who try to redirect their child's attention to whatever the adult is interested in.[29]

Before they can say, 'Hey, look at this!' babies start to lead episodes of joint attention by pointing or staring. In a study of fifty pairs of mothers and their thirteen-month-olds, the speed and frequency with which those mothers responded to their child either reaching for something, pointing at something or doing something to get their mother's attention was highly predictive of how much language that child would go on to acquire by the age of twenty months. But the key here is *play* responsiveness: how much time caregivers spend engaging in make-believe dolls' tea parties or teddy bears' picnics strongly predicted how much each child would *understand*. Children copy their parents' language, but they only develop understanding through shared *experiences*.[30]

Some parental sayings are counterproductive, though. The more a child hears instructions and injunctions (do this, don't do that ...) the slower their language skills develop.[31] This might be for one of two reasons: some instructions (especially those as basic as 'no', and 'put it down') aren't particularly complex and tend to refer to a single verb or object, so they may just be a less useful form of input. Or it may be that this kind of parenting style, which is predominantly characterised by adults controlling a child's behaviour, is less likely to lead to those episodes of infant-initiated joint attention that are so important for language learning.[32]

Professor Catherine Tamis-LeMonda and her team videoed forty-five minutes of activity at home from each of forty mothers and their thirteen-month-old children.* In that thirty-hour data set of interactions, mothers said 60,000 words in total to their children. On average, the mothers spoke about forty words per minute to their thirteen-month-olds during feeding and playtime, and about sixty words per minute during story times, bath times, dressing and other grooming activities. They mainly talked about body parts, food, what they were doing, what the baby was doing, objects around the house, animals, toys: concrete and immediate things in their baby's environment. However the *variance* between these mothers was vast, with some mothers speaking less than ten words a minute, even during book-sharing. The number of words each child heard during a day varied enormously, as did the type of speech: those that heard the fewest words were also the most likely to hear lots of instructions and injunctions.

Among even the extremely chatty mothers, there wasn't a lot of variety. Professor Tamis-LeMonda found that the vocabulary used was highly repetitive. There were predictable patterns of words used in each of the different settings she recorded. Unsurprisingly, bath-related nouns like 'tap' and 'shampoo' appeared almost exclusively at bath time, words for body parts and clothing were used when dressing, cooking verbs and food and utensil names were used at mealtimes and so on.

For me it still feels very fresh: that sheer repetitiveness. The refrains of 'now let's put your socks on your feet', 'look, the doggy is chasing the leaf', connected with the repetitive routines of infant

* It's important to bear in mind that the paper talks about the effect of 'maternal' speech but once again we have no idea if this is specifically maternal or *parental* behaviour. There's little reason to believe that fathers show particularly different patterns of behaviour based on their employment status – over half of the mothers in the study were working, and employment status was only weakly correlated with how much talking the mothers did.

care can make that first year of parenting feel like Groundhog Day. But that very repetition plays an essential role. Until Professor Tamis-LeMonda's study, no one was entirely sure *what* mothers talked to their children about all day and, while it comes as no surprise that the participants in the study spoke about what they and their baby were doing, what they could see, what was happening around them, this is the first data that supports the hypothesis that children acquire an understanding of language from the use of repetitive 'scripts'.

In linguistics, scripts are rote or routine exchanges that we use multiple times a day[33] ('How are you?' 'Fine, how are you?' 'Can I take your order?' 'I'll have a triple shot macchiato please, and your sugariest snack').* These patterns form a kind of meaning of their own and we don't bother to unpick the individual words for their sense: we get them in context. The mothers in Professor Tamis-LeMonda's study were, in the main, accompanying the same actions with the same words over and over, making meaning through context.

Professor Tamis-LeMonda also found many occurrences of repetitive padding phrases like 'look at the ...' 'what a big ...' 'do you see the ...' Research shows that these repetitive phrases really help, by cueing up a baby's attention. Professors Anne Fernald and Nereyda Hurtado at Stanford University showed 24 eighteen-month-olds pictures of pairs of familiar objects: a baby and a dog, a car and a book, a shoe and a ball. They then played a recording of a woman saying these nouns in one of two ways. In the 'noun in isolation' condition, the recording said, 'Baby!' 'Doggy!' 'Ball!' and so on, followed by, 'Do you like it?' In the sentence frame condition, the recording said, 'Look at the [*noun*]' instead. Babies who heard the isolated noun, followed by, 'Do you like it?' were slower to look towards the correct picture (and less accurate at identifying which picture was the right one) than the babies who heard the 'look at the ...' preamble. That frame gives a clear signal

* See the chapter on sleep for why that has become a rote response for me.

that a noun is coming. Giving consistent, repetitive cues, and leaving the noun until last, are just some of the ways we adapt our speech for infants.

At some point, we have to help babies to go beyond scripts and frames. The great advantage of language is its power of *abstraction.* How do we get from talking about the things in front of us right now to talking about things that are distant in time or place? Infant-directed speech characteristically changes again, in order to train young children in the art of abstraction. And for that to happen we need to use a bit of imagination.

When you read with a small child, or play an imagination game, you start to introduce them to one of the most magical features of language: the ability to talk about things that aren't in the here and now. Wonderful things start happening when parents 'direct eating words to infants during a pretend "tea party" [or] when they talk about animals and outdoor things during booksharing where pictures stand for real world referents', says Professor Tamis-LeMonda. Imagination and reading are an 'early bridge to decontextualized language – talk about the "there and then" rather than "here and now"'. And that abstraction is what distinguishes human language from other forms of communication, human and non-human alike. Symbolic communication – using words to stand in for objects – is what underpins all of our culture. Far from being frivolous, our first steps in abstract thought take place during teddy-bear picnics and while having picture books read to us.

Welcome to phonemes: the Lego bricks of language

By the end of their first year, babies have become specialists in the *phonology* of the languages they hear from their caregivers. Phonology is the set of primitive sounds (called *phonemes*) that your language contains. Every language has 'phonemes', including sign languages, which are built on finite sets of hand shapes, hand positions, hand movements, body positions and facial expressions.

Babies are born as almost 'universal listeners' with the capacity to understand and produce any set of language sounds. But over the first twelve months, babies begin to ignore differences that aren't common in their own language. The sounds that they hear often have their neural connections reinforced, and the sounds that they don't hear have their synapses pruned.

In terms of spoken English, anyone who has done phonics with their kids will be familiar with the phonemes rather than the letter names. In UK schools at least, kids aren't likely to be taught that the letter 'A' is said '*ay*' as in 'hay'. Instead they're more likely to be told that 'A' says '*a*' as in ant. This is so effectively drilled into children and parents alike that it can be hard to remember letter names rather than letter sounds. I've lost count of the number of times that I've spelled my name over the phone as 'eh, muh, muh, ah' because of the hours spent with phonics rather than the alphabet. But an explicit system of phonics is helpful, especially in a language as irregular as English where *i*, *y*, *i_e*, and *igh* can be (but are not always) pronounced the same way: I, fly, nice, and high, for example.

This is one of the reasons why early reading to children is so important, and why doing the silly voices is not only fun but *extremely* helpful. Take the Gruffalo: snake hisses his sibilants, owl hoots her vowels, fox is – well, fox is an Etonian when I'm reading it so there's a lot of laconic drawl. But they all say 'A Gruffalo! What's a Gruffalo?' When you do the silly voices you give your child what's called a 'contrastive data set' – 's' can legitimately be hissed through the teeth (snake), 'wh' can be sighed through the lips (posh fox), and 'o' can slide between notes (owl). Thanks to Julia Donaldson, this 'contrastive data set' gives young children exposure to sounds in a wide variety of accents and speech styles. It's also a great chance to do your naff regional accents in front of an uncritical audience, so go for it. After all, you don't have long to train your children in phonemes.

Needing to master more than one set of phonemes can slow the acquisition of language. Parents of bilingual kids sometimes stress over the reported delay their children experience in the growth of their vocabulary, and the couple of years' lag they have in reading in either language. Here in the UK, policy-makers, too, are concerned about the growth in the number of children in school for whom English is a second (or third) language. And it is the case that those children who arrive at school with little experience of conversation in the language of the classroom do tend to struggle more than those of their peers who have heard that language exclusively. The evidence shows that bilingual children can struggle to understand (and to make themselves understood) in those crucial first few years of school. But more recent research shows that there are huge advantages to bilingualism that could more than make up for the initial, brief language gap.

One of the most widely known advantages of early second-language learning is the ability to pick up more languages with greater ease later in life. Some of this is purely physiological: the wider the repertoire of phonemes you can produce and discriminate between, the better your chance of mastering the sounds of other languages. The effect is especially pronounced if one of your languages happens to be tonal, like many South East Asian, sub-Saharan African, and Pacific languages.* The way that children learn tones is different to the learning of phonemes based solely on vowels and consonants.[34] Trying to pick up a tonal language after adolescence is a huge challenge for those of us who only ever use pitch for emphasis and not meaning.

What's more, from the age of about seven onwards, children who are raised multilingually find it easier to memorise entirely new words than do their monoglot peers. The effect holds even when the 'words' are completely arbitrary.[35] From slow beginnings, the vocabularies of multilingual children in all their languages begin to grow at an accelerated rate and, by the age of nine, it is impossible

* In fact, only the WEIRDest languages *aren't* tonal. Languages with 'tonemes' account for around 70 per cent of the known set of languages in the world (Yip 2002).

to tell the difference in reading age between monoglot and polyglot children, even if they only began learning one of those languages at school.[36] Children who are raised bilingually are also at an advantage when it comes to executive function, having had lots of practice dealing with those early frustrations, and of suppressing the 'wrong' language when speaking with others.[37] They are also much more sensitive to breakdowns in communication, and are better at repairing them, as well as better at recognising non-verbal cues about emotions.[38]

Sadly, it's not enough to plonk your child down in front of a foreign-language radio station. We only learn language through use, and it's the amount of conversation we have (and how early we have it) that really shapes how proficient we become.[39] The reason so many adults fail to learn a language is because they don't like to make mistakes, and refuse to speak a language until they 'know' it. But these kids show us that speaking a language is the only way to know it. While it is harder as we get older, learning new languages is possible if we swallow our pride and make a lot of mistakes.

Children who grow up using multiple languages have a steep hill to climb, but the early struggles are more than made up for by the wealth of ways in which their brains adapt. Far from fearing a bilingual explosion, there are many reasons why we should embrace it.

To cut down on the sheer number of phonemes they need to master, babies manage to figure out the phonetic repertoire of their own languages before they begin to talk. Different spoken languages have different phonemes. To native English speakers 'r' and 'l' are clearly distinct. To native Japanese speakers, both sounds are indistinct from one another, as well as from the consonant sounds in 'ra', 're', 'ri', 'ro' and 'ru'.* But even in our

* To feel the difference, say 'r' and feel where your tongue curls back to touch the middle of your palate. Now say 'l' – your tongue taps the front of your palate instead. In Japanese, 'ra', 're', 'ri', 'ro' and 'ru' are said with

own language, the sound of any particular phoneme depends on the facial anatomy of the person saying it,* what mood they're in, whether they are speaking to you on the phone, face to face, through a screen, from another room, or whether they're shouting or whispering. Yet despite these challenges, children figure out which set of sounds they'll need to tell apart long before they learn to speak.

Spoken languages also vary wildly in their phonetic repertoire, so it takes a bit of training to prune all the myriad possible phonemes down to the set we actually use. As well as the r/l intermediate sound that we lack in English, there are Hindi variants of sounds that monoglot English speakers hear only as 'd' and 't'. In Angola, Namibia and Botswana there are several languages that have around *fifty* different 'click' sounds made using different positions of the lips, tongue, teeth and throat. In North American First Nations languages, there are various phonetic 'clicks'. While this variety is bewildering for the language learner, it's a boon for developmental research.

Take Hindi with its two types of 'd' sound: one made with the tongue at the front of the palette, similar to the English 'd'; and one with the tongue at the back of the palette, a sound not used in English. At birth, all babies can tell the difference between these two consonants, no matter what language their caregivers speak. But by one year old, almost all babies with non-Hindi-speaking families have lost the ability to hear the difference.[40]

Professor Janet Werker of the University of British Colombia has done a lot of the work to uncover exactly when this pruning takes place, which shifts a child from a universal listener to a specialised speaker. But because we can't ask seven-month-olds to *tell* us when they hear a difference between two sounds, she

---

the tongue almost halfway between the two points. 'Thank you' is neither 'arigatō' nor 'aligatō' but somewhere in between.

* I had my front teeth crowned the best part of a decade ago. I'm still trying to get used to the way I say 'f' and 'th' today.

had to come up with a paradigm that even the smallest of infants could manage but that also works for older children and adults. The sucking amplitude test, commonly used with newborns, was not going to work with kids on solids.

Instead, Professor Werker devised the 'head turn procedure'. On one side of the room she placed a smoked Plexiglas box with what she describes as 'electronically activated animals' inside. 'Electronically activated animals' may sound terrifying but she kindly shared some photographs of the original experiments: the 'animals' were a toy bear that played the cymbals and a toy rabbit that played the drums. Professor Werker's team trained five-and-a-half-month-olds to turn their heads towards the box whenever they heard a change in the sounds being played. If they looked at the right time, the box would light up and the animals would be made to perform.

The babies, children and adults were played strings of isolated phonemes, like 'ba, ba, ba, ba, ba, pa, pa, pa, pa, pa ...' If they responded by looking at the box when the phonemes changed this indicated that they could hear the difference. As well as distinctive English phonemes, Professor Werker and her colleagues played sequences that switched between 'T-a' (where the 't' sound is made with the tongue against the teeth) and 't-a' (where the 't' sound is made with the tongue against the roof of the mouth). Adult Hindi speakers and all babies under six months were equally adept at spotting the difference, but nine out of ten non-Hindi-speaking adults couldn't spot the change.

Professor Werker then recruited children between the ages of four and twelve. It had been hypothesised that we lose the ability to discriminate new phonemes around puberty due to the sensory reorganisation that blows through teenage brains, so she expected to find a drop in the children's ability at some point during the period usually spent at primary school. Instead she found that *all* the school-age children did just as badly as the non-Hindi-speaking adults.

Back to the drawing board, then. This is how science (and parenting) progress: not in neat epiphanies, but in constant, painstaking observation, resiliently starting again when things don't go as expected.

To create a new test set, Professor Werker recruited two elders of the community of Nthlakampx speakers, native to Northern Canada. This endangered language includes the two phonemes, 'k'i' and 'q'i'. The first of these is said in a way that is similar to the English-language 'k' sound: the back of the tongue hits the roof of the mouth, preventing air passing through the top and forcing it alongside the tongue. In contrast, 'q'i' is produced by pressing the back of the tongue against the uvula, forcing the air up and over. I'm attempting this in a café – I take my action research seriously – and am concerned that someone may be compelled to attempt the Heimlich manoeuvre if I carry on mangling the sound so violently. This sound is incredibly rare in world languages and, as there are currently only 200 living speakers of Nthlakampx, the children were unlikely to have heard it in their environment.

This time Professor Werker and her team recruited participants who were aged between six and eight months at the start of the experiment and tested them again between eight and ten months, and between ten and twelve months to see how each individual child's abilities had changed over time. The youngest infants could reliably spot the difference between 'ba' and 'da', between 'T-a' and 't-a', and between 'k'i' and 'q'i'. By ten months that ability had already begun to diminish, and by twelve months it had dropped to adult levels.[41]

The genius of Professor Werker's approach is that we can be sure that this isn't a generational thing. Following these children and observing the decline in their individual skills demonstrates that the youngest babies weren't great at the task just because they happen to be exposed to a wider range of languages. What we see in this data is the progressive loss of ability to discriminate between phonemes that aren't in their native language. This selective specialisation happens to us all, and it happens *early*.

WEIRD languages aren't differentiated by tone. We only use tone for emphasis or pragmatics (the difference between 'I've had a drink' and 'I've had *a* drink'). Two-thirds of the world's known languages have some kind of tonal component that distinguishes between words. For example, Mandarin vowels are tonal: ǎ starts high, dips, then rises again; ā is said on a single tone; and à starts high and ends low. In Chinese, *mǎ* means 'horse' and *mā* means 'mother' – a difference that us non-tonals struggle to hear, let alone produce.

Tonal languages, by the way, are *splendid* for punning – which can be incredibly handy when trying to get around the censors. When I received my author's copy of *Swearing Is Good For You* from the Chinese publisher, I had no idea why it had a pink alpaca on the front. Some strange and interesting internet searches later, I discovered that the picture is of a 'grass mud horse'. This fantastical creature's name in Mandarin is *cǎo ní mǎ* (草泥马) which sounds close to *cào nǐ mā* (肏你妈) or 'fuck your mother'. So far so appropriate for a book on swearing. But the grass mud horse has a dissident history. In China, 1 July is Party Day, a holiday that celebrates the founding of the Communist Party. In 2012, brave and cheeky internet users declared that 1 July is also 'Grass Mud Horse' Day. Censors were not impressed. As for me, I'm *thrilled* to be represented by the cheeky 草泥马.

As well as having fewer opportunities for outrageous puns, those of us unfortunate enough to grow up learning a non-tonal language also do worse at pitch recognition tasks. Four-year-old Mandarin speakers are far better at spotting changes in the pitch of musical notes than their English-speaking counterparts. They don't do any better at spotting changes in *timbre*, however, which suggests that it is indeed the tonal aspects of Mandarin that are important, rather than Chinese children somehow being exposed to more music overall.[42]

You didn't really hear that

Within those first twelve months of life, infants are busy picking up the Lego blocks of their language despite all the noise in the environment. Infant-directed speech has plenty of features that help with this, as we've seen, but our baby-directed chatter still happens in environments that are full of other people speaking, music playing, and the wipers on the bus going swish, swish, swish. Perceptually, there's a lot of brainwork required to filter out parental signal from background noise. Children learn to do this early: even before a child reaches their second year, they can learn the meanings of entirely new words, as long as the voice telling them the new word is at least 10 dB louder than the background.

Even if, as an adult, you miss something, you have the ability to rewind a little. Adults use a short buffer, a seconds-long memory of things just heard, to help decipher it. This specialised type of short-term memory, called a 'phonological loop', allows us to mentally rewind and thus have a second go at parsing something we might have just missed. But kids have a much shorter phonological loop – it takes at least a decade of life until it is about as long as an adult's mental voicemail. One of the studies that determined the length of phonological memory in children was done by Professor Emily Sumner of the University of California, Irvine.[43] In the paper 'Cake or broccoli? Recency biases children's verbal responses', she and her team report what happened when they asked twenty-four preschoolers a bunch of either/or questions, like, 'Does Rory (a cartoon drawing of a bear) like apples or bananas?', sometimes including made-up words, as here: 'Should we call this toy Stog or Meeb?' Across the board, the children consistently gave the second option as their answer for the vast majority of the sentences. What's more, the greater the number of syllables in the sentence, the more likely it was that they would choose the second option. This suggests that the 'buffer' of available sound memory in kids is limited to just a few seconds at most.

In an experiment with forty toddlers, Professor Brianna McMillan and Professor Jenny Saffran of the University of Wisconsin-Madison played recordings of the names of two new objects, a 'tursey' (a spotted blue oval with a frilled edge) and a 'coro' (a red four-pointed shape).[44]

These words were embedded in sentences like, 'The tursey is on the table', and, 'The boy dropped the coro'. Children saw a picture of either the tursey or the coro as the sentences played.

As long as the background noise was at least 10 dB quieter than the voice teaching the object names, the children were able to learn and later identify a tursey and a coro from a line-up of other brand-new shapes. But if the difference between the background and the instruction was only 5 dB then they didn't learn these new words.

But here's where it gets *really* interesting. In a second experiment, professors McMillan and Saffran introduced two new shapes, pif and blicket. This time children heard similar sentences (the blicket is on the table, the pif is under the tree) but they didn't see the shapes. Instead they were played a video of nature scenes at the same time. They were exposed to the word but not the meaning.

Then, the team played the *same* sentences while showing the shapes to the children, but this time with a background noise difference of just 5 dB. And this time, the children *did* learn the new words, despite all the background distraction. Infants seem to treat sequences of phonemes in rather the same way that some people hoard kitchen utensils.* Just knowing that a word exists in your language seems to be enough to prime very young children to learn that word so that when it finally appears, they'll spot it, even if the context is challenging. Whatever is going on around them, babies are trying to make the most of the first few months of linguistic input. No matter how daft, or bored or repetitive you may feel, every dolls' tea party, every 'Heads, Shoulders, Knees and Toes', or *We're Going on a Bear Hunt* is playing a vital role in introducing your child into the mysteries of language. They don't need an innate grammar module – but they do need your help, so keep on talking.

* I might *need* a melon baller one day. Probably the day after I throw it out ...

Baby's first word

Babies may be born non-verbal communicators, but some time in their second year something usually happens that seems to usher in a new era: baby's first word. This phenomenon of 'baby's first word' is actually something of a recent fashion. Until men of letters started keeping (and publishing) their diaries, there were few known records of what baby's first words might be.

Professor Linda Pollock of Tulane University studied ninety-one diaries that had been preserved from the sixteenth to nineteenth centuries. Only nineteen out of ninety-one diaries recorded anything that children said, and only nine of them mentioned first words at all. With infant mortality so high, children's language doesn't seem to have been a parental preoccupation in this period.

But something happened at the start of the Victorian era that changed the way we think about children's language, and that started the fad of recording 'first words'. In 1877 Charles Darwin published decades' worth of his diaries (simultaneously in German, Russian and French). In these diaries he recorded his first son's first word, which had been uttered in 1839. This word was 'mum', but according to Darwin this didn't mean the maternal parent. Instead it meant 'food' or 'give me food'.

When Darwin finally published those diaries nearly four decades after he first wrote them (the reaction of his by then thirty-eight-year-old son to having his infant babbles and bowel movements published is not recorded) other natural historians began keeping diaries of their own. Gentlemen's diaries now became respectable sources of scientific data, and the study of child development became a respectable branch of human biology. 'This new zeal for psychological knowledge has taken possession of a number of my acquaintances,' psychologist James Sully wrote in 1881. 'These are mostly young married men to whom the phenomenon of babyhood has all the charm of newness.' The hope shared by many of these naturalists was that infants and children would show how we evolved by recapitulating all the steps of evolution that brought us to this supposed Victorian pinnacle.

This trend soon caught on among the middle classes, who were newly fortunate enough to be able to keep most of their offspring alive beyond five years of age. In the 1910s there began a fad of 'baby books' that continues to this day. (This has recently morphed into packs of 'milestone cards' that commemorate 'baby's first ...' everything, apparently. The idea is that you prop the appropriate card next to your baby – 'today I am one week old', 'today I crawled for the first time'– and then snap a photo and share it on your Insta, maybe. There's even one for 'I slept through the night'. I suspect that our daughter will be old enough for her own social media accounts before she qualifies for that one.) The first generation of these books didn't ask for a first word but did have space to record your offspring's birthdays, Christmases, diet, clothing and sleep. Later ones started to ask for 'baby's sayings' or 'vocabulary at eighteen months' but one particularly gushing one begged you to record: 'What were the first wonderful words?'

But first words are rarely words. They are what writer Michael Erard calls 'the intersection between a baby's intention to mean with an adult's willingness to comprehend'.[45] He gives the example of the Mo Willems book *Knuffle Bunny*. Throughout the book, little Trixie is trying to tell her father that she's dropped her favourite toy. 'Aggle flaggle klabble!' she cries, and 'That's right, we *are* going home,' says oblivious dad. But a few pages later, when the toy is found, she exclaims 'Knuffle bunny!' and *this* is what her father recognises as her first words, despite Trixie's desperate attempts to communicate throughout.

It's a sweet story and a useful reminder: language doesn't have a crisp beginning with a first recognisable word: our babies are communicators from the moment they're born – it just takes us a little while to start talking the same language. In the meantime, with pre-verbal (or non-verbal, or unconfident) children, you need to pay very close attention. Be as patient as you can, and stay curious about what your child needs you to know. Get down to their level, follow their eye line, try to put yourself in their shoes as much as possible. When you find yourself caring for a child who is still mastering the art of talking – or a distressed or frantic teenager – all these habits will help you make sense of whatever they are so desperately trying to communicate. A little patience, and a little focus, can cut down on a lot of frustration.

6

From Speaking to Reading: How Kids Learn to Express Themselves

Despite the somewhat arbitrary nature of 'baby's first word', few milestones in a child's life garner as much attention or applause as that initial utterance. But why does that first 'mama' or 'dada' command so much interest? Partly it's the parental vying – the 'friendly' rivalry about who gets named first – but mostly we care because language means so much to us as a species. When we teach our children to express themselves, we're including them in one of the most obvious hallmarks of being human.

As Professor Erika Hoff, director of the Language Development Laboratory of Florida Atlantic University, points out, a typical infant brain has the capacity to *learn* language, but it is the people around them that do the teaching. In the previous chapter we looked at the multiple ways in which babies communicate – and how they come to understand us when *we* use language. But in order to become a fully fledged conversational partner, children need to learn a very specific set of behaviours, with complex rules that allow humans as a species to form an infinite variety of declarations, questions and requests.

So what are the building blocks of language? Linguists generally split language into five areas of study: phonology, vocabulary, morphology, syntax and pragmatics.

We delved into phonology in the previous chapter: children tend to specialise in the set of their parents' native phonemes long before they begin to speak. Once they have the phonology of their native language nailed, all spoken language becomes a mix-and-match game with those sounds. The set of words that you know how to use in such a way that other people understand you is your *vocabulary*. When building vocabulary, there are some shortcuts to be found in *morphology*. In English, endings like -s, -ing, -ed, -er are more or less taken for granted by adults, but kids pick them up with some characteristic irregularities.

So how do children learn these components of their language? All the evidence shows that we as parents have an incredibly important role in ensuring that our children learn language. In particular, if you want your kids to talk to you, you have to listen. They'll soon have plenty to say.

Whatever their first word might have been, babies tend to pick up new words at about the rate of one a week until they master around fifty words. At this point something astounding happens: an explosion of vocabulary takes place, with one- to two-year-olds capable of picking up one or two new words per day. This then accelerates again, with two- to six-year-olds capable of learning up to ten words a day. No amount of emotional blackmail by the Duolingo Owl could get me to learn that many words that fast these days. This explosion explains how six-year-olds can master an estimated 14,000-word vocabulary by the time they reach their seventh birthday.[1]

But even 14,000 words can only take you so far. Morphology is what really unlocks the power of language over other forms of communication. Combining symbols according to regular rules leads to being able to say far more things far quicker than if you had to learn every new symbol in turn. In that previous sentence I used seven morphemes: combin*ing*, symbol*s*, accord*ing*, rule*s*, lead*s*, be*ing*, quick*er*. If we didn't have morphology – if we had completely unrelated words for speed rather than quick, quicker, quickest (and the adverb 'quickly') – then we'd have to make at least four times the effort to learn how to express a sentence like the one above.

In every language there is a trade-off between whether you indicate things by word order and extra words, or whether you add suffixes or prefixes. There are languages that use auxiliary words to change meaning (like traditional Chinese, Japanese) and languages that allow you to pile on up to eight morphemes on a single stem (like Russian). So in Japanese there is no plural morpheme, but there are auxiliary counting words. Instead of saying 'the cat' and 'the cats', you say *itsupiki no neko* (one cat) '*ni-biki* no neko*' (two cats), *ikutsu ka no neko* (some cats) or just '*neko*' (cat/cats) – and just expect that the listener will figure it out from context. Children master the rules that are appropriate to their native language from context, usually by their sixth birthday. What's more, they're learning how to make sentences that make sense. For that they need a sense of grammar.

The syntax era

As toddlers are building vocabulary and its morphological variety, they're simultaneously figuring out syntax: the way we put those words and compounds together. In English we favour *subject-verb-object* – James ate the chocolate. About a third of languages follow this pattern, whereas half prefer *subject-object-verb* (*James hat die Schokolade gegessen*). Children need to learn how to pick up the meaning that comes from the *arrangement* of all those sounds-that-make-words-that-make-compounds, and once again the special way that we talk to children helps that to happen.

For native English speakers, subject and object are differentiated by where they are in the sentence (either side of the verb), and for (most) plurals we just add an 's'. For the native Russian speaker,

* Don't be seduced into believing that *itsupiki* and *ni-biki* means 'one' and 'two' across the board in Japanese. Not a chance! There are different counting words for flat things, long things, containers, small animals, birds, fish. In fact there is even a different counting system for fish in a river and fish on a plate. My husband and I studied Japanese together for a while. I think the shared sense of bewilderment was great for our relationship.

it would be natural for the subject and object, as well as plural versus singular, to be indicated by a stack of morphemes. If I was a native Japanese speaker I'd expect subject and object to be marked by position rather than morphemes (albeit *subject-object-verb* in Japanese rather than *subject-verb-object* in English), and I'd expect to use special words called 'particles' to indicate plurality. This partially explains why learning a second language in adulthood is so tricky: it's never a case of simply learning new words – you need new grammar rules too. In childhood you're not just learning the phonemes, the vocabulary and the morphemes of your language, you're internalising rules about how language should *work*.

Young children pick up grammar with what seems like enviable ease. So much so that even two-year-olds can tell the difference between a word when it is used as a verb ('we *house* the horse in the stable') and as a noun ('the horse's *house* is the stable'). Long before they regularly produce sentences that are this varied, they understand and can tell the difference between these similar-sounding words.

Is it the context of those words in the sentence that allows children to discriminate between these roles? Or are there local cues in the way the word sounds that can help to determine what a speaker means? To test this, Professor Alex de Carvalho, now at the Sorbonne, studied sixteen children aged between three and a half and five.[2] The team recorded sixteen sentences, which were constructed around eight near-homophones that can be interpreted as verbs or nouns. For example, *la* ***ferme*** (the farm) and *elle* ***ferme*** (she closes). They had a native French speaker record sentences where these words play one or the other role, for example: *la petite ferme est très jolie* (the little farm is very nice) and *la petite ferme la fenêtre* (the little girl closes the window).

These sentences were played to the children, but everything after the word *ferme* was masked: the video of the actress speaking was blurred, and the sound was obscured with static. The children were then asked to pick one of two pictures displayed on-screen – a picture of a toy farm, and of a girl closing a toy box, for example.

The forty-month-olds did pretty well, picking the right picture about two-thirds of the time, and the five-year-olds did even better, with an average success rate of 85 per cent. Remember that all they heard was *la petite ferme* ... and then static, but by the time these children had finished a year of school, most of them could tell the difference between a noun and a verb just because of the clues in the *prosody* – the stress and intonation used by the speaker. Even in degraded contexts (where the subject or object of the verb or the target of the noun isn't clear) words can still be recognised *as* verbs or nouns because the music of our speech gives whacking great hints as to the grammar of what we're saying.

But children do take a while to master the irregularities. Some more persistent overgeneralisations hang around in the development of morphology and syntax for several years. Between the ages of two and six it's pretty common for children to over-apply the morphological Lego bricks that they've just learned. Some particularly charming ones in the literature are 'spy*er*' (someone who spies), 'cook*er*' (someone who cooks), '*un*squeeze' (loosen) and 'sitt*ed* and draw*ed*'. Syntactic overgeneralisation in English tends to be a case of making the intransitive transitive, resulting in such gems as 'Don't giggle me' (don't make me giggle) and 'I don't want any more grapes; they just cough me' (they'll make me cough).[3] Over time, children start to learn about exceptions, but for uncommon words, it's often the case that these irregularities last a long time.

In fact, some of these constructions are only ungrammatical by *convention*. Why shouldn't we ask someone to unsqueeze us if our coat is too tight? Or to have cookers as well as footballers and designers? At the same time that they are learning a language, young children are hugely inventive coinage machines. We clamp down on some of their wilder inventions largely because we want them to be easily understood: managing the balance between self-expression and accepted convention is a constant tension.

It's worth noting that second language learners carry on making these sorts of mistakes into adulthood. This suggests that these mistakes aren't developmental – there isn't an age at which we become grammatically adept. In fact, if you've tried to learn a new language after adolescence, you're probably keenly aware that the plasticity you need has started to dry up: developmentally we become *less* good at learning new languages as we age.

The biggest (and saddest) difference between learning a language as an adult and as a child is how sympathetically people hear your overgeneralisations (and how mortified you are by them). When listening to children, adults tend to 'recast' what they've said: 'I sitted and drawed all day.' 'Oh! You sat and drew all day? How nice!' As adults we no longer benefit from this forgiving (and informative) type of child-directed speech, which is probably one of the many things that slows down our language acquisition: the attempt to teach language in an explicit manner deprives us of the kind of feedback that helped us master the implicit rules that govern our own language.

But we still don't know if that is because we become less sensitive to input after puberty, if our brains become less plastic, or even if we just become more self-conscious about making mistakes and thus less likely to learn by the trial-and-frequently-hilarious-error that small children engage in. It's most likely that there is some combination of all three factors at play.

When we learn a second language as adults, nobody talks to us like children any more. To see whether child-directed speech helps adults to learn languages, Professor Roberta Michnick Golinkoff and Professor Anthony Alioto recorded a female Mandarin speaker talking about pictures of ten familiar objects in either infant-directed or adult-directed speech. The voice actress was asked to simply read the sentences *as if* talking to an infant or an adult.

English-speaking adults who had never learned a word of Chinese before were shown pictures of the objects in question, while hearing the recorded sentence pairs. They were then tested on whether or not they could choose the correct object from a pair of pictures when they heard the Mandarin noun in isolation.

Even though they had heard identical sentences of Mandarin,

only those volunteers who heard them spoken in an infant-directed way showed signs of learning the words, with 73 per cent of them performing better than chance. The results showed that the adults who heard adult-directed versions of the same sentences were frankly just guessing on the multiple choice test.[4] So if you want to learn a language get someone to speak to you like an infant!

Being pragmatic

Finally, to get by in the world, children need to learn *pragmatics*. As humans, we've built this incredible skill known as language and then used it to find ways of obscuring what we mean. There are all sorts of reasons for doing so: from being funny, to avoiding direct conflict, to allowing someone to save face. As a result we don't always use the most direct way of saying what we want, think or feel. 'It's chilly in here,' can mean, 'Please close the window.' 'No, sure, that's a *terrific* idea, darling,' can mean, 'Stop balancing on one leg on that wobbly stool before you fall off: I don't have time to go to A&E today, thanks.' Nevertheless, children learn these special rules very early on.

Mastering vocabulary is important, but the precise meaning of a word can be tricky to pin down. In our house, the five-year-old devastated the three-year-old by describing her as 'wicked' – the five-year-old knows 'wicked' as a near synonym for cool. For the three-year-old, wicked is the witch who dies at the end. Somehow, children need to pick up not just the words, but their multiple, fluid, contextual meanings.

Even more challengingly, we don't always say what we mean and mean what we say. Child-directed speech is considerably more straightforward than adult-directed speech but research confirms that it isn't without irony. In fact WEIRD children as young as four are pretty good at spotting sarcasm, scoring an average of 80 per cent on irony-recognition tasks. Astonishingly, these same four-year-olds tended to score only 20 per cent on theory of mind tasks, whereas five- and six-year-olds had shown a significant improvement, scoring 40 and 45 per cent respectively, but with no increase in sarcasm detection.[5] Although children develop their theory of mind significantly in their first couple of years in school, this doesn't seem to be necessary for the understanding of sarcasm and other forms of irony, at least not in the early years when their insight into what other people might be thinking is still tenuous at best. Instead, they've probably learned the skill from all the times that they've heard their parents being ironic.

Professor Natalia Banasik-Jemielniak of the University of Warsaw studied the CHILDES (Child Language Data Exchange System), a huge collection of examples of speech by, and to, children. She looked at fifty hours of recordings of parents (mothers, in this case) interacting with their children, all aged between two and four, and she found several kinds of irony. Some were used by clearly exasperated parents and were directed at the child. One example that Professor Banasik-Jemielniak offers up is that of a three-year-old who kept making annoying noises while his mother was preparing dinner, to which she said: 'William, would you like to do something while you're waiting for your pancakes, other than make all these lovely sounds?' I'm sure I've said similar things when frustrated or tired.

But Professor Banasik-Jemielniak found that while children hear a lot of irony, they aren't the main targets. Quite often they are unwitting co-conspirators in passive-aggressive lettings-off-of-steam. In the same study, she gives this example:

Child (pretending to speak for her doll): 'I don't want to go to my house.'
Mum: 'You don't want to go to your house?'
Child: 'No.'
Mum: 'That's a shame. Maybe that's because you think the kitchen will never be done. Mommy thinks that too.'

Professor Banasik-Jemielniak points out that though some families were much more irony-prone than others, irony is generally a coping mechanism. Not every family used hyperbole or rhetorical questions, but those that did tended to use them to signal frustration or fatigue. Initially, kids seem to acquire irony by mimicry. Any emotive language is notable, which is why children tend to pick up swear words with terrifying ease.

But the use of *inventive* irony takes about another decade to develop. In adolescence the theory of mind starts to intervene when it comes to making sense of what people might *really* mean. We know this from a study by Professor Ting Wang, now of the Icahn School of Medicine at Mount Sinai, who used fMRI to study the brain activity of early adolescents and adults as they tried to make sense of two-panel cartoons. For example, one sequence showed 'Bryan' and 'Dina' blowing up balloons. In one condition (the sincere condition) the second panel shows that Bryan has successfully blown up his balloon. In the second condition (the sarcasm trials) he's managed to burst his balloon. In both conditions Dina says, 'Nice going!' In one of these conditions, Dina is clearly being a sarcastic little madam. The participants had to push one button when they saw a sarcastic response by one of the comic characters, and a different button when the answer was sincere. The adults did slightly (but not significantly) better at spotting sarcasm. But what *was* significant was the different brain areas that were in action as they did the task.

A series of fMRI scans of the twelve adults and twelve adolescents showed that adults preferentially used structures that process face and voice cues. In contrast, the adolescents tended to show greater activity in the medial prefrontal cortex (MPFC) – the area of the brain that is most commonly active when performing theory of mind tasks.[6] Adolescents seem to still rely on what the person speaking might be *thinking*, whereas adults seem to bypass this in favour of cues from tone of voice and facial expression. This seems to indicate that, first of all, you're not imagining things – your teenager really is inventively sarcastic – and that by adulthood our use of sarcasm has become slightly stale.

Quality, quantity, direction: what helps?

So beyond teaching our kids to be sarcastic, what are we doing that makes it so easy for them to pick up languages? Is it just that they have such spongy young brains? There is some evidence that children's brains are uniquely advantaged when it comes to learning a language but, like everything in science, the full picture is complicated.

No child can learn to use language if they're not given the opportunity to take part in conversations with people who care about them.[7] Children who are born deaf but with hearing parents tend to invent a repertoire of signs to help them communicate with their caregivers, but these signs don't come close to being a fully fledged language.[8] We learn language from existing speakers, but we *create* language by consensus: even the addition of words like the noun *wasteman* or the verb *to MacGyver* only emerge because enough people need to communicate new concepts (or refine old concepts). Language is fluid, and that fluidity is driven by consensus that comes about when we communicate.

For most children, caregivers are their first teachers. I hear our daughter say things that sound just like me and like other members of the family. Her 'that's okay!' is just like mine, and I feel a warm sense of reassurance when she says it. Sadly, her 'in a *minute*!' is also just like mine, and it gives me a stab of guilt every time I realise that this is how I sound to her. Children learn by imitation and, for their first decade at least, research shows that children need (and borrow heavily from) the speech of parents, grandparents and other caregivers.

However, this apprenticeship is not equally distributed. In most cultures that have been studied, parents with higher socio-economic status speak more, and use infant- and child-directed speech with their young children. Socio-economic status (SES) is a broad brush that paints over a lot of details, but it's usually defined as 'different basic conditions of life at different levels of the social order', and is usually derived from the level of education of a child's mother: a loose proxy of a very complex phenomenon.

SES is correlated with access to healthcare, healthy food, time to exercise, job security, the quality of your housing, and the amount of time you have available to spend on the job of being a parent.

When Professor Catherine Tamis-LeMonda and her team plotted word rate per participant in that groundbreaking study, she found that the higher someone's social class, the more loquacious they were with their children.[9] It's not entirely clear what is going on, but those systematic inequalities that I mentioned above are likely to account for quite a lot of the difference. Parents with fewer worries, more time and better health are more likely to chat with their children than are parents who are stressed, exhausted or sick.

However, there is some suggestion that the SES relationship with word count is changing. Sadly, that's not because life is getting any easier for those on low or unpredictable incomes. Rather, the number of middle- and upper-class parents who are spending more time on their mobile devices is eroding the amount of time spent in talk and play with young children at all points on the SES spectrum.[10]

Nevertheless, there have been consistent differences recorded among low-, middle-, and high-SES families in the word count shared with children. The most influential of these studies dates from the 1990s, and it suggested that there was a 30 million word gap between the most well off and least well off families by the time children get to preschool.[11] Multiple studies since then have confirmed that professional parents speak more to their children than do working-class parents, and that working-class parents speak more to their children than those parents who receive public assistance.[12] The wealthier your family is, and the more years of education you've been able to participate in, the more likely it is that you'll have the wherewithal necessary to spend time reading, playing and having teddy bears' picnics with your toddler.

This difference has an impact on a child's development: at the age of two years and nine months, the average child from a middle-class family has a mean length of utterance (MLU: the average number of words they string together) of about three words, and they start using prepositions like *in* and *on*. Children in lower-income families take another year to reach the same stage of linguistic development.[13] By the end of the reception school year, children in low-income families have the same MLU as their middle-class peers had acquired before leaving nursery. This matters, because lower verbal fluency, and the diminished confidence that goes with it, has a huge impact on kids when they go to school. This early disparity tends to grow wider as children grow up.

Politically, the trend has been to assume that lower SES families are 'failing' their children, and then to throw remedial resources at groups deemed 'at risk'. But what happens if we widen the spotlight and ask *why* there might be more space for child-directed interactions in better-off households? Does higher SES correlate with not having to do your own cleaning or shopping? Probably. Does it equate with spending less time worrying about keeping a roof over your head, heating it, lighting it, furnishing it, repairing it, filling it with food, toys, books and clothes? Almost definitely. Does lower SES correlate with being chronically ill? Beyond doubt, especially in countries where health and social care are cut to the bone. If the 30 million word gap does exist – or something like it, at least – we owe it to the future to ensure that all households have the chance to have that teddy bears' picnic. In the UK we have the 'Every Child a Talker' programme that aims to backfill the deficit – but how about 'every parent supported to be a listener?' Wouldn't that be a better intervention?

The one factor that outweighs all others when it comes to children discovering language is *how much reading* you do together. If you are worried that you've not been talking with your child enough then the answer is as close as your local library. Playing together with toys leads to lots of speech but reading leads to even more. Caregivers use more words, and use them in more complex sentences, when reading aloud to their children than when playing with them. What's more, the way that parents talk when reading is much more relaxed than in general, with far fewer instructions or prohibitions – there is generally less need to say, '*Don't* put that in your mouth!' or, 'Put that *down*, you don't know where it's been.' Instead the conversations tend to be about what the funny bunny is doing, or why Cinderella's slipper is the only thing that *doesn't* change back at midnight (it's a *massive* plot hole and I'm determined that it should bother the kids as much as it bothers me!).[14] Whatever age they may be, a bedtime story is a great way of spending some quality language development time with your kid.

It doesn't matter *how* you read as long as you read. The amount of *time* spent reading seems to matter more than all the silly accents, meta-commentary or even variability in the stories you tell. In the UK, the charity BookTrust does a fantastic job, ensuring that every child has at least some books. Libraries, too, are an invaluable community resource. And Dolly Parton is, frankly, saintly, not just for giving us the film *9 to 5*, but for the thousands of books her Imagination Library gives away each year. Making sure that every parent has the time, the confidence, and the resources to read with their child would make the single biggest difference to child language skills when they reach school.

Books are magic,* but they're not the only way in which children hear stories. What about recorded speech, whether audio alone or with video? Unfortunately, research shows that passively listening to the TV or radio doesn't do much for language at all. While older children and adults might pick up *facts* from videos or podcasts, the brain structures that help us to *use* language develop while we *interact* with people. For example, pre-recorded language – most commonly on television – is heard by many children whose parents can't or don't speak to them in that language, but there's plenty of evidence that this doesn't result in these children learning to speak.[15] In fact the total amount of TV that children are exposed to is *negatively* correlated with their language development. While it's unlikely that Netflix is zapping the language out of your child's

* For example, I'm speaking in your head *right now*. Spooky!

brain, it *is* likely to displace other forms of play, interaction or reading – all of which have a proven positive effect on a child's linguistic development.[16]

There is one exception: some three- and four-year olds have been observed picking up specific vocabulary from educational programming that is designed to be watched by preschoolers – especially when they watch with a caregiver.[17] My daughter and I have learned a heck of a lot about marine biology from *Octonauts*, and a syllabus worth of materials science and engineering from *Do You Know?* From the biology of whale sharks to the manufacture of fishcakes, we've picked up some very specific vocabulary! But this only works when the programmes spark discussions with adults, older children and, occasionally, peers, so you need to watch along and discuss what's happening on-screen.

Into the abstract

Remember that the first year of infant-directed speech is made up of a very limited and highly repetitive vocabulary. Infant-directed speech carries on for between thirteen and twenty months. During that time, talking with children is still a somewhat repetitive narrative about the daily routines that are taking place. But after this, *child*-directed speech starts to develop. This version of caregiver chat begins to include something called 'decontextualised' language.[18] So rather than 'here are your feet, here are your socks ...', child-directed speech contains far more explanations, imagination and narrative than infant-directed speech. Examples of explanations are things like, 'Oh, we can't put them in the bus because the bus is full of blocks,' or, 'Because the lights have to be on for the remote control to work'. Imaginative play examples include, 'I'll save you from the wicked sister,' and, 'We have to have the police come and make an accident report now.'* Narrative is talk about things that happened in the past or

* The study's authors don't give the context in which this was said, but

will happen in the future and includes examples like, 'He is going to look in your nose and your throat and your ears,' and, 'Oh yes, we have popcorn in the movie theater, remember?' There's also far more give and take, with children supplying an increasingly large proportion of the talking.

Professor Meredith Rowe of the University of Maryland studied fifty pairs of parents and children, first meeting with them when the child was either eighteen, thirty or forty-two months old (roughly infants, toddlers and preschoolers). She then met them again twelve months later to see how their language was progressing. The range of the quantities of words spoken was huge, with some parents speaking just a few hundred words to their child in a ninety-minute period and others almost 10,000. But the proportion of the different *types* of language seemed to vary systematically. Parents of toddlers and preschoolers started to vary their vocabulary, and about 6 per cent of the words they used were 'rare' (defined as those that a Year 4 schoolchild wouldn't be expected to know). And the characteristics of child-directed speech seem to change most dramatically in the third year. Professor Rowe spotted distinct differences between the toddler and preschoolers cohort when it came to decontextualised speech: preschoolers heard far more explanations and narratives than did toddlers. Play has become more complex too by the preschool age, with more role playing. The abstractive power of language and the imaginative activity of games go hand in hand and strengthen one another.

Is it the quantity or the variety of child-directed speech that matters the most? That depends on a child's age. Children who started in the eighteen-month-old cohort gained more vocabulary if their parents spoke more words, regardless of the type of words used. But those children who had reached thirty or forty-two months were far less sensitive to the *quantity* of their parents' speech: perhaps because by this point they'd started to produce

---

I'm assuming that two toy cars may well have been involved in an RTA (rambunctious toddler accident).

more of the language in the conversations themselves. Parents' levels of input tended to drop between the toddler and preschool groups, suggesting that conversation has become more of a back-and-forth affair between kids and their previously monologuing parents. But the *type* of language makes a big difference by the age of three or four. A wider parental vocabulary led to faster learning in the toddler group, while more decontextualised speech – especially in the form of explanations and narrative – predicted more gains in the preschoolers.

As we've seen, decontextualised language and imaginative play go hand in hand. Not just because imaginative play involves made-up creatures and faraway lands. As we've already seen, role-play creates opportunities to try out familiar social settings, or to share memories and explanations. These are abstract without being fantastical, and they seem to be an essential part of the development of a child's social brain as well as their language. In WEIRD settings, fathers and mothers alike tend to get involved in their child's play universe, and the more they do so, the faster the child's language and social skills develop.[19]

In fact, close readings of this sort of socio-dramatic role-play shows that kids already understand a surprising amount about authority and power dynamics before they leave nursery. In an adorable set of studies reviewed by Professor Susan Ervin-Tripp, it's apparent that preschoolers have internalised the typical speech patterns of the two types of professionals that they are most likely to have met.[20] While they typically don't use the 'I put it to you ...' of the lawyer or the sharp inhale that means 'this'll cost you' of the electrician, they are keen users of the 'well ...' and 'let's see ...' that are typical of the doctor's visit, and the 'okay' and 'now then' of their nursery teachers.

When play-acting, children take status markers depending on whether they're playing the doctor or the patient, the teacher or the child, and they also mimic not only the physical characteristics of these roles (like deep voices or pointing and gesturing) but the 'discourse markers'.

All children learn language through mimicry and play-acting. That's not just vocabulary and grammar. Language games unlock the social and cultural structures that children live in. When you play with them, you (perhaps unintentionally) shape how they'll navigate the world. Without being explicitly taught, children notice that 'well', 'okay' and 'let's see' are most common in the speech of high-status people (doctors, teachers) while lower-status people (patients, children) use 'uh' more often.

It's not just these cookie-cutter phrases that children learn. Whether French- or English-speaking, toddlers also tend to use longer and rarer words when play-acting as doctors and teachers than they do when playing the roles of patients or pupils. Examples that Professor Ervin-Tripp collected include exchanges like these, where the high status and rare words are underlined:

Child (pretending to be a doctor): 'Uh <u>well</u> i think you have a <u>hernia</u>.'
Adult (pretending to be a patient): 'What's a hernia?'
Child: 'It's a <u>sickness</u> like a <u>disease</u>. [pause] <u>Well</u>, she's dead.'[21]

This isn't a purely anglophone phenomenon. When the study was repeated with francophone children, there were strikingly similar results. French discourse markers include *eh bon*, *bien*, and *mais*, in the same sort of places that anglophone people use 'well, okay, so ...' French children are equally adept as their English-speaking peers at mimicking the social tone of discourse, saying *bien* more frequently when playing higher-status roles, and *eh* when in lower-status roles.

How do we know what to tell others?

Preschool and early school-age children sometimes seem to understand far more about the world than they actually do, partly because they're such fantastic little mimics. But do they really understand what's going on when they talk, or when others listen?

It was long believed that we needed a sophisticated theory of mind in order to have meaningful conversations with each other. Understanding how much someone else knows or what they might already think are really important when it comes to minimising miscommunication. However, more recent research suggests that a fully fledged theory of mind is *not* necessary. Even preschoolers are surprisingly adept at identifying what kinds of things go without saying. In an experiment that involved 74 three-year-olds and 74 five-year-olds, experimenters selected age- and sex-matched pairs of children who already knew one another.[22] The experimenters then told the children about fictitious animals called 'selks'. Selks are animals that drink purple soda, eat rocks and sleep in water. One-third of the pairs were told this information together. For another third of the pairs, each child was told the information independently. And for the final third of the pairs, only one child was taught about the selks.

The children then had to choose what to give to the selks: a banana or a rock, a carton of juice or a bottle of purple soda, a pond or a sandpit. Where the children had been taught about the selks together, they simply got on with the task without giving each other much in the way of explanations or justification – they knew and took for granted their 'common ground' about the preferences of selks. Where they were taught separately, or when only one of the children had learned about the selks, they were much more likely to talk to one another about *why* the selks needed the rock/soda/pond or didn't need the banana/juice/sandpit with phrases like 'the selks eat rocks' or 'these animals sleep in the water'.

You might be familiar with this phenomenon of toddler-splaining: 'Mummy, we need to clean our teeth so they don't stay dirty,' or, 'Daddy, those cups can't go in the washing machine because they'll break.' It can either be adorable or frustrating depending on your level of patience. But for preschoolers at least, it's very difficult to imagine others going through a process of learning something unless you learned it together. There are so many discoveries that you and your child can share while taking a walk, playing games, visiting a library or sharing a book. Making these discoveries together not only builds their language and their knowledge of the world, it also strengthens your relationship. Because language underpins everything.

What language allows us to learn

As we've already seen, the degree of linguistic confidence that a child has by the time they enter reception class is a strong predictor of how large their vocabulary will be at the age of thirteen. The most important determining factor seems to be how good we are as caregivers at conversing with our children. But don't reach for the flash cards. Linguistic competence is not just a measure of the number of words they internalise, it's how those words help support their ability to think abstractly.

One of the earliest tests of abstract thinking involves letting children feel objects that are hidden inside boxes or bags. They then see some of the same objects. If they can correctly match objects that they felt but didn't see with identical examples that they can see but not feel, we know that they have 'abstracted' something about these objects. A fluffy object feels fluffy to touch and looks fluffy to sight: at an early age you connect these two different senses and give them a third, abstract label.

Being able to use language to apply abstract labels to senses data seems to have a mutually reinforcing effect on abstract thinking. Professor Susan Rose of the Albert Einstein College of Medicine and her colleagues studied 148 children. Each child was asked to feel unusual objects in a bag and then select the picture that most closely matched that object. Her study followed children from the age of three to thirteen and she found that those toddlers who were better at matching an object that they'd felt (but not seen) with one they'd seen (but not felt) turned out to be linguistically stronger than their peers ten years later. And across the two groups, those who did best at the task also did best with language.

Is it the ability to name an object that helps with recognition across the senses? Or is there something about being able to integrate different kinds of data that gives children an advantage in language? Higher performance might just mean that a child's brain is better able to make connections in general, and that their ability to match words to objects, actions or qualities in the world is just that little bit better, meaning that they can pick up vocabulary faster. Or it might be that knowing more words, particularly more adjectives, helped the children do better in the cross-modal task. Being able to verbalise – even in your head – that something is rough or smooth, bendy or straight, spiky or round, certainly helps with this task.

Other studies suggest that the ability to use 'describing words' helps with practical tasks. For example, children who are better at using prepositions also have better spatial awareness. Professor Hilary Miller and her colleagues at the University of Wisconsin-Madison recruited forty-one (predominantly white, middle-class) four-year-olds to see whether children's use of 'spatial words' (like the prepositions 'under', 'over', 'next to', and so on) as well as movement verbs like 'rotate' or 'mirror' were correlated with an ability to think spatially.[23]

The children who had been more comfortable using the spatial vocabulary were also the ones most likely to do well on the spatial reasoning tasks. Researchers had long hypothesised that spatial vocabulary might help with spatial cognition because it gives people the ability to describe objects spatially to themselves (an ability known as encoding) and the performance of these children in the experiment supports that hypothesis. What's more, *teaching* children spatial words makes them better at spatial tasks.

Language allows us to reason about all kinds of abstract things like temporal order, causality, relatedness and consequences; a set of concepts familiar to anyone who has ever read a story that starts with 'once upon a time' and ends with 'and they all lived happily ever after'. We can eavesdrop on the development of these abstract concepts by listening to children when they tell their own, made-up stories. From a very young age, the progression of children's storytelling gives us a window into the development of their understanding of causality. Most three-year-olds are emerging storytellers. For example, my daughter is at that adorable age where she'll use every ounce of her not-inconsiderable guile to make sure that she gets to stay up as late as possible. If I refuse to tell her yet another story, this no longer results in tantrums. Oh no. Now they result in *her* telling *me* a story. They are delightful, inventive, and as convoluted as she can make them, for maximum sleep-delay. And somewhat typically for a preschooler, they don't necessarily make a lot of sense.

In what is now quite an old study, play specialist Professor Brian Sutton-Smith and developmental psychologist Gilbert Botvin collected many hours of children's made-up stories. They found several differences between the types of stories told by three-year-olds, six-year-olds, and nine-year-olds.

A typical three-year-old's story, collected in 1977 (the year that I turned three and was probably inventing similar literary gems) went: 'A little duck went swimming. Then the crab came. A lobster came. And a popsicle was playing by itself.' There are characters, and they seem to be related (at least until the popsicle arrives) but there's no narrative flow: the events just happen, one after another.

By the time children turn six, they make up stories that actually have some element of plot. For example, this story hangs together pretty well:

Once there was a little girl. She went walking in the woods and soon it was dark. It was so dark that she couldn't find her way back home. She cried and cried. An owl heard her and asked if she was lost. She said yes. The owl said he would help her find her way home. He flew up in the air and looked around. After finding out which way to go he said, 'Okay, follow me.' Then he led the girl out of the woods and showed her the way home. When she got back home she was so happy. She gave the friendly owl a kiss and thanked him and told her parents she would never go walking in the woods again by herself. The end.

But even at age six, stories tend to have very few characters.

What's more, according to professors Sutton-Smith and Botvin, this little girl's narrative was unusual for a six-year-old's – at least in 1977 – because she talks about the main character's *feelings*. Those sorts of observations were more likely to show up in the narratives of the nine-year-olds. As were Batman, Spider Man and Wonder Woman.[24]

This study hasn't been replicated in the last four decades, but storytelling is surprisingly stable across generations (for example, fairy tales mutate, but relatively slowly). Despite changes in children's literature, which is slowly starting to focus on subjects other than middle-class kids and their dog having smashing adventures,* more recent studies suggest that this pattern of increasing sophistication in children's *own* storytelling has held pretty stable.[25] While the characters may change from generation to generation, the pattern of complexity in the length and coherence of stories, and the detail included, rises as children become more sophisticated in their interactions in the world.

Throughout childhood and adolescence, the development of thought and language seem to go hand in hand. An increase in sophistication in one leads to an increase in sophistication in the other. Thinking about things more analytically, or more abstractly, allows for mental leaps that go beyond the immediate and concrete. Those debates with your tween or teen about takeaway for dinner, the benefits of using the car versus walking, how late they can stay out, whether they can watch a particular film – the more you engage with them and get them to make their case, the faster their linguistic skills will grow. It's not a *row* – it's a healthy apprenticeship in the cut and thrust of reasoning and rhetoric. I do hope that reframing is *loads* of help the next time you spend an hour debating the impact of the trip to Grandma's house on the

* *Swallows and Amazons* is, however, the best children's book ever written. This is a hill on which I will die. Who *doesn't* want the kind of benignly neglectful parent who lets you go boating with the telegram 'BETTER DROWNED THAN DUFFERS IF NOT DUFFERS WON'T DROWN'.

polar ice caps. Just remember that the urge to yell, 'Because I SAID so! Now GET IN THE CAR!' is a sign of your child's burgeoning linguistic prowess.

Better?

Didn't think so.

Communication, communication, communication

Arguments aside, enjoy the flourishing of your child's communication prowess throughout their development. While the gains might not be as dramatic as they were in those first few years, language and communication skills are still developing well into their teens. Professor Marilyn Nippold of the University of Oregon reviewed the way that adolescent language changes between the ages of ten and fifteen. While conversations with friends increase dramatically in frequency and duration through this time, there's no evidence that these conversations displace ones that young people have with their parents.

At this time, adolescents do start to prefer to discuss their worries, and their embarrassments, with friends rather than parents. This is probably a significant part of why parents sometimes feel that they 'don't know' their teenagers any more. But when it comes to major life choices (deciding whether to abandon a course of study, for example) teenagers still say that their parents' advice has the most weight. It may not look like it, but your teenager is still paying very close attention to you.

Patterns of speech also start to change – as children go from ten to fifteen years old they're more likely to be able to sustain a topic of conversation, with fewer abrupt subject changes in recorded conversation. Children pick up rarer words, or start to use more complex constructions. They get more confident in the use of idiom, analogy and metaphor, and they get better at the social parts of language: learning to have proper, back-and-forth conversations with their peers and parents alike.[26] They're also more likely to start adding those phatic 'I'm listening' phrases like

'Really?' 'I know what you mean!' and to interject with questions to keep a conversation going. In short, they start to converse more like adults.

Part of this is mere socialisation – late adolescents start to spend more time around adults, and adults have largely dropped any effort towards child-directed speech at this point – but it's also a sign of increased executive function: the ability to focus for longer periods, and to share someone else's perspective. Throughout adolescence, children and young adults also start to use more complex sentence structures, join together multiple ideas, and talk about things figuratively. Your conversation still matters, as your child starts to decide who they are in the world. So keep talking, keep *listening*, and give them as much respect and as clear an explanation as you'd like in return. Your habits will rub off on them, for better or for worse.

7

Unicorn-Robot-Firefighter-Princesses: Why Stories and Play Are the Best Thing You Can Share with Kids

To really examine how brains develop you have to leave the world of fMRI scanners and carefully designed stimuli and dive into the messy, unconstrained world that kids actually inhabit. What might appear to be the most chaotic part of childhood, the process of make-believe play, is what really allows children to develop a sense of order about the world. It's also the first opportunity to witness your child's developing curiosity and creativity.

As they begin to be able to move under their own steam, around the end of their first year, babies will pick up things and explore their possibilities: something that educational psychologist Anita Hughes calls the 'what else can I do with it?' stage of exploration. Then, just before the beginning of their third year, Hughes notes a change in the way children play again. What she terms the 'what can this become?' stage is the next creative leap for most children. A drum becomes a hat, a cup becomes a drum.[1] This 'silly' play, a trait we share with several other great apes, is what allows us to see things not just in terms of their qualities but also their *possibilities*. The playful sense of exploration is what has turned rocks into tools, strings and skins into instruments, marks into pictures, pictures into words, words into abstract ideas. Forget mysterious black obelisks: play is what uplifted us as a species and allowed us to develop culture.

Play is naturally educational, and doesn't need to be engineered by adults. Nevertheless playing-to-learn has become big business even though research shows that complicated, highly designed toys aren't any better at helping children to learn than simple objects like a bucket of sand, or a bowl of water and some cups. That's because the 'what can this become' stage is our first training in creativity, so having objects around that let children invent their own ways of using them is at least as crucial – possibly more so – than having toys and games with rigid rules and detailed directions for their use.[2]

That said, 'educational toys' have a long history: the orator Quintilian, in the first century of the common era, seems to have invented the phonics flash card: 'I quite approve of [giving children] ivory letters to play with, as I do of anything else that may be discovered to delight the very young, the sight, handling and naming of which is a pleasure.'[3] But more straightforward 'playthings' have been around much longer still. For as long as we've been documenting the lives of children we see drawings, sculptures and carvings of them at play. In Egyptian sarcophagi and Roman gravesites, children are buried alongside small dolls made of lead, rattles made of pipeclay, and balls made of linen and reeds.[4]

One of the biggest challenges for archaeologists and historians is that children don't just play with toys. They'll make up games and stories, and they'll play with whatever is to hand. Even in this current era when the toy market in the UK alone is worth in excess of £3 billion per year, children still enjoy games like 'pushing my baby sister around in the laundry basket', gaining a valuable understanding of friction, momentum and rudimentary first aid.

One modern development, online play, has caused a fair amount of concern. Some commentators have warned that the internet has been destroying children's health and well-being for the last two decades. But as millions of people who have grown up with the internet now demonstrate, being online can also be a useful part of social development. Among adolescents (and many adults) online chatting takes on an element of role-play, with make-believe, fun and creativity making up a large part of what teens do online.[5] Far from being an entirely new way of relating, a chat laden with poop emojis is very similar to the kind of lunch-break hanging out or note-passing silliness of my own school days.[6]

But online play is not enough on its own. There are important physical elements of play that develop dexterity, strength and social skills. Whether that's learning the fine motor skills obtained by making models out of dough, or the interpersonal skills of playful conflict games like tag or 'everybody's it'. Almost every mammal species plays some form of fighting or chasing game, and rough-and-tumble play seems to be a necessary part of developing every mammal's adult brain. In recent years, research has shown that trying to create risk- and conflict-free environments for children can backfire, leaving them short on essential social skills from coordination to confidence.[7] As a parent it can be terrifying (or hilarious, depending on your disposition) watching your child coming down a slide face first, or seeing a child's sibling or friend doing something that is either a vigorous hug or a gentle throttle. But we need that kind of limit-pushing, daring play early on in our lives – and sometimes during adulthood, to be honest – in order to blow off steam, test our limits and develop our skills.

What is play?

In the UK at least, early years education is driven by the idea that play is the way for children to learn.[8] But when it comes to checking what the research says, we quickly run into a problem. Not since I wrote a book about the science of swearing have I had such difficulty in working out what various different scientists *mean* when they study a phenomenon. As with swearing, play is hard to define: both are phenomena that are variable, contextual and culturally specific. And both are seen as being a bit frivolous, despite being core parts of what make us human.

For starters, we can't simply classify certain types of activity as 'play'. For example, is fishing 'play'? It might be if you're dipping for tadpoles rather than being on a trawler crew. What about play-acting caring for a 'hurt' peer versus learning to give first aid?[9] And in my own case, sometimes writing is playful and sometimes it's a complete slog.

So if it's not the *activity* that defines something as play then is it the *intention* that determines whether we're playing? Some researchers have attempted to categorise play. Common categories include social play, object play and locomotor play (roughly speaking: playing together, playing with things, and playing around).[10] But these classifications can easily overlap – I can play socially with a ball while developing my locomotor skills. Or a toddler can use a teapot to have a pretend tea party, imagining themselves to be somewhere or someone different (object play) while taking turns and negotiating with friends (social play) and practising the skills of pouring water into a cup (locomotor play). These categories don't actually help us much.

Other theorists talk about play as being either hedonic – enjoyable for its own sake – or eudaimonic – enjoyable because you're developing or using an aspect of your competence. Playing a piano piece that you know well might be hedonic, but putting in an hour's practice at the keyboard is more likely to be eudaimonic. Cooking something quick and tasty may be mainly hedonic, while a more challenging gastronomic tour de force may be eudaimonic, but again, there's plenty of overlap to muddy the definition.

Is play simply a matter of 'taking part in games'? In reality, many games are anything but 'playful'. By their nature, games require a set of rules and constraints (otherwise they aren't games, they're anarchy). They usually have some sort of scoring system, too. Far from being the light-hearted and inventive 'play' of a teddy bears' picnic, 'play*ing*' a game is usually surprisingly structured. Yet, in education, games are often offered up as a form of play, in order to try to engage kids in learning. Using maths games as a teaching tool works *because* there are rules and order. But are kids being *playful* with maths there? It's more likely that educational games aren't play so much as what Professor Amy Bruckman of Georgia Tech referred to as 'chocolate-coated broccoli'.[11]

In contrast to constrained and predictable rule-based games, the *American Journal of Play* defines play as 'multifaceted, diverse, and complex. It resists easy definition and engages many disciplines.' One play advocate, Professor David Elkind, defines play as a 'form of exercise for creative dispositions – for imagination, for curiosity, for fantasy'.[12] This is a lovely definition, but it seems to exclude the physical play that children need. Nice as it is, Elkind's definition is perhaps a bit too narrow for our requirements.

Some authors have even taken the wildly imaginative step of asking *children* what they think counts as play. In 2002, Professor Justine Howard of the University of Swansea asked 111 three- to six-year-olds to sort a set of twenty-six photographs into two piles. These were photos of the volunteer children taking part in activities at school and nursery, and Professor Howard asked them to sort the photographs into 'play' and 'not play' categories. Photographs that showed them in sandpits, with toys and outdoors were consistently categorised as play. Drawing and painting were ambiguous, with some children classing them as playful and others saying they were work. In a finding that wounds my soul, all other paper-based activities – like reading and writing – were classed as work.[13]

Can we pin down something as nebulous as play when even its main practitioners disagree on the details? Play is complex, and complex phenomena need complex definitions, and – for me at least – the most convincing description of play comes from Gordon Burghardt, professor of ecology and evolutionary biology at the University of Tennessee. He sets out five criteria that play should meet, in order to properly be considered 'playful'.[14] There are still some exceptions and borderline cases, but see if this looks like play to you:

1) **Play is behaviour that isn't immediately needed for survival** – a play fort offers no *real* defence, a drive in a toy car doesn't *really* get you anywhere. But this part of the definition also includes things like choosing to walk an extra stop

because it's a nice day and you can't face a crowded bus, or having a frivolous meal out as opposed to cooking something economical and nutritionally balanced at home. Personally, I *like* that about this definition because it makes me realise how many elements of frivolity there are in my day.

2) **Play is spontaneous, voluntary, deliberate and rewarding in and of itself** – so play isn't, in this definition, a PE lesson, or a drama lesson, or the act of walking an extra stop because your bus broke down, or buying takeaway because your oven blew up. This feels pretty cautious to me: while I wouldn't say that I personally found cross-country runs intrinsically rewarding, I know that some of my peers did. Maybe play is something that, even if it's not *voluntary*, is something that we don't need to be induced, bribed or threatened to do. By this definition, zero-sum games, where the object is to be the winner, also don't count as 'play' – the motive is to win rather than to play the game in and of itself. Knocking a football around is play; trying to score the goal that takes your school team to the finals is, perhaps, more akin to work.

3) **(Child's) play is incomplete, exaggerated or precocious** – to play at being doctors, kids don't go through six years of medical school. They also get bored and wander off halfway through bringing me the crucial biscuit that they prescribed for my ouchy toe – at least in my bitter experience. Tea parties with teddies are frequently exaggerated in our house: the pouring of endless cups of 'tea' would put anyone's nan to shame. And very young kids don't have to be induced to 'help' in the kitchen. A toddler with a broom is a beautiful and breathtaking sight to behold, rather like a volcano that's just started to smoke: the potential for ruin is ever present, but that's just what makes it so hard to look away. Sadly, as adults, this rules us out of being playful in the strictest sense. It's hard to imagine anything that I'd voluntarily do that was precocious. I mean, don't get me wrong, when it

comes to groaning when I get up from a chair, or complaining that a restaurant is too loud, I am definitely acting as if I were roughly three decades older, but I wouldn't say this was voluntary or enjoyable; I'm just coasting downhill fast.

4) **Play behaviour is repeated (lots!)** – I've lost count of the number of times that I've been a patient to my daughter's doctor. I can't tell you how many tea parties I have attended. My daughter the 'chef' is a nightly fixture of dinner time thanks to the BBC's marvellous *My World Kitchen*. Play doesn't wear thin with repetition – at least for the juvenile participant. For very young kids, repetition-with-minor-variation is the whole point. The reassuring 'script' of a tea party or a doctor's visit gives them space to be inventive while being guided by some unseen frame. Just as a blank page is the least inspiring sight for any writer, a complete lack of structure doesn't do much to prompt playfulness. A level of context that is both supportive and flexible is ideal and those half-understood rituals of adulthood make for great play scripts. Watching my daughter be 'me' on the 'phone' is hilarious: 'Yes? Mmmhmm. Okay, can I call you later? Mmmhmm. Okay later yes? Thankyoubye.' She has no *idea* what the other side sounds like, but she has 'getting out of this social interaction as fast as possible' completely *nailed*.

5) **Play happens when you're happy and relaxed** – for kids and adults alike, play isn't something that happens when you're hungry, angry, stressed or sick. Schools have recognised this, with breakfast programmes and free school meals to address the distraction of an empty belly, and mindfulness and well-being programmes to help children feel secure enough to learn through experiment and through play. Curiosity and play are – metabolically speaking – a luxury. But for our children, playing *is* their job. And making sure they have enough resources to enable them to play is our job, not just as parents, but as a society.

The benefits of play

While juveniles of any species are playing they are a) expending energy, and b) not seriously contributing to the security of the group (by hunting, guarding, parenting ...) so there must be some advantage for play to be so widely observed across multiple species.[15] According to the late Professor Patrick Bateson of the University of Cambridge, play is 'developmental scaffolding. Once this job is done, it largely falls away.'[16] Juveniles of most primate species play. Chimpanzees, bonobos, gorillas and orangutans raised in captivity will play at bathing, cooking and feeding dolls.[17] They also pretend that things are other things: Koko the gorilla would put her bottle on her head while signing 'hat', for example – the kind of thing toddlers do all the time, often with pants.

For most adults, the only time we engage in imaginative play is when we play with kids.[18] If you are a storyteller, inventor, improviser, actor or artist you may be seen as belonging to a special category of person, but these kinds of playful activities are in fact essential for our emotional and social well-being. In his book, *Play*, former Children's Laureate Michael Rosen makes the impassioned case for play at all ages. Play 'helps us live with change, to enjoy it and use it,' he writes. 'Being in the state of mind that says "I wonder what might happen if I tried this" and then not worrying or being afraid of the outcome, is a state of mind that can cope with the unexpected.'[19] This sounds like something we all need more of, whatever our age.

It's not known exactly when pretend play ends or why. It's certainly more common in early childhood, but it drops off around the tween era: perhaps because school is more demanding, perhaps because of an increase in self-consciousness, or perhaps because pretend play isn't needed any more, as theory of mind matures.[20] However, the popularity of games like Dungeons and Dragons, online role-playing games, and even fan fiction and meme generating shows that the playful creation of characters is not something that is completely abandoned at adolescence.

This drop in playfulness is a shame as play is absolutely essential as a learning tool. Simply changing the atmosphere to one that is more playful leads to faster learning and better skills. In one study of younger children, Dr Karen McInnes of the University of South Wales devised an experiment in which children were given jigsaw puzzles to solve. She used the definitions of play that had been developed by Professor Justine Howard, her co-author, in the study that asked children to classify photographs into those showing play and those showing work. From those definitions, Dr McInnes divided the thirty participants, all preschool or reception-aged kids, into two groups. One half were given the chance to 'practice' with the puzzles: they sat at a table, were told to spend their time trying to solve the puzzle, and an adult sat with them to keep them on task. In the second group, the 'play' group, the children were allowed to sit on the floor. An adult encouraged them to play with the jigsaw but didn't *tell* them to, and then the adult left the children to their own devices.[21]

At first glance the playful group looked less focused. They moved around a lot, fidgeting and shifting positions. But when the research team analysed the video recordings of the children in these eight-minute play or practice sessions, it became apparent that the supervised children were also distracted. They spent more time talking about things other than the puzzle than the playing participants did. They also tended to make repetitive but unhelpful moves like picking up and putting down the same piece over and over. In contrast, in the play condition, children mostly talked about the puzzles, and their reasoning about the pieces. The playful children tried far more systematic problem-solving strategies than did those children who were assigned to the more formal condition. The children in the practice condition were persistent, but they persisted with incorrect moves as often as they did with correct ones. The children in the play condition were far more likely to quickly abandon trying to fit a wrong piece, and to move on to another piece. Being allowed to be playful also seemed to give them licence to be more forgiving of their own mistakes, to recognise them and move on.

But did these behavioural differences have a noticeable effect on the children's speed when it came to testing their puzzle-solving skills? Those in the formal practice condition shaved fifteen seconds off their pre-practice time, while those who had *played* with the puzzles were now forty seconds faster. One week later, when the team tested the children again, the practice condition children solved their puzzles twenty-eight seconds faster than they had the first time, while the play group managed to reduce their time by one minute and thirteen seconds. So while play might look unfocused and unstructured, and formal practice might look neat and planned, those appearances belie the outcomes.

In many cultures around the world, parents don't 'play' with their kids – or at least they don't indulge in *imaginative* play.[22] But in every culture that has been studied, children are often given something to play with and then left to their own devices. This playful period of copying and experimenting is an apprenticeship in useful, practical skills they will need as adults. In the Amazon, for example, some children are allowed to play with (extremely sharp) knives. Learning not to cut themselves is considered an important part of their apprenticeship, and Pirahã parents have no problem letting their children learn this by trial and (occasionally painful) error.[23]

Playing with your parent's tools may be less dangerous in most other cultures but children's play diets everywhere involve some elements of behaving like grown-ups. In our own home, that currently manifests as a fascination for doing the washing-up and the sweeping (score!); in other cultures, children play at food preparation, hunting or farming. Professor Artin Göncü and Professor Suzanne Gaskins observed four-year-old Yucatec children spending much of their days 'working' next to their mothers. These children are playing, in that they are 'happy in mastering the act of tortilla making through symbolic re-enactment of that script', where 'symbolic re-enactment of that script' is academic for 'pretending to make a tortilla'.[24]

But Göncü and Gaskins noticed that children from more

industrialised communities play different sorts of games: WEIRD kids – especially those in nursery settings – 'work through issues about separation from [their] parents in symbolic play in the classroom'. I know that my daughter regularly plays at 'going to work' while she sends me to 'nursery', and, as I write this section in the great lockdown on 2020, she's playing a lot of 'we can't go shopping because of the coronavirus' games. She doesn't *seem* worried by this, but she does seem to be trying to make *sense* of the behaviour of the adults around her. This natural experiment is fascinating (and exhausting) as we watch the children we care for negotiate a huge social change. I am thankful – and slightly envious – of how well they make these adjustments by play-acting.

As well as the WEIRD games that children play at nursery, WEIRD parents are more likely to give their kids broken laptops or defunct mobile phones than to give them old farming implements or tortilla presses. But in WEIRD societies, kids are less likely to need to learn to gut a fish and more likely to have to say, 'I'll have that on your desk by Friday.' As a result, WEIRD parents also take a much more active part in role play with children.[25] This parental play is – just like the tortilla making – an apprenticeship in life skills: here's how you visit the doctor, here's how you speak on the phone, here's how you host your friends. Even fantastical settings – superheroes, robots, princesses and dragons – allow parents to pass on their beliefs about 'correct' values: collectivism or individualism, bravery or caution, generosity or individual ambition.

Role play like this also gives children the language they need to talk about feelings, or to negotiate over resources. In a review of several decades of play research, Professor Deena Skolnick Weisberg at the University of Pennsylvania identified several ways in which play helps with language.[26] First, children learn best when they are allowed to exert some control and follow lines of investigation that interest them. In play, children are usually allowed to take that lead even when there are adults involved.

Second, the *kinds* of language that are used in 'socio-dramatic' play – role-playing everyday social interactions – tend to be more complex and require much more sophisticated turn taking and listening than most other types of language that children use. For example, children negotiate roles ('I'll be the shopkeeper and you be the lady'; 'My cat is poorly; will you be the vet?') while role-playing. The language used in play also has lots of nice abstract language, referring to imaginary cats, cafés or cornflakes. In addition, children talk more about things they need or want, and give more explanations, during these games than they do in other types of conversation.[27]

This kind of role play also seems to have an essential role in socialising children. Children who play games with 'emotional content' ('You're sad, I'll look after you'; 'You're scared, I'll comfort you') are more popular with their peers than those who don't.[28] Children who spend the most time in pretend play, particularly where they get the chance to play-act and talk about emotional states, are the fastest to develop empathy, to behave sympathetically, and to be able to cope with their own big feelings.[29]

For the first few years, WEIRD families spend a lot more time in parent–child play than other cultures. But siblings and peers quickly take over from parents as the playmates of choice for our children. By the age of three or four, most WEIRD kids have become like their non-WEIRD contemporaries in that they will choose to play with peers over parents. By the time your child is ready for school, a whole load of their language, values and ideas will come from play with other children, so enjoy the invitations to the tea parties, or the demands that you heal teddy's hurt-ed foot, while you can. This is the closest you're ever likely to get. Your child will soon have playmates of their own.

Plays well with others

In the middle of lockdown, I once again became one of my daughter's preferred playmates. In our blended family, she has a slightly older 'sister' with whom she can play half the time. But when she's the only child at home I am roped into games that can become very confusing. 'Pretend you're the mummy and I'm your child', she'll say, offering me the same play gambit that she'd otherwise offer her peers. She needs social play, even when that play is essentially the same as day-to-day life. As we saw with the jigsaw experiment, context counts.

Dr Karen McInnes's' jigsaw study also demonstrated that kids get plenty of benefit from playing alone. But having a playmate exercises some very different parts of the brain. At some point in human development, playing with others begins to generate more activity in parts of the brain that are involved in planning and decision making, as well as those involved in empathy and theory of mind.

One of the most compelling pieces of evidence for this conclusion comes from an experiment led by Professor Jean Decety from the University of Washington, Seattle. A dozen twenty-somethings (six women and six men) played a simple computer game while lying in an fMRI scanner. The game had to be simple because a) you can't use anything more complex than a set of fingertip controls while lying in a tube about the width of an industrial washing machine, and b) you have to try to play the game while bombarded with a sound not unlike said industrial washing machine on a fast spin cycle, and laden with bricks.

The game was something like a hybrid of Tetris and Connect Four. The volunteers had to recreate a simple pattern they'd been shown on-screen by shifting yellow disks that fell from the top of the display. They did this by using their fingers to press buttons that would move the disk to the left or right. Disks would appear at the top of the screen every two seconds, alternating between yellow and blue.

There were three kinds of matches played by each volunteer. In the 'playing alone' trials, the blue disks fell at random – nobody controlled where they would end up and it was just chance whether or not the blue disk would help (by providing support for) or hinder (by blocking) the player's ability to place the yellow disks. In the 'competition' trials, one of the experimenters would join in the game from the fMRI control room. They would control the blue disks and try to block the player in the scanner from completing their pattern. In the 'cooperation' trials, the experimenter would use their blue disks to help the person in the scanner make their pattern.

The cognitive challenge of each game is more or less the same, no matter whether the blue disks fell at random or whether they were piloted by the experimenter. As a result, the researchers could compare the activity in the solo trials with the activity in the trials with an opponent or collaborator. Any activity that showed up in all three types of trial is due to the baseline demands of moving pieces around by pressing buttons while lying in a loudly banging tunnel. Subtracting the metabolic activity in the solo trials from brain activity in the other trials allowed the researchers to deduce what additional neural activity appears when we play with (or against) someone.[30]

It turns out that it doesn't matter if the human player was trying to help or hinder the volunteer: in both conditions, the same parts of the brain were hoovering up oxygen – a clear sign of neuronal firing. When compared with the solo trials, one of the busiest regions in all the volunteers' brains was the orbitofrontal cortex. Previous research suggests that this part of the brain is important when it comes to linking our emotional states with our understanding of risk and reward: people who have suffered damage to this region of the brain don't tend to experience sadness, anger, frustration or fear when they lose in a gambling task, for example.[31] In the healthy volunteers in Professor Decety's experiment, the orbitofrontal cortex showed far greater activation when they played against another human, which suggests that the stakes feel higher in social play than they do in solitary games, even if the actual game is exactly the same.

Furthermore, the volunteers in Professor Decety's experiment showed far greater activation in the anterior insula while playing socially. This part of the brain is involved when we're experiencing empathy, or undertaking a type of thought called metacognition: thinking about thinking. Playing with others gives a workout to the part of the brain that tries to model another person's thoughts and feelings. When we play alone, there's no need to think of others at all.

Keep in mind that at no point did the opponent appear on the screen: the volunteers were simply *told* that someone was playing against them. So, in rather hopeful news, playing against someone remotely is enough interaction to exercise our social cognition. Online games, be they chess, *Fortnite* or *Animal Crossing*, are likely to keep at least some of our interpersonal skills sharp.

There's little data on when we begin using these social brain structures to play with others, but once we need playmates, we really do start to *need* them.[32] In a study from the early 2000s, adults were invited to play a game of 'cyber ball' – an online game of virtual 'throw-and-catch' that involved 'throwing' by selecting someone's name from a list. In one condition, the volunteers weren't able to play because the game 'crashed' and in another condition they weren't able to play because nobody ever threw the 'ball' to them. Professor Naomi Eisenberger and her team from UCLA and Macquarie University analysed fMRI scans that were taken when the participants were included in the game and compared them to scans taken when the same participants were excluded either deliberately or by *force majeure*. When the volunteers felt deliberately excluded, activation increased in an area of the brain called the anterior cingulate cortex: the area that also registers physical pain. Professor Eisenberger, together with another team from UCLA and the University of Oregon, repeated the test on a group of 23 twelve- to thirteen-year-olds. Again, they saw that the parts of the brain that sense pain lit up when being socially excluded, and that the greater the activity in these parts of the brain, the more distressed the adolescents felt at being left out.[33] Being excluded literally hurts.

That doesn't mean that your child is in danger if they experience *some* solitude. Playing alone is a healthy and necessary part of a child's play diet. 'Reticent' behaviour – watching others playing without joining in, is something that all children do from time to time. As long as your child isn't in the position of being so anxious that they *never* want to play with others then don't worry about the occasional bit of wallflowering.[34] And as with eating, pressure can be counterproductive. If your child seems anxious about making new friends, don't push them into 'getting involved'. There are even social benefits to just being in the same physical space as other children without necessarily interacting. For young children especially, 'parallel play' – playing in a similar way, alongside other children – is a low-stakes, non-threatening way of making friends.[35]

As children grow up, their need for play doesn't diminish, though they may have fewer opportunities for playfulness because of school pressures or increased family responsibilities. It's probably worth making time for play for your adolescent, though. A small study in the US found that those children who were involved in sports or who maintained hobbies in early adolescence reported a mild effect on school results and behaviour from those two activities.[36] And don't forget that adolescents (and adults) can also benefit from imaginative play.

Imaginative play in adolescents is barely studied, perhaps because there's a strong social pressure for most adolescents to wean themselves off what seems like such a 'childish' pursuit. Two playful activities common among adolescents, fan fiction and role-play gaming, are sometimes viewed with derision. (I know that tabletop gaming added to my extreme lack of cool and I will disclose my fan fiction *nom de plume* only under extreme duress or significant inebriation.) But these playful, fantastical worlds are full of opportunities for social and imaginative play, giving teenagers – and many adults – a much-needed outlet.

Fan fiction writers are usually pseudonymous, not least because many of them are young women writing pretty vivid smut. But in my experience, long-lasting and authentic friendships are made through writing fan fiction, as writers respond to each other's imaginative leaps and build further with their own. Fan fiction is – at its best – a collaborative sandpit.

Professor Angela Thomas of the University of Sydney studied one 400-strong online community called Middle Earth Insanity, which was founded and administered by two adolescent girls 'Tiana' and 'Jandalf'. Their community created stories, songs, poems and other forms of art inspired by the fantasy genre; the tales of Middle Earth and *Star Wars** in particular. People develop strong attachments to their 'beta readers' – those who are persuaded, or volunteer, to read and suggest ways of improving a draft, and to offer encouragement. The pairings in these trust-based relationships often go on to write 'joint fic' or 'pair fic', which emerges as online, asynchronous role play, as each participant takes on part of the story.[37]

Professor Thomas points out that the (predominantly) teenage girls in the Middle Earth Insanity community end up improving their writing skills no end. But they also develop aspects of their emerging personalities. Writing fan fiction allows the participants to try out new types of identity, often role playing or writing 'gender-swapped' versions of male characters from Sherlock Holmes to Luke Skywalker. Fan-created versions of characters like 'Femlock' (female Sherlock) allow adolescent girls to create a world where they can incorporate all the atavistic traits of 'boy heroes' into female characters. And successful creations are rewarded by the community through comments, reviews and fan art.

There is an irrepressible enthusiasm in most fanfic communities, which extends to raising up other authors, nurturing newbies and celebrating one another. And yet, since its inception in the 1970s, through photocopied fanzines and fringe meetings at conventions, this kind of largely adolescent, largely female play is rarely studied and rarely acknowledged, and is seen as only marginally less weird

* *Star Wars* is *not* sci-fi, even though it happens in a Galaxy Far Far Away. Even George Lucas calls *Star Wars* a 'fairy tale' – it has a princess and a farm boy, for Yoda's sake!

than another popular form of role playing storytelling: Dungeons and Dragons.

If fan fiction is predominantly female authored, Dungeons and Dragons is predominantly (though not exclusively) a place for teenage boys and young men to engage in imaginative play. In the late 1980s there was a D&D-related moral panic, in which the game was blamed for a rash of suicides and murders. This panic sparked a wave of research, which showed that D&D players are a surprisingly mixed (and mainly well-balanced) bunch.

Professor Armando Simon of the Social Sciences Division of Edison Community College in Florida studied eighty-six players of D&D, aged between fifteen and thirty-five. He found no correlation at all between the amount of time spent playing D&D and these participants' emotional stability: D&D players were no more or less fucked-up than the rest of the population.[38]

In fact, as with fanfic, D&D (and other role-playing games) can have a positive impact on the well-being of adolescents.[39] Professor Aubrie Adams of the University of California, Santa Barbara, found that participants in an online D&D community were likely to offer help and assistance, behave democratically, send lots of 'friendship maintenance' messages, and were concerned with ethical themes of fairness and justice (albeit of the largely retributive flavour of justice that is possible when you have a fire-belching staff).

In the last three decades, the internet has made it possible for adolescents to engage in imaginative play in ways that their parents never could. As yet, there's not a great deal of research into what the mass writing of Holmes/Watson fic or the mass participation in *Minecraft* is doing to shape our children's cultural and social development, but the signs look promising. Adolescents (and adults) who indulge in fantasy and imagination seem to be well -adjusted, happy, thoughtful people. Even if they are warlocks on the weekend.

Play fights

What do you do when your little angel suddenly starts fighting with their friends, getting involved in social media scraps or playground punch-ups? It's important to find out what's going on: bullying is harmful both to the bully and the bullied. Sitting down and finding out *why* the fighting is taking place is an important first step in helping your children find another way to resolve their conflicts.

But sometimes rough-and-tumble fighting, or aggressive-looking games, are actually harmless. As long as they're fun for *everyone* involved, they seem to be an essential part of growing up. Immature mammals across the entire animal kingdom fight or play hunt when they're little. And among those species that have been studied – most often marmosets, because they are aggressive without being dangerous, and they're small enough to keep in a lab – the pups that play fight the most go on to be the best at hunting when they mature, but don't show any signs of becoming bullies. This suggests that the play fighting and play hunting help those skills to develop.[40]

Some degree of *playful* aggression is a normal part of an immature brain's development. Rats that are never allowed to play fight never learn how to identify and defend themselves against real aggression. Either they demonstrate a kind of ratty paranoia, seeing aggression everywhere, or they fail to notice the warning signs of aggression in other rats and are entirely defenceless when attacked.[41]

The amount of aggressive play in (non-human) offspring is actually pretty startling; 80 per cent of a rat's playtime, for example, is spent 'fighting' on average.[42] Throughout the animal kingdom, including in our own little region, play fighting peaks around the middle of immaturity and drops off as animals 'settle down' into their position in the group, which suggests that these juvenile fights help to establish the eventual social pecking order of that generation.[43] As the frontal lobe matures, the amount of time spent play fighting tends to reduce.[44] But it seems to be the case that play fighting *causes* the frontal lobe to develop, rather than that the development of the frontal lobe reduces play fighting. We don't so much grow *out* of play fighting as we grow through it.

Our kids aren't rat pups or baby marmosets, though. Does play fighting matter in a society in which dominance isn't established by hunting or fighting, but by other, varied measures like wealth, education, the car you drive, the clothes you wear and so on? Perhaps not, but there certainly doesn't seem to be anything unusual about kids taking the time to play fight: according to Professor Emeritus Fergus P. Hughes of the University of Wisconsin-Green Bay, some pretend aggression in imaginative play is perfectly normal – as long as that aggression is only one of the types of social behaviour your child plays at. Most children spend as much time pretending to be a teacher or a doctor as they spend pretending to be a vampire, soldier or monster.

You can tell whether a child is play fighting because, once you get past the apparent aggression, you can see signs of joyfulness – many primates have a 'play face' that they display when play fighting.[45] Play fighting is gentler than the real thing: kids, kits, cubs and pups all pull their literal and metaphorical punches in play fights. As a result, participants rarely get hurt, and when accidental injuries do happen, there are usually apologies (from humans) or displays of grooming behaviour (in other mammals) to restore trust and soothe hurt feelings.

Children (and other juvenile animals) are good at judging how much fight is too much fight. Most well-adjusted animals will limit their strength when put with opponents that are younger or smaller than themselves.[46] In humans, verbal teasing also tends to be limited to the degree of 'toughness' we think that someone can comfortably take (and dish out).[47]

As well as being more gentle than real violence, play fighting seems carefully calibrated to be *reciprocal*. The players will swap between being the 'goodie' and the 'baddie' and back again multiple times.[48] Children who are skilled at playful conflict also have an advantage when it comes to the skills needed for effective communication, cooperation, and the understanding of others' intentions.[49]

Of course, not all aggression is playful. According to Professor Hughes, you can tell the difference between play fighting and 'instrumental' aggression. Instrumental aggression is when someone hits, scratches, bites or yells to get something that they want. The best way of dealing with this in your children is to acknowledge their feelings, but to explain other, better ways of asking for a turn, or of waiting or finding something else to play with.[50]

Human society is far more complex than the relationships between lab-reared marmosets or rats. As adults we're expected to achieve our goals by more than physical dominance. Our children are adept at mirroring the techniques that we use as adults, be that negotiation, persuasion, leadership or inspiration. If you want your children to thrive, try to model the influencing skills you want them to acquire, whether that's assertiveness, confidence, compassion or charisma.

Technology panic

Even when we know that it's all pretend, we're often uncomfortable when we see children acting aggressively. In particular, the last three decades have seen multiple waves of panic about the impact of video games on children's emerging psyches. But with the first generation of gamers now old enough to have become parents themselves, is there really any cause for concern?

Since the mid-1990s there have been dire prognostications about the social skills and physical and mental well-being of 'digital natives'. In 1997, developmental psychologist Frank Putnam warned: 'I predict that in ten years we will be faced with a group of socially withdrawn teenagers who are "addicted" to living in their virtual worlds.'[51] But does this make any greater sense than panicking about the kids of the sixties becoming addicted to pop music (the first UK singles chart was compiled in the 1950s) or Victorian children getting hooked on soccer (the Football Association was founded a mere 160 years ago)? In fact there was a genuine fear that there would be a spate of youths 'addicted' to reading during the mid-eighteenth century, in the wake of the appearance of new forms of 'amusing' books for children.

Does this latest set of technologies really stifle playfulness, or is this a case of 'we didn't have that when I was young'-itis? The US think tank, Alliance for Childhood, certainly considers computers to be harmful. They published a white paper that concluded that any form of digital technology is developmentally inappropriate for children and is incompatible with healthy childhoods. 'Computers are perhaps the most acute symptom of the rush to end childhood. The national drive to computerize schools, from kindergarten on up, emphasizes only one of many human capacities, one that naturally develops quite late – analytic, abstract thinking – and aims to jump start it prematurely,' the report reads.[52]

But the authors of this report have conflated the skills needed to *develop* software – abstract, analytic thinking – with the skills you can practise while *using* software. Just like paint and paper, a recorder or drum, a puppet or a book, computers open up ways of being creative and playful for children and adults alike.

Thankfully, there's plenty of recent research that looks at the possibilities that online experiences afford (and that even-handedly assess the real challenges that exist, too – from a potential loss of privacy to digital inequality). According to Professor Jeffrey Goldstein of Utrecht University, 'The stereotype of the typical gamer as an inactive, overweight, socially isolated adolescent is false on all counts.' A preponderance of studies show that most gamers play in moderation (one to two hours a day, compared to an average watching time, in the general population, of three to four hours of television per day). They're also slightly more likely to take part in sport, and have plenty of friends in 'real' life as well as online. Oh, and they tend to be thirty years old on average, with an age range that encompasses primary-school children to retirees.[53] What's more, adolescents who play *cooperative* video games are likely to behave generously and to report feeling closer to their friends – although competitive video games have the opposite effect.[54]

The notion that computers in and of themselves are responsible for producing a generation of obese, socially stunted, linguistically challenged outcasts has, by now, been roundly debunked. That doesn't stop the regular headlines about the dangers of 'screen time' and the imagined epidemic of unhealthy and maladjusted kids. Research shows that *parental* screen time, and its damaging effect on the amount of time we spend in conversation with our kids, is much more likely to have a lasting, harmful effect on child development. The more time you spend on your screen, the more time your child is likely to spend doing the same.[55] If you're worried about the use of devices, make sure that you're as aware of the time you yourself spend staring at a screen as you are of your kids' device dependency. There are significantly more instances of depression and defiance among children whose caregivers are distracted by their screens while parenting, while those parents who are more present tend to have happier and more cooperative kids.[56]

Around half of primary-school-age children have had some experience of playing in online virtual worlds. Professor Jackie Marsh of the University of Sheffield studied 175 children in a primary school, based in a predominantly white working-class housing estate. Among these five- to eleven-year-olds, just over half of them had spent time in child-friendly virtual worlds like Barbie Girls, Club Penguin, Neopets or Webkinz. She interviewed three small groups of children who played in these environments to find out what sorts of things they got up to. She found that, for most of them, their online lives were extensions of their offline lives: they spent time there with the same friends as during playtime at school. They hung out online with school friends in the way that people of my generation used to wait until the dot of 6 p.m. – the start of off-peak calling charges – to phone our friends, tying up our parents' landlines with gossip, jokes, plans and stories.[57] Children in these virtual environments are doing something similar, only with more friends at a time, and with greater scope for playfulness.

As well as competing in online structured games in these virtual environments, the children in Professor Marsh's study spent plenty of time in imaginative social play. In Club Penguin, for example, most of the children enjoyed dressing up as penguin pirates or penguin mermaids. They liked weaving intricate stories, sometimes with the help of game designers who would set up virtual events and scavenger hunts in the environment. But just as often the children would make up their own 'games'.

Professor Marsh reports one of the seven-year-olds in the study acting out the sort of grown-up behaviours he'd seen at home: 'Me and my friends and my cousins and strangers who come to my party, we all went to the disco room and then when we were all drunk we went back to my house and had a little lay down.' Of course they were no more 'drunk' than my daughter is a princess or a 'swording knight who murders bad dragons'. 'Brendon' and his friends were role playing together, acting out the risky and dramatic ideas they have of what it's like to be a grown-up.

Role playing isn't the only playground pursuit to follow on from the schoolyard to the virtual world. The excruciating note-passing 'my-friend-says-she-likes-you' rituals of early crushes also takes place in these worlds. 'I like reading messages and falling in love with girl penguins. I have got about five girlfriends. You have to win a love heart and then you can send them to them,' said one suave seven-year-old.

There was plenty of scope for naughtiness too: 'I, like, dance around and check if they've been looking after their puffles [a kind of virtual pet],' said one seven-year-old girl. 'And if they've got security cameras, I throw snowballs at them and block them.' This extremely petty vandalism has few 'real world' consequences, but is exactly the kind of playful aggression seen in teasing or play fighting in the physical world. The technology may be new, but the social promise and pitfalls of a bit of juvenile rebellion are not so different to the ones our own parents and grandparents grew up with.

Of course, sometimes things stray from the realm of play to the territory of bullying, just like in the real world. And sometimes those kids whose parents can afford to buy them in-game credits end up with fancier pets and costumes than those who don't, just like in the real world. The prevailing culture can be regressively gendered, heteronormative and overtly consumerist, just like in the real world. And there will be fallings-out, heartbreaks, gossip, factionalism and meanness. Just like in the real world.

Rather than looking at technology as some alien landscape that is luring in and corrupting impressionable children, we should view it as an extension of the playground, where social rules are tested, and relationship skills are built. Be there to listen to your child: they may be dressing up as a penguin, but in all other respects, a lot of what they're going through is just like the stuff we experienced in all its skinned-knees-and-broken-hearts intensity.

Let's play

I hope I've made the case that play is serious business. Play is where our children learn. Not just in the structured 'educational games' or with the over-engineered 'educational toys' that may well amount to just so much chocolate-covered broccoli. From cops and robbers to Dungeons and Dragons, play helps develop language, numeracy, physical skills and reaction times. But it's also critical for developing softer skills, like communication and negotiation. All over the world, our children imitate adults and older peers as part of a social apprenticeship: play fits our children into the adult world in which they'll eventually have to take their place.

But that's not all that play is. Play is a sign that we have enough. Enough food, enough security and enough energy to allow ourselves to be creative and to indulge in behaviour that isn't the bare bones of survival. In the first few weeks of the coronavirus pandemic, many of us found ourselves bereft of time, resources or any sense of security. In those early weeks in particular, people found it hard to write, to play music, to paint, to joke. Creativity dried up as insecurity set in. But in my own case at least, it was the kids who showed me how necessary play is. As they adjusted to the new normal, they invented new games, scatological songs, fantastical stories. They demanded indoor 'camping trips' and breakfast 'picnics'. Their appetite for the non-essentials never waned and – joy of joys – I'm slowly rekindling my love of making up daft songs or building dens from sheets and clothes horses. Play isn't necessary to survive, but it is a necessary part of what it means to thrive.

We could do better. In the UK, poverty and stress lead to the loss of time and space to play. This isn't just sad, it's tragic. Hungry, stressed children in hungry, stressed families miss out on so much of the brain-building benefits of play. We owe it to all children to hold open the space for this most entertaining but essential activity – to demand that they all have enough food, enough time, and enough security to play.

8

What's On Your Mind: Learning to Understand Other People's Thoughts – and Our Own

When babies arrive in the world they have no idea how or why people do things. They don't even have the ability to understand how and why *they* do things. If you need convincing, spend some time on YouTube enjoying the delightful facial expressions of babies being startled by their own farts.

Over time, human beings start to understand that people don't just act randomly: they have beliefs, desires and intentions. And, in WEIRD societies at least, we discover that those mental states may be at odds with our own, and even at odds with reality. But our theory (or theories) of mind aren't just models of what other people *believe*. We also develop mental rules of thumb that allow us to predict or explain the behaviour of people around us, or even to justify our own thoughts and beliefs to ourselves.

Unless you're a raging solipsist, you tend to assume that other people have just as rich a mental life as you do. This 'folk psychology' or 'theory of mind' is what allows us to play our part in a culture that is built around communication.

Humans also overgeneralise, ascribing human-like intentions to living and non-living things alike. See how we ascribe malevolent motives to our cats, cars or computers. We're even prepared to believe that abstract, animated shapes have feelings and desires. In a 1944 study, Fritz Heider and Marianne Simmel of Smith College created animations that contained a large, hollow rectangle, a large triangle, a small triangle, and a circle. The circle and triangles moved around the screen, sometimes bumping into each other, sometimes entering or leaving the rectangle. But the people who *watched* the film saw a bully (the big triangle) chasing a smaller person (the small triangle) who is trying to protect another person (the circle). Some went further, assigning gender roles to the shapes, with several volunteers 'explaining' that the big triangle was a man trying to assault a woman (the circle) and that the smaller triangle was another man trying to protect her. These objects were simple black paper cut-outs on a white background but still, the brains of those volunteers watching the film turned them into characters with beliefs, desires and intentions.[1] The more traits an individual has from the autism spectrum, the more likely it is that they will describe the animation as no more than a set of moving shapes. This result suggests that neurotypical people are using the same mechanisms when they imagine mental lives for inanimate objects and when they try to understand what another person is thinking.[2] Calling the Wi-Fi router a recalcitrant dickbag is simply an overgeneralisation of the feelings we have about people.

At some point, most children learn that thoughts, knowledge, wants and feelings are mental states and that, though they may be caused by things in the world, they are ours and ours alone: we have to make an effort to communicate what's in our heads to others, and we have no access to their mental states unless they communicate those thoughts with us. Most of the time, most of us understand that what other people think, know, want or feel is different to what is happening in our own heads.

For example, Professor Henry Wellman has been collecting a corpus of 'mind talk' from children for a couple of decades.[3] At two years of age some children understand the difference between negative and positive feelings, and realise that two people can feel different things. He found examples like these:

'Father: [Your brother] is mad at your daddy.

Two-year-old: But I'm happy at my daddy!'

This understanding – that others have thoughts that are different to our own, and that are hidden from us – is called theory of mind. For much of the twentieth century it was thought that the emergence of these abilities followed some kind of innate, pre-planned developmental trajectory. But more recent research, in non-WEIRD cultures, suggests that theory of mind changes depending on where you're brought up. The society you're raised in and its rules of politeness determine when you develop some of the abilities that go to make up theory of mind, and indeed whether you develop some of those abilities at all. Though the first step – mimicry – seems to be universal.

Around the world, babies attend to the faces and postures of their caregivers and random strangers alike, as everyone who has been on the receiving end of the frank – and frankly disconcerting – baby-stare knows. During this time, babies are busy mirroring and modelling our facial expressions, movements and tone, to try to make predictions about how we, their caregivers, are likely to behave. They'll copy laughs, cries, shouts and smiles as much to see how these things feel to them as they do to see the effect on other people. This mimicry is a fundamental step in becoming part of human society: the abilities that allow us to see each other – and ourselves – as explicable, if not always predictable.

What are these abilities and how do we develop them? Thankfully, there is over half a century of developmental research into that exact question. And it turns out that 'theory of mind', far from being a single, unified thing, is actually a complicated repertoire of interlinked mental behaviours. It's a whole set of rules and models that we deploy in order to make other humans seem less random.

One of the first experiments to show that we're not born with this knowledge dates from the 1980s and is called the Sally–Anne test. In this experiment, young children are shown two puppets, Sally and Anne. Sally puts a marble in her box and leaves the room, then Anne takes that marble and hides it in her own box. When Sally comes back the children are asked, 'Where will Sally look for her marble?' Over the age of four, most neurotypical children understand that Sally will look in her own box, while under-fours tend to say that Sally will look in Anne's box. The youngest children don't seem to understand that Sally can't possibly know that the marble has been moved.

It's such a simple set-up that it has been replicated in other settings, including Japan, Canada, Austria, the US and Hong Kong.[4] And while this test was originally designed for use with children, chimpanzees, bonobos and orangutans have taken part in similar experiments (involving a human in a King Kong suit playing the part of 'Sally', rather than a puppet).[5]

Our closest cousins in the animal kingdom know that it is possible to know something that another individual doesn't know. They understand that – in terms of beliefs at least – mental states are unique, subjective and private (if not explicitly communicated). The apes showed signs of suspense and anticipation, looking back and forth between ape-Sally and the original box, which suggests that they know that 'Sally' would look in the wrong place.

The one downside of the popularity of the Sally–Anne paradigm is that it has become almost synonymous with 'theory of mind'. But it shouldn't be: theory of mind is a toolbox made up of lots of different types of knowledge and heuristics that we use to try to make sense of the behaviour of those around us.

Welcome to the world: it has people in it

Newborn babies arrive on a planet that already has about 7 billion other human minds that are busy thinking, feeling and acting. In their lifetime they'll get to know somewhere between a few dozen and a few hundred of those other people pretty well. But, depending on where they're born and where they choose to live, they may meet anywhere from thousands to hundreds of thousands of other people in the course of their lives. Some they may 'meet' remotely – through voice, video or text. And they'll need to decide quickly what these people might be thinking or planning to do. If every new colleague or client or fellow commuter was a brand-new mystery to be solved, life would be even more stressful than it is anyway. For people on the autistic spectrum, new people *may* need to be figured out from scratch each time. For neurotypicals, there are a handful of quick and dirty heuristics that we use to decide what might be going on in other people's minds. These rules of thumb aren't always right, but they're usually enough of a guide to allow us to get along without causing too many fights. So what are these heuristics?

Professor Henry Wellman and Professor David Liu of the University of Michigan devised a five-stage model of the development of theory of mind. Taking several decades of research from all around the world, they identified five different 'theories' that children develop.[6]

The first experience that most children get about 'other minds' is the fact that two people can want different things. While it's important for a child's *needs* to be met, their wants are another thing entirely. Especially when that's wanting mummy's cup of coffee, or wanting the knife that granddad is using to chop onions. I know that my daughter figured out pretty early on that she could *want* to stay awake in direct contradiction to my incredibly earnest desire that she please, *please*, go the fuck to sleep.

It usually takes a little longer to reach stage two: the recognition that people can have different beliefs about things. My daughter was frankly obsessed with the fact that Uncle Mike *doesn't like bananas!* She is firmly in the 'bananas are great' camp, and their divergence of opinion has so far been commented on roughly several trillion times. She pointed out bananas in shops, bananas in books, bananas on TV, all so that Uncle Mike's curiously different attitude to bananas could be restated with equal parts concern and incredulity: 'I don't think you'd like this shop, Maimai. It has *bananas* in it.' 'Oh no, Maimai! This boy has a banana!' At three years old, the idea that she and Uncle Mike thought different things about something as ubiquitous as a banana was *fascinating*. Not since Boris Johnson's insistence that the EU was about to mandate a standardised curve has anyone got so much mileage out of this starchy yellow fruit.

Although this is often referred to as 'stage two' in the development of theory of mind, is it always the second insight that kids achieve? Here we encounter one of the first clues that theory of mind is shaped by culture and experience, rather than being a straightforward developmental unfolding for which we're preprogrammed. Studies from Iran and China show that the 'diversity of belief' stage generally develops at a later stage in those countries. The understanding of people's ignorance or false belief happens just as fast, if not faster in these countries, but where cultural values stress collectivism, harmony and agreement, kids don't get as much chance to experience discussions of divergent-but-equally-valid opinions.[7]

Accepting that people's beliefs can differ may be limited to the 12 per cent or so of us who live in WEIRD societies. The Pacific islands, with their diversity of languages and cultures, make for an invaluable natural laboratory. Studies of members of some Pacific island cultures show that an understanding of differing beliefs never seems to emerge, even among adults. In studies among children growing up in rural communities in Vanuatu, even fourteen- and fifteen-year-olds do no better than random guessing on false belief tasks.[8]

Why should this be? Isn't an understanding of others' mental states such a valuable skill that all social primates should have one? After all, even some non-human primates like orangutans *do* have an understanding of others' false beliefs. However, social cohesion is even more important, and privacy norms seem to override the desire to predict other people's mental states in some human cultures.

Certainly this is one of the most distinct differences in cultural values between Melanesian families and westernised, industrialised families. WEIRD families are much more likely to talk about individual beliefs and desires ('Oh, you wanted the dog! I thought you wanted the frog, sorry!') whereas rural populations on Vanuatu have strong social conditioning against speculating about others' mental states. It would be like asking someone's salary in the UK: inconceivable!

The third theory that most WEIRD kids develop is called 'knowledge ignorance' – otherwise known as 'how can you *not* know that'. As adults we sometimes fall into this trap, assuming that our partner knows we're nearly out of bin bags and will pick some up, or believing that *everyone* understands the offside rule. This is a cognitive bias called the 'curse of knowledge' and when you find yourself in a row that boils down to 'how was *I* meant to know that?' versus 'how could you *not* know that?' you've been caught out by it.

Very young children are universally cursed this way: they assume that adults *must* know everything that they know (and more). It's not a bad heuristic to start with – most caregivers set out to answer as many of their children's questions as they can. But, eventually, they learn that there are things that we don't know – the date of one classmate's birthday, another classmate's favourite colour, whatever flavour of phonics mnemonics they have at nursery or school this year. Around the age of four or five, WEIRD kids start to get cynical about their parents' omniscience.

Children's surprise at our ignorance is equal parts touching and insulting. My daughter has just reached that age where my lack of knowledge about something actually makes her furious. Recently she had a minor meltdown over the fact that I couldn't explain what 'war bears' are. I eventually figured out that she had misheard me saying that 'warm air' makes hurricanes (I had a cold) but for a few stressful minutes, her demands for an explanation of 'bears! Bad bears! That do bad things? What are they?' nearly had both of us in tears of mutual frustration.

In the end, she'll figure out that I don't know everything, and that it is entirely possible for her to have knowledge in her head that isn't in mine. And when that day comes – probably very soon – I'll miss being viewed with the same reverence as some oracular combination of Google, CBeebies and her teachers. But, on the whole, it'll probably be less stressful for us both.

The fourth stage in the development of most children's theory of mind is the realisation that not only can people be *ignorant* of something they can actually be *mistaken*. It's a subtle difference but think of it this way: you can be talking to someone who doesn't know anything about the offside rule – that's ignorance. Or you could be talking to someone who assumes you mean the offside rule in football rather than netball: that's a mistake.

Some of the most famous theory of mind experiments – like the Sally–Anne test – examined whether children could reliably say where a person might look for something that had been hidden while they were out of the room. Small children are certain that the absent person *must* know where the ball has been moved to. Older children begin to understand that the person might still believe that the ball is in the last place that they put it. This ability, the understanding that others might make a mistake because they have *false beliefs* about the world, is a fascinating landmark, not least because it seems so fundamental to understanding how the world works but it takes so long to develop.

Until this understanding develops, the mismatch between their knowledge and yours is another major source of frustration for children in those preschool years. Sometimes you really need to get down to their level and ask them what *they* believe in order to figure out what they expect you to know. Ask them for an explanation and you might find yourself really surprised by how much they *have* noticed. Particularly about things like the existence of a spare packet of biscuits in the cupboard, or the presence of an ice-cream van in the neighbourhood. I'm speaking from bitter experience here as someone who has come across to my child as intransigent and uncaring when it comes to sharing treats, rather than merely *ignorant*. Eventually kids will work out when you're incompetent rather than malevolent, but that takes time.

The final stage in the development of our mental models seems to be the understanding that we can hide our feelings from one another. For WEIRD children at least, this is a very late stage of development of theory of mind. As babies, one of the first things we figure out is how to understand someone's apparent emotional state. Later on in childhood, one of the last things we learn is that faces can lie.

While WEIRD kids usually master all these theories about the minds of others by the time they leave primary school, it's important to note that it takes far more effort for them than it does for us. Adolescents are *still* figuring out how to make sense of other people *automatically*. From fMRI studies, it's clear that the brain structures used by adolescents to work out what we're thinking and feeling are different to the ones that we use as adults. In the way that you instantly know the answer to 'five plus five' but your small child has to use their fingers, older children have to use parts of the brain involved in social and causal reasoning to try to calculate what the heck the rest of us are up to.

Thinking and feeling: understanding emotions

As adults we tend to have a *fairly* reliable idea of how other people are feeling. We can tell if the boss is in a bad mood, or our partner is worried. We can tell when the kids are excited or our friend is glowing with pride. But we aren't born with this ability. In fact, studies show that the first attempts to make sense of someone's emotional state are purely physical. Like most primates, our emotional intelligence begins as a process of monkey see, monkey do.

Most human babies are stunningly adept at mirroring facial expressions. Within their first couple of hours, they'll start to consistently copy the facial expressions of their caregivers.[9] I remember wondering if our two-week-old was having some sort of seizure one evening. I was cleaning my teeth with my baby on my lap. She was looking up at me, pulling her mouth into the *wildest* shapes, gurning like a veteran clubber on their fourth disco biscuit. I went to spit out my toothpaste so I could call for my husband, partially out of concern, partly out of a desire to say, 'Are you *seeing* this shit?' But as I did so it hit me: she was mimicking my toothbrushing face. It turns out that – devoid of context (and teeth) – the facial expressions inherent in dental hygiene are pretty extreme.

So while I have no idea what emotional states were induced by watching me brush my teeth (or floss, or apply mascara) there's plenty of research to suggest that babies learn about feelings from the way *they* feel when they copy our expressions. By copying us they induce a similar emotional state in their own bodies.

Research on adults suggests that facial expressions affect human emotions. Sure, you smile when you're feeling good but smiling also *makes* you feel more positive, all other things being equal. Frowning makes everything seem just that little bit shittier. For example, when volunteers were asked to hold chopsticks between their teeth either lengthwise (which forces the zygomatic muscle – the muscle that pulls your mouth into a smile – to work) or end-on (which causes the corrugator – the frowny muscle – to contract) EEG readings of their brain activity showed that the chopstick-induced frowners had stronger brain activity when they were shown pictures of frightening, enraging, upsetting or disgusting things. What's more, the volunteers *said* that these pictures were more upsetting while they frowned than they were while smiling.[10]

Copying our caregivers' facial expressions, and linking those muscle movements with the emotions we feel in response, creates a feedback loop in the infant brain, where feelings and facial expressions become almost one and the same. This explains why, following Japan's cultural norms, babies born to Japanese parents learn to associate emotions with facial expressions that use more eye-muscle cues and far less mouth movement, expressions which read as subtle to Westerners. Dominant cultural norms are also the reason why North American babies learn grins and pouts from their caregiver's lower-face expressions. And why British children eventually learn how to say 'So sorry' when what they mean is 'Get out of my fucking *way!*'

Mimicry is the foundation of emotional intelligence but as children start to become verbal, the way we talk about thoughts, wants and feelings helps to shape their emerging theory of mind. The amount of time spent playing together has a huge impact on how quickly a toddler's theory of mind develops. 'Playing along' – actively using your imagination with a child, or talking with them about the game you're involved in – speeds up their understanding that people can have different beliefs, desires and intentions.[11] The children of parents who use more phrases that relate to beliefs ('Doggie thinks you have her ball'; 'I know where it is'), desires ('Doggie wants her ball'; 'Teddy would like a cake') and emotions ('Teddy is sad that Doggie won't share'; 'Doggie is angry that Teddy tried to snatch the ball') have theories of mind that are one or two *years* in advance of the average by the time they reach school.[12] Having an older sibling around has the same effect, given that big brothers and sisters are rarely reticent about telling the little ones what they think, want or feel.[13] Younger kids don't do anything to improve their older siblings' theory of mind, however, suggesting that even if they are telling the older ones what they want, the older ones aren't listening.

In a year-long study of children between the ages of two and three, Professor Jane Brown and Professor Judy Dunn of the Pennsylvania State University noticed changes in the frequency and sophistication of children's use of emotional descriptions and justifications.[14] They wanted to know what children said about feelings and they found that, by the age of two, North American children start expressing their feelings with words rather than tantrums.

I still recall with intense pride the moment in a busy restaurant when our kid, then two years old, clearly stated: 'Mummy, get me out of this *fucking* high chair.' Whenever anyone asks me if parenthood has changed my attitude to swearing, I tell them this, and I stand by my belief that a clearly enunciated profanity is better than a screaming, food-flinging tantrum any day of the week. Strong language helps temper strong feelings, cutting down on the need for a physical outburst, so I found it pretty rewarding to see it happen in practice.

Professors Brown and Dunn also discovered that between the ages of two and three children start to use language not just to express their feelings but also to *change* the emotional states of their parents, friends or siblings. By three years old, most neurotypical WEIRD kids have started to use language to tease, provoke and comfort other people. But Brown and Dunn also found that the level of emotional literacy began to vary widely between children at this age, and that the children of parents who talked to them about feelings at the age of eighteen months were more skilled when it came to talking about and understanding feelings at the age of six.[15] Somewhat disappointingly, they also found that parents and older siblings were far less likely to talk to boys about feelings than they were to girls. I find this tragic: as a society, our stunting of boys' emotional growth starts early.

Research also shows that, by the age of six, many children start to gain *some* understanding of the fact that we can hide our emotions, although this ability doesn't really mature until the second decade of life.[16] Professor Paul Harris and his colleagues at the University of Oxford presented children with stories like these:

'Diana's big brother is teasing her. She knows that her big brother will keep teasing her if he knows how she feels.' And: 'David sees an old lady walking down the street wearing funny clothes. He knows that she will be cross if he doesn't hide the way he feels.'

They then asked the children how they think David and Diana *feel* and also what kind of facial *expression* they might have. By the age of six, children already understand what David or Diana might be feeling, but they are also smart enough to know that a smile might hide sadness, and that a serious face might hide the fact that someone is dying to laugh. Somewhere before the teenage years, in British children at least, we learn the art of putting on a brave face or politely hiding a smirk. In short, children learn to predict how other people might react if they laugh or shout or cry. Based on this, they learn to hide what they're thinking or feeling if the other person might be sad or angry as a response.

It's worth thinking about the sophistication of this. At six, children are starting to understand not only their own feelings and the feelings of others, but also how those feelings might *interact*. They also learn that feelings can be hidden, for the greater good. This is a lot to learn so early on, but life as a member of a social species can be really hard without these skills. A little white lie can help avoid conflict or pain for us social primates. Which means we learned to lie as a species. Which in turn means that kids need to be on the alert for people telling them massive whoppers. So how do children figure out that what someone says and what they actually *think* might be at odds?

I think you think

Remember the Sally–Anne experiment? This is sometimes called the false belief understanding test and in some variants it goes something like this. A toddler is told that a teddy or a ball is the experimenter's favourite toy. The toy is then put away in a toy box by the experimenter. While the experimenter leaves the room, a second member of the team takes the toy out of the box and hides it somewhere. If you ask a toddler where they think the first experimenter will search for the toy when they come back in, they'll usually say that the experimenter will look in the hiding place. Those toddlers have the 'curse of knowledge' – they can't understand that the experimenter doesn't know that the toy has moved.[17] By the age of five, however, most of the offspring of WEIRDMOMS will have figured out that the experimenter will look in the 'wrong' place (the box). They've reached a stage of development in their theory of (other) minds that allows them to understand that people can believe things that just aren't true.

At the same time, WEIRD children are beginning to understand *why* someone might make a mistake. In Australia, at least, four-year-olds have started to understand the difference between a mistake (a false statement based on a sincere belief) and a lie (a statement that conceals a true belief). In a slightly gross experiment, Professor Candida Peterson of the University of

Queensland spread Vegemite (wait, it gets worse) on a piece of mouldy bread. While she did this, a toy bear was either 'watching' or 'not watching'. In the 'not watching' scenario the bear was 'reading' a book with its back turned. When another toy asked Bear if the sandwich was good to eat, Bear replied, 'Yes.' The children could tell whether the bear made a *mistake* (because it hadn't seen the bread before the Vegemite was applied) or was *lying* (because it had seen the bread and knew it was bad). They reserved their ire for the mendacious toy, letting the merely ignorant bear off, even though the other toy suffered the consequences of a mouldy sandwich in both cases.[18]

What Professor Peterson found is fascinating: here is a complex, multilevel set of reasoning tasks going on in the heads of these preschoolers. Firstly, they can tell whether or not Bear *knows* that the bread was mouldy. From that they can infer whether or not Bear is *lying* – saying something false, where the truth is known – or mistaken – saying something false where the bear honestly believed this to be the case. They then judge Bear's actions based not on the *outcome* – the other poor toy eating a mouldy sandwich – but on Bear's *intention*. That is a lot of abstract reasoning from little humans who haven't even learned to tie their shoelaces.

By the time they reach preschool age, kids in WEIRD societies start to use their theory of mind to keep track of who knows what. They learn to be aware when something might be new information, or a new experience, for someone else.[19] Professor Michael Tomasello and Professor Katharina Haberl of the Max Planck Institute for Evolutionary Anthropology recruited seventy-two children from a German city, half of whom were around twelve months old and half around eighteen months old. One of the researchers played with the child using a pair of toys. After a short while they left the room. At that point the other researcher started to play with the child and added a third toy to the game. Some time later, the original playmate came back and said, 'Wow! Look! Look at that! So look at that! Just give it to me, please ...' (only in German).

The eighteen-month-old volunteers pretty consistently handed over the new toy, showing that they understood without being told that the adult was most likely to be interested in the toy that they hadn't seen before. In contrast, only around half of the twelve-month-olds seemed to understand this, with the rest handing over one of the old toys.

Most of the eighteen-month-olds had the ability to a) figure out that people generally think that new things are more exciting than old things, and b) remember which toy is new from the point of view of the grown-up who has left the room. That ability to take the perspective of someone else without directly experiencing it for yourself is a really important part of what makes us so successful as a species.

Do you see what I see?

While the awareness of different knowledge and opinions happens by school age, the understanding that we *literally* have different perspectives on things seems to arise much earlier in life. In fact we can't be certain exactly when it emerges, because it is present in most of the youngest participants in experiments on perspective-taking. So far the experiments that test the ability to recognise that other people have a different view of the world require the ability to at least bum-shuffle into a different position without falling over in an entertaining but scientifically uninformative heap, so we don't have data on anyone under a year old.

The data we *do* have comes from a study in which Professor Sarah Dunphy-Lelii and Professor Henry Wellman recruited 56 fourteen-month-olds and 56 eighteen-month-olds to come and sit in the lab. While they were there, Professor Dunphy-Lelii would look at a brightly coloured picture and say, 'Oh wow!' (A lot of developmental science is feigning enthusiasm around small children. As is a lot of parenting.)

When there was a physical barrier in the way, blocking the child's view, these infants would move around to be able to see what Dunphy-Lelii found so exciting, even if that required quite a lot of energetic shuffling.[20] That expenditure of energy is a sure sign that they knew that Professor Dunphy-Lelii had a different field of view. It's also a clear sign that they knew *how* to change their point of view to try to match hers, in order to see what had elicited the 'wow!' Infant and toddler FOMO is real, as evidenced by how often they insist on following you to the toilet.

As well as understanding that they might not be able to see what someone else sees unless they move, children also understand that other people can't necessarily see what they see. By eighteen months, children will turn a picture towards an adult so that the adult can see it better, and by two years of age they'll even turn the picture around completely, giving up their own ability to see in order to let someone else see better. *Hiding* things, however, comes much later. Children generally don't seem to be able to work out how to position something so someone *can't* see it until they reach at least three.[21]

That might be because of the difference in our experiences of being shown stuff and having it hidden. It's obvious when someone *shows* you something, but – by definition – it's much harder to spot when someone is hiding something from you. This gives kids fewer opportunities to mimic stealth, except during games like hide and seek where we *explicitly* teach our children to trick us. And even then, we usually know to look under the cushion on the sofa because a) that was where they hid the last thirty times, and b) they don't *fit* under the cushion, just like the last thirty times!

But the difficulty of *imagining* things from another person's point of view stays with us throughout childhood and beyond. Even adults regularly make mistakes when responding to instructions given by someone with a different point of view. We know this thanks to Dr Iroise Dumontheil and her colleagues at UCL and Birmingham University.[22] They devised a simple computer game in which 177 volunteers – all female – were asked to move objects they saw on-screen, based on instructions they were given. On this screen the volunteers could see a set of shelves that look pretty much identical to the IKEA Kallax model: essentially a set of sixteen open-backed boxes. Each of the boxes had an object in it, like a toy plane, a ball, champagne flutes or a duck. In each round of the game, four of the sixteen boxes had grey screens at the back, which hid the contents from a virtual 'director' who was represented as an avatar 'standing' behind the shelves.

In the first set of trials, the director character told the volunteer to do things like 'move the small ball to the left'. This sounds pretty straightforward, but in some of the trials there would be a small ball that the director could see, and another, even smaller ball, that was hidden from the director by one of the grey screens. If the participant moved an object that met the description, but that was masked from the director by the grey screens, that was marked as an error.

It's worth pointing out that even adults struggle to do this consistently. These adults – aged nineteen to twenty-seven – still moved objects that the director *could not have seen* on about 50 per cent of the experimental trials on average. Older adolescents did even worse, getting the task wrong about 70 per cent of the time, while children between seven and ten years old made mistakes about 80 per cent of the time on average.

But what is *really* odd is what happened when these same participants tried the game without a 'director' character. In this version the participants were simply told to ignore objects in boxes with grey backgrounds. In this set-up, the number of errors dropped way down, with even the youngest children managing the task correctly 80 per cent of the time. The task was exactly the same, the objects were the same, the instructions were given in the same way – as text on a screen – and the same sorts of spatial and logical reasoning were required in both versions. The only difference was that the director-less version didn't require the participants to take another person's perspective into account. The game gets easier as soon as we take the suggestion of a theory of mind away.

This result seemed so astounding that I read and re-read the study looking for an oversight. Was the director trial always the first one? (It was not.) Was there any other distractor beyond the presence of a two-dimensional image of a 'director' on-screen? (There was not.) It seems that we simply struggle when we have to model other minds. And yet our theory of mind seems so effortless and so complete. (It is not.)

We constantly kid ourselves that we understand why someone is behaving in the way that they are, or that we know how someone will react to our behaviour. All this despite the fact that we regularly – even as adults – get this wrong. Your friend didn't love the film you recommended. Your partner wasn't thrilled with the surprise party. We're constantly making mental models based on the idea that people are only slightly different from ourselves but, in WEIRD societies at least, we're consistently awful at envisaging someone else's point of view. The younger your kids, the harder it is for them to remember that the contents of their frame of reference are wildly different from yours. And to be fair, you're only slightly better at figuring it out than your kids. When you and your child have an inevitable mismatch of minds – and the inevitable tantrum that follows – it's important to give yourselves space for empathy. Stay calm and stay curious: ask yourself what it is that you might have missed.

Intention attention

Often when we argue with kids it's because we don't understand each other's motives. What do we intend when we demand they be home by a certain time, even though their friends can all (allegedly) stay out late? What do they intend when they're jumping on the sofa even though you've told them not to? Understanding motivation can help diffuse a lot of tension.

Thankfully, children seem to learn about intentions from an early age. Exactly how soon do children figure out that we're not just randomly waving our arms around, that we are actually trying to achieve something? It's tough to design an experiment for this:

asking a nine-month-old, 'What do you think I'm doing right now?' isn't likely to yield a publishable data set. Instead, researchers tend to measure how long infants spend staring at something: the assumption runs that expected events are somewhat boring and don't hold a baby's attention for long, while unexpected events are interesting, and babies will stare for longer while they attempt to figure out what the fuck just happened.

A nice example of this set-up is the 'indirect reach' paradigm. In this type of study, babies watch an experimenter – either in the room or on video – attempt to reach over a barrier to grab a toy. The presence of a barrier demands some elaborate contortions on the part of the experimenter. Then the barrier is removed and the experimenter reaches for the toy again. At what age do babies react differently to an experimenter reaching directly for the toy versus repeating that same elaborate gesture that the barrier required? If the babies were getting used to the *action* that the experimenter performed, then the elaborate reach will be an uninteresting rerun and not attract much staring, while the direct reach – a new action – will attract stares. Conversely, if the baby gets that the *intention* was to reach the toy, then they won't show any surprise at the experimenter reaching for the toy directly once the barrier is removed. They will, however, subject the same experimenter to a long, hard, WTF stare if they contort themselves again on the way to picking up an easily reached object.

It turns out that babies as young as nine months old (the youngest age tested so far) show surprise when an adult goes out of their way to perform an unnecessary and awkward arm movement in pursuit of a goal – they can distinguish between the adult's actions and their intention despite their tender age.[23] This puts babies on a similar level to macaque monkeys. They too express surprise when they see a human experimenter take a convoluted route to picking up a grape, unless there's a barrier in the way that demands such a stretch.

But what happens if they've never seen the experimenter successfully reach the toy? Can human babies *infer* an intention from an incomplete action? Professor Amanda Brandone repeated the experiment with Professor Henry Wellman, but in this set-up, she tried to reach the toy over the barrier but failed. Then, when the barrier was removed, she either used the same elaborate arm movement, or reached directly, and this time she successfully got the toy. Twelve- and fifteen-month-olds were surprised by the roundabout arm movements made by the experimenter once the barrier was removed. The nine-month-olds, though, showed no particular surprise when the experimenter took the awkward route – they didn't manage to connect her original actions with the actual intention of reaching a toy. Until about a year old, most children don't have the theory of mind necessary to guess what someone might be trying to do, unless they've seen them achieve their goal.

However, from as young as nine months, babies can tell whether you're trying to do something (and failing) in contrast to whether you're simply refusing to do it. Professor Tanya Behne and her colleagues at the Max Planck Institute set up an experiment where they played with toys while sitting at a table with babies aged between six and eighteen months. In some cases she would play with the toy while 'distracted' by a phone call and 'forget' to share with the baby. In other trials she would try (and 'fail') to get the toy out of a clear box. At other times she would tease the baby, offering the toy and then taking it away, or just playing with the toy herself. Professor Behne made the babies wait for thirty seconds while she pretended to be distracted or stuck, or while she refused to share with them. The six-month-olds got equally frustrated in all conditions, but from nine months and upwards, the babies began to bang the table, shout or look away in frustration – but only when Professor Behne was *refusing* to hand over the toy: a thirty-second wait for a stuck or distracted grown-up is acceptable, while a thirty-second wait for a selfish grown-up is not.[24]

Experiments on chimpanzees yield similar results to those done with the nine-month-olds, with the apes walking out on experimenters who teased or refused to hand over food, but showing far more patience to those experimenters who were 'distracted' or who 'got stuck' in the process.[25]

By the middle of their second year, children also seem to be able to figure out if something is *accidental* rather than intentional. Professor Malinda Carpenter, now of the University of St Andrews, designed some Heath Robinson-esque 'toys'. These contraptions had things she could pull or twist or flip. She also had fairy lights, a party blower and a pop-up toy. These surprising objects weren't really connected to her contraptions, but in the experiment, Professor Carpenter made it seem as if they were.

Using some clever sleight of hand, as she dexterously played with the mechanisms she switched on the lights, or activated a pump to blow the party whistle, or made the toy pop out of its box with her left hand. Once the infants had got the idea that a couple of Professor Carpenter's toys had exciting results, she showed them the third 'toy', but this time she carried out two movements. For example, one of her devices was made from an old bird feeder, and it had a ring that could be pulled and a lid that could be moved up and down. With some of the infants she moved the lid then said, 'Whoops', then pulled the string and said, 'There'; with others she swapped the 'whoops' and 'there' actions – just to make sure that neither action was somehow naturally easier to copy.

Then she handed the toy to the child and said, 'Your turn'. The children were significantly more likely to imitate the action after which Professor Carpenter had said 'there' than the one where she had said 'whoops'. Even though she kept her face as neutral as possible, and showed no surprise, the difference between her saying 'whoops' and 'there' was enough for her tiny playmates to understand that only some of her actions had been part of making the lights light, the whistle sound, or the toy pop up. This is phenomenally impressive: not only can these children copy a brand new series of actions, they have the mental model of exactly which actions she actually *intended* to make.[26]

As caregivers we often talk about what incredible little mimics our children are, but we don't always give them credit for how *selective* that mimicry is. From a very early age they stop mirroring the bizarre facial contortions of a parent mid-tooth-clean, and reserve their efforts for those behaviours we display when we're trying to achieve something. Take a moment and think about how much learning that has required: understanding how actions have consequences, understanding which consequences are actually *good*, understanding how some actions are simpler than others. By the end of their first year, babies have already become efficient students of adult behaviour, and they can only do that by understanding our intentions. Without our noticing, our children learn to make shrewd guesses at our motivations before they can even put those thoughts into words.

Our children are working very hard: they have to make much more mental effort than we do in order to model the thoughts and intentions of others. Brain scans show that, by our mid- to late twenties, most of us will have delegated much of the business of reasoning about others' mental states to specialised areas of the brain. Although adolescents may be able to *function* in a way that is almost indistinguishable from adults, the *way* they function requires them to draw on many more parts of their brain. By adulthood we tend to use the left frontal lobe to give us a 'quick and dirty' read of what someone else might be wanting, thinking or feeling. In contrast, adolescents still need to use the entire frontal lobe, while younger children recruit parts from all over the brain: it's a lot of effort for them to figure out what we're up to. They need to do a lot more reasoning to work out what might be going on in other minds.[27]

When your adolescent seems to be overwhelmed by social drama, or incapable of understanding how *worried* you were about them staying out late, or just so damned inconsiderate when they leave their washing-up in the sink, remember that they're still trying to figure out what makes other people tick. It's nothing personal – they need time to build up their theory of mind. But please don't worry. Most of the time kids *really* want to be kind.

9

The Kids Are All Right

'I have always relied on the kindness of toddlers,' said probably no one ever. Among WEIRD cultures at least, common wisdom dictates that young children are selfish, impulsive and thoughtless. Even the idioms 'terrible twos' and 'three-nager' tell us a lot about what we expect of children at the preschool level. It's no wonder that so many of us dread those years of meltdowns and stand-offs.

Put yourself in a toddler's shoes. It's uncomfortable, both literally and metaphorically. Here you are with all this new-found personhood, an understanding that there are things you want (and don't want), but your *agency* – the things you are *allowed* or able to do – lags far, far behind. Here I am, sitting in a coffee shop, having chosen what to wear, what to tick off my to-do list first, which cake to eat, what coffee I wanted. This is, admittedly, a luxurious state of affairs. It's no wonder that the great Covid lockdown brought out the toddler in so many of us, when so many of these little choices were taken away. Compare that with trying to get kids ready for school. They have little to no choice of what to wear, what to eat, when to eat it, what to study and in what order. It's no wonder they get frustrated when we ask (or tell) them to do just one more thing.

That's where we get this idea that toddlers and preschoolers are selfish. Sometimes they chafe – hard – at having yet another choice taken away from them. But when they have the chance to choose for themselves, children show signs of incredible kindness from as young as eight months. Even without a fully functioning theory of mind, very young children care about us. Deeply. They'll crawl out of ball pits and over obstacles to help an adult stranger in need. They care about justice, sacrificing their own resources to make things more fair. And they will even disobey our instructions in order to give us the help we *need* rather than the thing we asked for. Forget selfishness. Most kids, in most circumstances, have the capacity to be amazingly altruistic.

Altruism is putting someone else's needs above your own. It's not an exclusively human trait: numerous mammals behave helpfully towards unrelated members of their own species. And beyond mammals, the white-fronted bee-eater bird and the spiny plunderfish will protect other, unrelated offspring if the parent is incapacitated. Putting yourself out for others – even when there is no direct genetic advantage – seems to be valuable for many species.

But humans take altruism to a much higher degree than other species. Our civilisation as we know it could not exist without bonds of trust and reciprocity because someone has to be the first giver in any relationship. We need altruism to allow us to take that first step. And altruism starts with empathy.

Whenever we find ourselves experiencing feelings that are more appropriate to someone else's situation than our own, we are experiencing empathy. That involuntary wince when you see someone hurt themselves is fundamental to altruism – it's what motivates us to do things that benefit people that we're not related to. We want to minimise others' distress, because it distresses us to see them feeling bad.

You might expect – I certainly did – that in order to be empathetic you require a sophisticated theory of mind: that you have to have experienced another's situation, or something similar, and imagine yourself in it in order to understand how they might feel. But it seems that empathy is far less cognitively demanding than that, with the mirror system doing most of the heavy lifting.

The youngest children to have been studied were eight-month-old babies, but even they showed signs of worry when a caregiver pretended to injure themselves.[1] These are babies who have never walked, who can barely crawl, yet share the pain someone feels when they walk into something. And children's empathetic responses only get stronger over time, as they start to be able to do something to help.

Defining altruism: sharing, helping, making things right

Humanity's sense of empathy motivates children and adults alike to be altruistic: to help unrelated friends, strangers, or even people we never have and never will meet. But there are different forms of altruism. WEIRD parents normally try to nag their children into sharing, first and foremost. 'Don't forget to take turns on the slide!' 'Let the little girl play with the blocks with you.' 'Share the raisins with your sister, please.' But sharing *resources* seems to be the most difficult form of altruism to master. It's found very rarely in other species – among chimpanzees, food sharing hardly ever happens, and when it does it's more of a case of 'tolerated theft', according to primatologists. If you're rolling your eyes at the thought that your child is kind, it may be that you're looking in the wrong places.

That's because there is one form of empathy-motivated behaviour that toddlers excel at. They love to help. It's very difficult to spot when that behaviour begins: it starts so early and comes on so strong. My own daughter's nursery wisely leveraged this instinct, getting the children to tidy up after themselves between activities. There's even a jaunty song that goes with it and that works, *Manchurian Candidate*-style, at home. One of the first parenting gurus, Mrs Eliza Warren, author of the 1865 bestseller *How I Managed My Children from Infancy to Marriage*, reported that she'd do something similar: 'saying kindly – "Mamma likes to see the room tidy; let us all help to make it so." Then the little feet pattered about, and the little hands were ready to be useful; then a kiss was given to each, and such a joyful clapping and shouting at the end of our labour.' (#humblebrag #blessed)

Mrs Warren was leveraging the instinct to help that most children have. In fact, the helping instinct is so strong that it caused problems for Dr Felix Warneken, associate professor of developmental psychology at the University of Michigan. During a study designed to determine the influence that parents have on children's helping behaviour, each and every toddler helped Felix when he dropped pens, lost clothes pegs, or shut himself out of a cupboard. The data firmly indicated that the children all wanted to be helpful. It didn't matter what parents did, or even if they left the room. To uncover any difference at all in children's readiness to help, Dr Warneken had to devise an obstacle course to try to slow these little helpers down.[2]

But even the most helpful toddler is likely to struggle to share. Like chimpanzees, children (and adults) find it harder to give *things* than to give help. In 2012, Dr Warneken asked children to play games with a puppet. In the course of these games they'd be asked to either help the puppet or share marbles with it. Between the ages of two and a half and three and a half, there's no difference in how willing children are to *help* the puppet. But if the puppet has been mean, if they previously refused to share with the child, three-and-a-half-year-olds are unwilling to share, reserving their generosity for those puppets who had previously been kind. In contrast, the two-and-a-half-year-olds shared less overall, but they also don't punish the mean puppets.[3] Our ability to confidently give things without fear of being taken advantage of seems to be something that takes some time to emerge, with a greater cognitive demand associated with keeping track of who is likely to share-and-share-alike versus who is, frankly, taking the piss. On the whole, however, humans get more generous, not less, when they learn how to spot a selfish bastard.

Encouraging our toddlers to share might make us feel good – and make us look good on play dates – but we have to remember that they're still going through the process of figuring out who to trust. According to Dr Julia Ulber, a developmental psychology lecturer at Canterbury Christ Church University, 'A two-year-old child won't understand why they should share their precious dolly with another child as much as you wouldn't want to share your car with everyone who comes to your house.'[4] Dr Ulber points out that forcing children to share doesn't speed up their social development.

Kids are also surprisingly willing to make amends for their mistakes, as long as we don't shame them out of it. Children will make mistakes, break things or hurt people from time to time. It's inevitable. Even as adults, with all that theory of mind and executive function we have going for us, we sometimes upset people too. When children make a hurtful mistake, most of us want them to be capable of owning up, apologising and putting things right. Most very young toddlers know when they've hurt someone and they want to fix things. The way *we* make them feel about their actions makes a huge difference to whether they decide to help and make amends, or to run away and hide.

Dr Jesse Drummond and colleagues at the University of Pittsburgh found that children who felt guilt after breaking an experimenter's favourite toy, a monkey called Mr Beans, were really strongly motivated to confess to breaking the toy and to want to help mend it. But those children who demonstrated *shame* tended to avoid the experimenter afterwards, and were less likely to come forward to clean and help.[5] Kids are willing to say sorry and put things right, but only if they're not too ashamed to own up in the first place. Humiliating children for their mistakes doesn't stop them screwing up. It just encourages them to hide their screw-ups from us.

Kindness makes you feel good

Empathy and altruism may have benefits for society as a whole, but what's in it for our own kids? If you're worried that having an altruistic child means that you're raising a pushover, consider the benefits to their health and happiness.

Kindness makes us happy. Dr Elizabeth Dunn of the University of British Columbia and her colleagues surprised random people around campus with a gift of either $20 or $5. They then asked the recipients to spend that money on either themselves or someone else. While the amount of money that people received made no difference at all to how happy they felt, what they *did* with it made a big difference: those who spent the money on someone else reported happier moods throughout the day than those who had spent the money on themselves.[6]

Though sharing may be challenging for them, even two-year-olds get that 'warm glow' effect when they give. Dr Lara Aknin and her colleagues at the University of British Columbia recruited twenty healthy, full-term toddlers from local libraries, hospitals and community events in Vancouver, Canada. Overwhelmingly, these children showed greater happiness (as measured by experts coding video recordings of their facial expressions) when sharing a toy than they did while playing with it by themselves. What's more, they also showed significantly greater happiness when giving a treat of their own to a (demonstratively appreciative) puppet, than they did when receiving a treat themselves or watching someone else give a treat to the puppet.[7] What seems to motivate them is not any instruction or command to share that is issued by an adult. Instead they seem to be inspired by the positive feelings they get when they see how happy they've made someone else.

In fact, *not* being able to help can feel incredibly stressful. One easy way to measure someone's stress level is to measure how dilated their pupils are. Dr Robert Hepach and Professor Michael Tomasello at the Max Planck Institute for Evolutionary Anthropology, together with Dr Amrisha Vaish at the University of Virginia, set up a game for two- and three-year-olds to play with an adult member of the team.[8] They played together with a toy train that could deliver cups of coloured water, but the experimenters had sneakily rigged it so that the cup would 'accidentally' spill when the child had their turn to drive the train. The children's pupils dilated – showing that they were very stressed – when the spill happened. Afterwards, the children were told that the accident hadn't been their fault – that the tracks had been broken – and that there was still plenty of water to play with.

No child was sent home stressed, you'll be pleased to hear. The same can't necessarily be said for the experimenters who had to repeatedly upset 128 children. 'We keep playing the roles because we want to answer the scientific questions, but it can be a relief to put away these tough roles for a while,' says Dr Vaish.[9]

It's what happened in the middle of all this kerfuffle that was of interest to the experimenters. Sixty-four of the children were given the chance to help mop up the spill, while the other sixty-four didn't get an opportunity to help: someone else came in and mopped it up for them. Those children who were able to mop up the spill showed less stress – their pupils shrank back down as they helped – whereas those who didn't get that chance stayed stressed until they were reassured that it wasn't their fault.

The cognition of helping

As we heard from Dr Vaish, if you want to research child psychology, you need to hone your acting skills, whether that's pretending to be upset by a spill, or acting like a complete incompetent. At the beginning of his career, Dr Felix Warneken suspected that the conventional wisdom, which suggested that toddlers are completely self-involved, might not be correct. To explore just how helpful children can be, Dr Warneken has pretended to bump into, drop and break things thousands of times.

In one of his earliest experiments he would 'accidentally' bump into a closed cabinet while trying to put magazines inside (the experimental condition) or bump into the same closed doors while putting a stack of magazines on top (the control condition). He wanted to see if children could understand when help might be needed. About half of the eighteen-month-olds opened the doors for Felix in the experimental condition, but none of them went over to help in the control condition – showing that even very young children know the difference between accidents that get in our way and those that don't. What's more, they know if something is accidental or intentional and will only help in the case of accidents. In another set of Felix's experiments, the vast majority of children helped by giving back markers or clothes pegs that he had dropped on the floor, while ignoring ones that he threw deliberately.[10]

However, it is worryingly easy to unintentionally damage cooperation and helpfulness. Dr April Bay-Hinitz and her colleagues at the University of Nevada, Reno, randomised classes of four- to five-year-olds to spend a week playing either cooperative games, where everyone wins if you work together, or competitive games, where only one person can win.[11] When the children played the cooperative games, they showed much more helpful behaviour and kindness in the subsequent two weeks. But after five days of competitive-only playtimes, aggression went up significantly, not just during the games but throughout the school day. What's more, the children stopped helping one another, refused to share, and were just generally less nice.

Thankfully, the effect was reversible with a few days of cooperative play. Which is a relief because kids are *incredibly* clever helpers. In WEIRD settings at least, if adults ask for the wrong kind of help, children will disobey them and give them what they need, not what they say they want. Dr Alia Martin and Dr Kristina Olson from Yale University sat down individually with 19 three-year-old children, and asked them to pass them some things. The children had a choice of passing a real or a toy phone, a working or a broken cup, a real or a rubber hammer, and a new or a dried-up pen. The researchers knew from previous research by other psychologists that children as young as fourteen months are keen to help. But, Dr Martin points out, what we say to one another is often not exactly what we mean – and what we ask for is not always what we need.[12]

Yet even very young children seem to understand that want and need are different things. 'If you know the cup is broken, you might want to make sure that's what they *really* want: like hey that cup is broken, want me to get you another one? Or maybe you think they *do* want what they're asking for, but you don't think the thing they want is the best thing for them,' says Dr Martin. 'Adults do this kind of paternalistic helping with kids all the time, doing what we think is best for them in the long run even if it goes against what they want now.'

For example, if Dr Martin or Dr Olson asked the kids to pass them a toy phone so that they could make a call, or the broken cup so they could drink juice, the children almost always ignored what they asked for and gave them the working object instead.[13] However, if they asked for the 'non-working' object to do something that it was actually capable of doing ('Can you pass me that cup so I can cut out a circle of Play-Doh?' 'Can you pass me that phone to hold down these papers?') then the kids would hand over exactly what had been requested. This is really smart stuff. These children not only figured out what Dr Olsen and Dr Martin intended – remember that this needs a pretty well-developed theory of mind – they also trusted their own judgement about what might *actually* help rather than automatically obeying the grown-up. In fact they were so confident of their judgements that about a third of them *told* the experimenters why they needed to be given something else.

Hanging out with these little helpers (under carefully controlled lab conditions) led to some bonus insights into their cognition, because the children were so keen to explain what they were doing. 'Children pointed out *why* they weren't fulfilling the request exactly. For example, they'd say something like, "This cup is broken, I'll give you this one."' According to Dr Martin, 'this suggests that children were thinking about how to respond to the request rather than just choosing whichever object wasn't broken; they wanted to acknowledge what we had asked for and explain why they might not always be giving exactly that'.

What does this tell us about how their brains are working? According to Dr Martin, it suggests that even very young children can be attuned to people's intentions.

> I don't think my studies show that children understand all the nuances of how to read intentions from behaviour – even adults suck at it a lot of the time. But it does seem like they get the idea that intentions are not straightforward, that when someone says 'Can you give me that cup to pour the water' they have to think about whether the cup actually works for that person's ultimate goal.[14]

But if you want that sort of sophisticated help you'd better make sure you deserve it. Children are impressively smart when it comes to deciding who to help. Dr Amrisha Vaish and her colleagues also looked at whether someone who is nasty gets less help than someone who is nice.[15] In this study, she had children sit with two adults, one of whom was drawing a picture, making a clay model or making a belt or necklace. After the first adult finished their craft project a second adult – the 'actor'– asked to see it. In the 'helpful' condition, the first adult 'accidentally' dropped the necklace, damaged her clay bird or tore the picture, and the actor helped to fix or retrieve it. In the neutral condition, the actor just made a bland observation about the first adult's masterpiece. In the harmful condition, the actor said, 'I'm going to break this [or take it or tear it] now,' and either stole the belt or necklace, or tore up the bird or picture and threw it in the bin.

Later, the child watched the actor and another adult, whom they hadn't met, as they played a game involving coloured balls. It was rigged in such a way that both the players needed the last ball at the same time, and the child was asked to choose who to give the ball to. When the actor had previously been helpful – or even stayed neutral in the first part of the experiment – the children gave the ball to the familiar adult rather than the stranger. However, when the actor had been nasty, the children overwhelmingly chose to give the ball to the neutral stranger: the children chose to punish actors who had been cruel.

But is it just that the actor had made the first adult sad? To work out whether the *intention*, or merely the damage done, was the motivating factor, Dr Vaish repeated the experiment with an additional twist. This time the actor either tried – and failed – to ruin the first adult's project, or they 'accidentally' damaged it.

In this case, children withdrew help from the person who had *tried* to cause harm, even though they failed. Those who accidentally damaged the first adult's craft project weren't obviously punished for their clumsiness.

What does this all mean? Well, first of all you can't buy kids' loyalty by being helpful. When the actor was helpful, neutral or accident-prone, they were still likely to be helped. Luckily for me, children will forgive klutzy adults. But you can *lose* children's loyalty very easily just by having hurtful intentions.

'Even three-year-olds showed some ability to distinguish bad outcomes from bad intentions, and to withdraw their prosocial behavior from those with bad intentions,' says Dr Vaish. 'We knew from previous work that young children, and even infants, can read and respond to others' basic intentions, but it was believed to be much later in development that children incorporate intention information into their moral evaluations: the fact that we saw this effect at age three was quite surprising.'[16]

Preschool children in WEIRD settings have been seen making other moral judgements when it comes to helping. Hepach, Vaish and Tomasello looked at whether children will help people who they know to be cry-babies. In a 2012 study they recruited 48 three-year-olds to come and play at the lab.[17] Each child saw an adult in distress three times. One-third of the children saw the adult being harmed, either by being physically hurt or treated badly. Another third saw the adult being mildly hurt, either by being frightened or treated thoughtlessly. The final third weren't able to see what made the adult sad. While in the same room as these children, the adult would then (pretend) cry on three different occasions. The authors describe their acting method in the paper as 'having a furrowed brow, pouting lips, and whimpering'.

Once the child had seen this first adult – the actor – get upset three times, they then went off to play blocks with the second adult. The actor then went behind a screen and after five seconds started whimpering again. In the cases where the actor had previously demonstrated that they were a bit of a cry-baby – whimpering in the minor-harm scenarios – children were much less likely to break off their game to go behind the screen and check if they were okay. But in the other two conditions – where the children had either *seen* the adult get hurt, or they hadn't known *why* they were upset, about three-quarters of the children stopped playing and went to check. They've learned whose sounds of sadness they can easily ignore.

At the 'end' of the experiment, to say thank you, the child was given two balloons filled with air, while the actor was given one balloon, filled with helium. The actor then 'accidentally' let their balloon go, and 'demonstrated sadness'. (More whimpering.) The children very quickly gave a balloon to those adults who had previously been sad about major harms. The children were significantly slower to offer their balloons to people who had been sad for reasons that were either unknown or trivial. Even at three, children determine who is and is not deserving of sympathy depending on whether they think someone has a tendency to lay it on a bit thick, and whether or not they've had a bad day.

Being a cry-baby, or being a bully who damages someone's picture over and over again, can be exhausting. Dr Vaish needed to play at being a cry-baby, or act the bully, hundreds of times to get these results. 'Playing these roles can be taxing after a while, because when we pretend to cry or we destroy others' belongings, we do temporarily take on some of those characteristics, which can be a downer,' says Dr Vaish. And she and her colleagues have to do this while still collecting data and making sure that they're behaving as consistently as possible with every child.

> You get quite good not just at acting but at acting while monitoring and responding to what a young child is saying and doing at the same time. It keeps you on your toes! Some roles are tough, but others are lighter and more fun. And it's through this acting that we get to answer some really interesting questions about quite young children – questions that we couldn't answer just by interviewing children of these ages.[18]

When it comes to adolescents, it's easier to stick them in scanners or interview them about their behaviour. And it turns out that – while teenagers might seem inconsiderate at times – they still want to help. They're just less good at knowing how and when. Between the ages of eleven and sixteen, teenagers are less likely to notice that you're sad or frustrated. Children this age get slower at matching emotional faces with the words that describe them – happy, sad, angry – than when they were younger. Puberty seems to cause a decline in empathy, at least until the age of sixteen.[19]

This may be the result of some drastic rewiring in the brain around that time. A cascade of pruning takes place, which repurposes the network of brain areas that humans use for understanding other people's minds. All the neurotypical people studied so far seem to use the same four areas of the brain when mentalising – when thinking about what someone else may be thinking and feeling. While most humans use the same four parts of the brain to mentalise, the ones that dominate change distinctly as we age.[20] Up to the age of fourteen, children tend to rely most strongly on a part called the dorsomedial prefrontal cortex: lift up your fringe (if you have one) and tap the middle of your head just above the hairline – that's roughly where you'll find it. Adults, in contrast, rely more on the temporal cortex – back near your ears.

Also during adolescence, children become more scared of saying or doing the wrong thing. For example, studies show that adolescents are extremely sensitive to social risk. Between the ages of thirteen and twenty-four, people are more likely to take risks in a driving simulation task when they are with a friend than when they are alone.[21] This reinforces something that insurance companies have known for years – people over twenty-six years of age are more likely to crash when they don't have a passenger, people under twenty-six are more likely to crash when they do. When you look at brain scans of healthy volunteers who are in a driving simulator, you can even see different reward centres lighting up depending on whether they are told that their friend, a stranger or their mum is watching. Rather sweetly, kids get a kick out of driving sensibly if they think a parent is watching them do it. For all it may seem like your teen doesn't care what you feel, they really do.

It's a culture thing: altruism means different things around the world

Studies like these are expensive, involved, and require specially trained researchers. You try whimpering in exactly the same way 250 times! So most studies are done in or near to university research labs that have – to date at least – been concentrated in WEIRD societies. That means there's a potential WEIRD bias in what we 'know' about behaviour. Even in relatively homogeneous WEIRD settings, not all kids behave exactly the same in each experiment – with some children willing to forgive a nasty adult, and others refusing to share even with someone in need – suggesting that these behaviours are common but not universal. But now there is an increasing body of evidence that hints at the weirdness of the kids of WEIRDMOMS.

For example, sharing is far from universal. Some things can be divided spatially – a cake, or a punnet of strawberries, or a sheet of stickers. But some things can only be shared across time – like who gets to choose the song on the car stereo, or who gets to wear the princess dress.* One of the most common ways that WEIRD families try to ensure fairness is by insisting on taking turns. It seems so instinctive to me that I don't think we even thought about it at home – when it comes to swings, shoulder rides, or scooters, I'd assumed that it was just natural to take turns.

But that isn't as universal a strategy as I once believed. Dr Esther Herrmann and her colleagues at the Max Planck Institute in Leipzig played a simple game with children from Germany and Kenya.[22] These 168 age-matched pairs of five- to ten-year-olds were given the chance to use a hook to 'fish' for beads to string on a

* Somehow, it's never my turn ...

bracelet. In the training part of the game, each member of the pair had a hook and a tube of their own. In the test part, each child had their own tube to fish from, but only had one hook between them.

The thing that most surprised the research team was that the children in both countries very rarely grabbed the hook from the child who picked it up first. But the difference between the German and Kenyan pairs was significant when it came to turn taking.

The majority of the German kids took turns from the outset, taking one bead then handing over the hook. Across the two trials, 95 per cent of the German pairs made sure that the beads were shared equally. Among the Samburu and Kikuyu children, turn taking – and even the idea of sharing equally – was far less prevalent.

The idea of 'having a turn' just seemed wrong to most of the Kenyan participants. Dr Herrmann showed videos of someone playing the same game and either fishing all the beads for themselves, or sharing the hook so that the other child could get half of the beads. When asked who was playing the game correctly, all the German children said the child who took turns was playing the game correctly. In contrast, 75 per cent of the Kenyan participants said that the child who monopolised the hook was playing the game right.

Dr Herrmann and her colleagues point out that Kenyan children understand about taking turns: they are taught to take turns when it comes to games like hopscotch or skipping. Adults, too, will take it in turns to use a tool. But in the dominant culture in Kenya where these experiments took place, material things are widely shared, though not in a calculatedly reciprocal way, or even in a way that tries to be scrupulously fair. Rather, if someone asks for something and a family member or neighbour can spare it, it will be given. Unlike in WEIRD settings, the sharing of *things* is a common way of helping.

For these children, monopolising the fish hook wasn't selfish – it was a sensible strategy. If someone is good at getting a resource then they should be allowed to maximise it. Everyone will benefit as a result because there will be more to go around. Taking care of one another doesn't always mean taking turns, or sharing things immediately.

And the joy of sharing does seem to be widespread. Dr Lara Aknin and her team repeated their experiment (where children had the opportunity to share their treats with a puppet) on Tanna Island, Vanuatu. They recruited twenty children as similar as possible in age distribution to the children in her original experiment in Vancouver. Again, the children got much more of a kick out of sharing their treat with the puppet than receiving a treat themselves.[23] The presence of the same effect in urban Vancouver as in rural communities in the Pacific doesn't prove that the joy experienced when being altruistic is *universal*, but it does indicate that isn't limited to WEIRD cultures.

Also, the understanding that what people need is not the same as what they want seems to be fairly widespread. As a Canadian who has worked in the US and is now in New Zealand, Dr Alia Martin has had the chance to look at helping behaviour in a few different contexts. In her experience, 'the cognition behind paternalistic helping is probably pretty universal: after all, it's extremely useful to be able to think about people's goals and consider whether simply doing as asked will produce the best outcome'.[24]

But even if that *cognition* is universal, social norms change how (and when) that paternalism takes place depending on how socially acceptable it is to override someone. 'We may not agree with someone's decisions, but, just taking WEIRD cultures as an example, it is more acceptable to actually be paternalistic toward some people than others. For example, I'm more likely to tell my child he can't eat a third piece of cake because he might become ill, than to tell an adult friend,' says Dr Martin. When we spoke, she was busy analysing data from a study that compared children from the US and mainland China. In this data set, American four-year-olds were equally likely to override an adult or a child. In China, children would override the child but would consistently give the adult what they had asked for, even if it was a less useful object.

That's not the only way that acceptable behaviour varies around the world. For example, if we are helpful, should we broadcast our good deeds or keep them quiet? In a fun experiment, a team from China, Canada and the US somehow managed to persuade hundreds of individual seven- to eleven-year-olds to tidy up a classroom.[25] The team recruited 250 children from a range of social classes in China who all attended a neighbourhood elementary school. The experimenter led each child individually into an office under the pretext of giving them an intelligence test. However, the office had been set up beforehand. 'We wanted to make it similar to a messy classroom, so basically we crumpled up sheets of paper, then put [them] in the garbage can and dumped them all over the place,' explained Dr Kang Lee, professor of developmental psychology and tier one research chair at the University of Toronto, Canada.[26]

At this point, the experimenter started to drop some fairly heavy hints that they would like to see the room tidied up. For example, 'I sure wish someone would help me clean up this room. It would be so nice if this mess was cleared.' They carried on hinting this way until each child actually went about cleaning the room. They did this with each of the 250 children, which is a lot of hints to drop.

According to Dr Lee's co-author Professor Gail Heyman, professor of psychology at the University of California, San Diego, there was a big difference in willingness to help between the Canadian and Chinese schoolchildren.[27] Despite their nice-guy reputation, the Canadian children were actually much less likely to spring into action as a clean-up crew. In contrast, she encountered a strong cultural norm in China that encourages children to help clean up their classrooms. But are the Chinese children just trying to make themselves look good? That's unlikely, because when they were asked who cleaned the room they lied their arses off, denying they had helped.

'The idea is that lying is always seen as bad, but it turns out that this is not true,' said Dr Lee when I spoke to him by phone:

We tell white lies to each other to be polite – this is a kind of prosociality as well: to not hurt other people's feelings. We usually refrain from telling the blunt truth. Here in North America, people tend to say, 'oh, your haircut looks great, your gift is wonderful, your dinner is delicious', even though they're all not, right? So this is one kind of prosociality we teach our kids, even though it goes against our teaching about honesty. It's messy, but somehow kids learn all this, starting from two years of age.[28]

For example, in societies where modesty is prized, children start to weigh up the importance of being known to be good, and being thought to be modest. For example, a group of British children were asked to rate the responses of a (fictional) child who had been praised for making a good catch. At about eight years old, British kids have already internalised the idea that a modest answer ('oh, I was just lucky') is more likeable than a self-enhancing response ('it's because I'm good at sport').[29]

By the age of ten, British children can even explain *why* they think self-deprecating responses matter: junior-school-aged children already understand that no one likes a show-off here in the UK, to my immense *chagrin*.[30] Yes, I use words like *chagrin*. With an accent too. I'm afraid that I'm an incurable show-off.

But even I will downplay the effort it took to make a cake, or the expense I've gone to over a gift or a treat. British adults are almost universally familiar with the phrase: 'What, this old thing?' Cross-cultural expert Dr Lee points out that in Britain we tend to preserve our modesty by lying by omission rather than by explicitly concealing things we might be proud of. In other cultures, however, children learn early that explicit modesty lies are important.

In China, Japan and Korea, a modesty lie is the lie you tell to not stand out because you want to be an unsung hero. 'In those cultures you don't want to brag about your personal achievements, or the good deeds you have done,' Dr Lee explains. 'In a collective society, you want to maintain and promote group coherence over individual achievements. You don't want anybody to be different. So if you have done something good, that makes you different from others.'[31]

In the classroom-tidying study, once the child had done the tidying, the experimenter told them that they'd done a good job, and then left saying that they had to get something from their car. At this point the teacher would return, saying, 'I'm so sorry for my messy office ...' and would then break off, act delightedly surprised and say, 'Oh! Someone has helped me by cleaning up my office!' followed by, 'I wonder who helped clean it up for me?' If the child didn't say that they had done so she would then ask, 'Do *you* know who cleaned my office up for me?' And if they still didn't claim the credit she would say, 'Did you clean up my office for me?'

Most of the Chinese children either lied or kept silent about their good deed until they were asked directly if they had been the one to clean the room. A quarter of the sixth-graders (11–12-year-olds) *never* fessed up, no matter how much they were pressed. If the teacher came in accompanied by several other children then the children were even more likely to keep quiet. In contrast, around two-thirds of the Canadian children told the teacher that they had tidied up the room before the teacher had a chance to ask about it. Canadians are notoriously nice and it seems that they're not backwards about telling you so.

If you find yourself thinking that one set of the children was 'right' and the other set were 'wrong', then that just shows that you are a product of your culture. The Chinese children weren't bad for fibbing and the Canadian children weren't bad for boasting. Dr Lee points out that modesty versus honesty play out very differently around the world. 'In Chinese society, if you get 100 per cent in the maths exam and your classmate asks how you did, you say, "Oh, I did okay ..." Chinese students will never tell you, "I got 100 per cent." In Canada, however, if you say, "oh, I did okay," but you actually got 100 per cent that would be horrible – you'd be a phony!'

But, according to Dr Heyman, being an unsung hero only goes

so far even for the Chinese children. They find other, subtler ways of making sure that people *know* just how unsung a hero they actually are. As Dr Heyman explains:

> In collectivist cultures like China, there is a much stronger emphasis on the needs of the group and group harmony. Calling attention to oneself disrupts this, so children in China are explicitly taught to try to be unsung heroes. However, I have other research suggesting that children in China also want to call attention to themselves and do so in situations where they are not *seen* as trying to call attention to themselves. For example, they may brag about their success at school, as long as that could credibly be interpreted as an implicit offer to help tutor other students.[32]

Saying, 'I'm good at maths,' would be rude, while saying, 'I can help if anyone is struggling with advanced trigonometry,' is just good manners.

Children are quick to learn the rules for success in the culture they happen to be raised in. 'The most surprising part is how we [say that] we teach our kids to be honest from a very, very young age, but somehow they figure out the rules about white lies and modesty lies,' Dr Lee tells me.[33] We don't explicitly instruct children to lie, but they pick up our example very quickly. 'We are really evolved to be in tune with each other; we are social animals. Lying and learning how to lie in different situations is one of the prosocial abilities that we develop over the first few years of life.'

Building a kinder human: what can we do to help?

Whether you're a child or an adult, putting someone else first can be really costly despite the warm glow we get from giving, or the stress of being unable to help. It takes time and resources to do something for someone else. So how do we encourage our children to make those sacrifices? It turns out that parents actually have very little explicit influence. When Dr Felix Warneken recruited parents with two-year-old children to a study of helping, all the groups of children were equally eager – to the point that it kind of messed up the experiment.[34] Because the children were all so keen, it wasn't possible to spot any variance between the conditions in the first attempt. To try to identify the *really* keen helpers, Dr Warneken set up an obstacle course of a ball pit and soft-play blocks that the children would have to climb over. Still, over two-thirds of them chose to break off their play and tackle the obstacles in order to help. The only group who showed a slight-but-not-significant drop in helpfulness was the set of toddlers whose parents had ordered them to help. To the surprise of no parent of a toddler anywhere, commands can be surprisingly counterproductive.

Rewarding kids for being kind doesn't help either. It can actually be detrimental because of something called the overjustification effect. Dr Julia Ulber, lecturer in child psychology at Canterbury Christ Church University, looked at the ways that children behave when their sharing is rewarded, praised or not acknowledged at all.[35] A set of 96 three-year-olds were asked to play games where it would be up to them to ensure that marbles were shared equally. They played against our old friend the puppet, who either said, 'If you share a marble, I'll give you a present,' or simply, 'I only got one marble. I want to have as many marbles as you. Will you give me one?' Later, the child was given six stickers and the puppet given none (because the experimenter 'had forgotten' to bring two sets of stickers). Those children who had been *praised* for sharing were kind enough to donate two or three stickers to the puppet. The ones who had been *rewarded* for sharing gave only one sticker on average. In fact, they gave slightly *less* than one sticker on average because five of the children in the reward condition refused to share at all.

What's going on here? Surely rewards are nice? The problem is that the reward might not be as nice as the feeling we get from being kind, and actually distracts from the warm glow. Dr Ulber explains that when children are already motivated to do something because it is intrinsically enjoyable, shifting their attention to an extrinsic reward can lead to them underestimating their own enjoyment of the behaviour. 'The overjustification effect means that the *expectation* of a reward can undermine children's initial, intrinsic motivation to do something.'[36]

That doesn't mean that it's time to go cold turkey on the toddler-crack yet. 'Material rewards like stickers might be essential in cases where children are very shy or inhibited, or when the intrinsic interest in the activity is very low. For example, who likes putting the rubbish out?'[37] And if you want to use rewards effectively, be on the lookout for opportunities to bestow them spontaneously, rather than using them as a goal to aim for. 'Rewarding children does not necessarily have negative implications if it happens unexpectedly, much like flowers have a greater impact if given outside Valentine's Day,' Dr Ulber suggests.

You've got a nerve

If you want children to be kind, the most important thing you can do is to help them feel loved and secure. The vagus nerve controls heart rate and breathing, among other things, and the better the nerve is at making subtle changes to your heart rhythm, the better you tend to be at managing feelings of stress and anxiety, and to feel safe in new situations.[38] Several studies have looked at the connection between altruism and the responsiveness of the vagus nerve – a characteristic sometimes called vagal tone. In a study of seventy-four preschoolers given a set of tokens that they could exchange for prizes, Dr Jonas Miller and his colleagues at the University of California, Davis, noted that those who had better vagal tone were also more generous.[39]

Is there a Joe Wicks for the parasympathetic nervous system that can help children tone up the vagus nerve – and maybe even bolster our own? Meet Dr Mariana Lozada, senior researcher at the National University of Comahue, Argentina. She studied groups of six- and seven-year-olds to see whether there were some activities that would help children become more altruistic.[40] Two classes of twenty children were recruited to the study. In the control group, the class spent thirty minutes a week learning about the environment, followed by twenty minutes doing art activities. In the intervention group, the class spent five minutes on breathing, relaxation and mindfulness exercises. Then they spent some time doing things that reminded them of feelings of security and belonging, like listening to stories about people being caring and kind, or remembering times that they had been helped. Finally, they played cooperative games with each other for fifteen to twenty minutes before doing the same art activities as the other class.

After ten weeks of these sessions, the children were given fourteen sweets and asked whether they'd like to share, anonymously, with another randomly selected child. Those children who had spent time on relaxation, mindfulness, thinking about kindness and playing cooperatively gave away twice as many of their sweets at the end of the ten-week course than they had at the start of the experiment, but the control group gave away the same amount as they had at the beginning.

Spending time being mindful with your kids may be effective, but it's our *daily* habits as caregivers that make the most difference. Dr Maja Deković, professor of child and family studies at Utrecht University, studied the popularity and the kindness of kids in junior school (between six and eleven years old).[41] Data was also gathered from those children's parents about their parenting style. An authorit*ative* style – firm but warm, and encouraging the child to think about their own and others' feelings and needs – was associated with children who were kinder and more popular. An authorit*arian* style – one where parents do a lot of telling off and forbidding – was associated with kids who were less popular and less prosocial. Of course the parents in the study might have been more authoritarian *because* their kids' behaviour was more challenging, while kinder kids are just *easier* to parent. But there's lots of other evidence that children's kindness can be influenced by small shifts in parenting style, like making the time to listen, ensuring that children know their feelings and needs matter, and being consistent but warm. This is all easier said than done when you're faced with a screaming five-year-old at the end of a tiring day, but building up your own vagal tone by practising compassion with (and on) your children is likely to work wonders in weeks. Try to take some time yourself to practise mindfulness, relaxation and gratitude. It's an investment in your future parenting.

Nurturing our children's nurturing instincts

Hopefully, this chapter has convinced you to be a bit more sanguine about just how kind your child really is. If they're not scrambling out of ball pits to give you clothes pegs, or willing to share their stickers equally with your friend's kids, they're not doing anything wrong and neither are you. Even in the experiments where toddlers have the chance to make themselves feel better by helping an adult who has dropped something, 35 per cent of children didn't manage to help. Some of them went to the person who needed help but didn't seem to know what to do, some were distracted by the ball pit (who wouldn't be?) or defeated by the obstacle course. And some were just too nervous to leave their parent's side. Think about the times you've wanted to help but have been too overwhelmed, too scared of saying or doing the wrong thing, or just not sure *how* to help. We all have clashing motives and sometimes we fail to act, no matter how much empathy we may feel. Our children are no different.[42]

But if you would like your child to be a little more gracious from time to time, forget nagging or rewarding – and certainly avoid shaming them. Children learn what we think is acceptable behaviour by watching how *we* treat people. That doesn't mean that there's no room for talking about altruism. 'Explaining behaviour and why it is important that we apologise, say thank you, and so on – it all helps. Talking about emotions positively influences a toddler's helping and sharing,' says Dr Ulber, and Dr Amrisha Vaish has consistently found the same in her research.

But never forget, we have all failed to share, or found ourselves too busy or distracted at one time or another. Dr Ulber has some really important advice: 'As parents we should have realistic expectations.' As with so much in parenting, it's scientifically appropriate to cut your kids – and yourself – some slack.[43]

Epilogue: How to Build *Your* Human

If writing this book has taught me anything, it's that kids need our attention, our patience, our willingness to communicate and our time. It's also made me realise how precious time is, and how many competing demands there are on our patience and attention. It's made me even more militant about the need to protect childhood: not from video games or social media, but from the pressures that make family life so stressful.

But it's also brought home to me that children's brains are *not* like our own. They have different processes and different structures. They notice different things than we do. They find learning easier, but they find regulating their emotions and maintaining concentration even harder than we do. Even at our most sleep-and-coffee deprived.

And it has reminded me that we are building *humans* – not robots. Each child is unique, even in the same family. Each family is unique, in its values, priorities, resources and experiences. We are humans building humans in all our infinite variety. Your tiny human is an individual, so let them be unique.

I've also realised that we, in WEIRD cultures, need to change the way we organise our societies. Because there are a few things that research has been surprisingly consistent in demonstrating:

1) Childhood shapes our lives profoundly. Even before babies are born there are things they have already learned. The more time and attention you can give a child, the better the chance they will become resilient, articulate and kind.

2) Attention is most beneficial when it is driven by curiosity rather than conflict. This might seem like a lot to ask when you're already tired, stressed or overwhelmed, but when your child does something that you don't understand (or don't like) try asking 'why?' And genuinely ask the question, don't set it as a trap. Prove to your kids that you care enough to listen to what they say and, over time, they'll trust you more, become more honest and open with you, and start making better choices. The more time you spend trying to understand your children, the better they'll understand themselves.

3) Drop the distractions. It just isn't possible to figure out what your child needs from you at the same time as answering an email from your boss/reminding a client to pay an invoice/doing the online grocery shopping. Trying to juggle sends the message that your child isn't worth your full attention. Don't half-arse two things, whole-arse one thing. Even if sometimes that thing doesn't seem important. That's because ...

4) Play is serious business – especially when children are in charge. It's so important to show an interest in what your child is playing with and to follow what they are interested in. If you spend time observing a child and follow their interest and attention early on, they'll pick up language, social skills and confidence far faster than if you try to formally educate them. A teddy bears' picnic will do more for a young child's language than any amount of flash cards.

5) Parenting like a scientist takes resilience. Things won't go perfectly all the time. That's because – and I can't stress this enough – you are building a *unique human being*. Nobody has done exactly what you are doing *right now*. It also takes time,

energy and curiosity. Sometimes the asymmetry between kids' resources of time, energy and curiosity and your own can seem like a colossal universal joke at the expense of all caregivers. Building humans is bloody hard work.

6) All of which means that we – as a society – need to support everyone involved in raising a child. Not by telling people how to care for children, but by giving people the time and space to raise children. Social policies that lead to longer or more uncertain working hours for less pay, that place families into smaller and more precarious homes, that reduce the time and space available for play, are doing vast harm. If we want future generations to grow up happy and healthy, then no child should be raised in poverty. That includes poverty of time, poverty of emotional support and poverty of security, as well as financial poverty.

While I haven't tried to give you the recipe to create a contented kid or an attentive adolescent, I hope I've helped you to understand *why* your child might be sad, angry, confused or sullen. And I hope that understanding helps you find patience: patience with your child, and patience with yourself. Building a unique human has unique challenges. Don't be afraid to ask for help. And don't be afraid to reject advice. Stay open-minded, curious and patient – treat your relationship with your child like the often-frustrating, always-fascinating experiment that it is and know that this never-to-be-repeated experience belongs to you and you alone.

And please: Don't Panic.

Acknowledgements

My love, thanks, apologies, and admiration to my family – Team Science Baby. We may not have a baby any more, but thank you for always being willing to science the shit out of things together, even when it's hard. And thank you for the gift of time to write, cups of coffee, maps to the kitchen, superhero drawings, and all the hugs. I love you all so much.

My thanks to every neglected friend to whom I owe coffee and long conversations. Sorry I have been at the bottom of the word-well. I miss you!

My immense gratitude to every researcher named in this book. And to all those who took time out to be interviewed, an especial thanks for letting me intrude on your time. Specifically, thank you to Professor Gail Heyman, Dr Kang Lee, Dr Julia Ulber, Dr Amrisha Vaish and Dr Felix Warneken. I have tried to be as accurate as possible, but any mangling of their findings is my fault entirely! And to Susanne Hillen for her splendid eye for detail!

Thank you so much to Carrie Plitt, the most supportive and stellar agent. I am so lucky to have you. And thank you to Rebecca Gray: your enthusiasm and incisiveness keep me going and I'm so excited to be working with you again.

And a final thanks to booksellers, librarians, and you, the reader. Communication makes us human. Thank you for keeping the conversation going.

References

Adams, A.S., 2013. Needs met through role-playing games: a fantasy theme analysis of Dungeons & Dragons. *Kaleidoscope: A Graduate Journal of Qualitative Communication Research*, 12(1), pp. 69–86.

Aknin, L.B. et al., 2015. Prosocial behavior leads to happiness in a small-scale rural society. *Journal of Experimental Psychology: General*, 144(4), pp. 788–795.

Aknin, L.B., Hamlin, J.K. & Dunn, E.W., 2012. Giving leads to happiness in young children. *PLOS ONE*, 7(6), p.e39211.

Alter, A., 2017. *Irresistible: The Rise of Addictive Technology and the Business of Keeping Us Hooked*, Penguin Press.

American Psychiatric Association, 2013. Diagnostic and Statistical Manual of Mental Disorders: DSM-5, 5th edition, p. 5.

Ambridge, B. et al., 2013. The retreat from overgeneralization in child language acquisition: word learning, morphology, and verb argument structure. *Wiley Interdisciplinary Reviews: Cognitive Science*, 4(1), pp. 47–62.

Anam, T., 2019. 'For five years we dreaded every meal': my infant son's struggle with food. *The Guardian*. Available at: http://www.theguardian.com/society/2019/apr/09/for-five-years-we-dreaded-every-meal-my-infant-sons-struggle-with-food [accessed 4 December 2019].

Anbuhl, K.L. et al., 2016. Early Development of the Human Auditory System. In *Fetal and Neonatal Physiology*, 5th edition, pp. 1396–1410.

Anders, T.F. & Taylor, T.R., 1994. Babies and their sleep environment. *Children's Environments*, 11(2), pp. 123–134.

Arbib, M.A., 2005. From monkey-like action recognition to human language: an evolutionary framework for neurolinguistics. *The Behavioral and Brain Sciences*, 28(2), pp. 105–124; discussion pp. 125–167.

Ball, H.L., 2003. Breastfeeding, bed-sharing, and infant sleep. *Birth*, 30(3), pp. 181–188. Available at: http://dx.doi.org/10.1046/j.1523-536x.2003.00243.x.

Banasik, N., 2013. Non-literal speech comprehension in preschool children: an example from a study on verbal irony. *Psychology of Language and Communication*, 17(3), pp. 309–324.

Banerjee, R., 2002. Audience effects on self-presentation in childhood. *Social development*, 11(4), pp. 487–507.

Barac, R., Moreno, S. & Bialystok, E., 2016. Behavioral and electrophysiological differences in executive control between monolingual and bilingual children. *Child Development*, 87(4), pp. 1277–1290.

Barbehenn, R.V. & Peter Constabel, C., 2011. Tannins in plant-herbivore interactions. *Phytochemistry*, 72(13), pp. 1551–1565.

Barnes, S. et al., 1983. Characteristics of adult speech which predict children's language development. *Journal of Child Language*, 10(1), pp. 65–84.

Bateson, P., 2010. Theories of Play. In A.D. Pellegrini, ed., *The Oxford Handbook of the Development of Play*, Oxford University Press.

Batsell, W.R., Jr et al., 2002. 'You will eat all of that!': a retrospective analysis of forced consumption episodes. *Appetite*, 38(3), pp. 211–219.

Bauer, R.H., 1993. Lateralization of neural control for

vocalization by the frog (*Rana pipiens*). *Psychobiology*, 21(3), pp. 243–248.

Bay-Hinitz, A.K., Peterson, R.F. & Quilitch, H.R., 1994. Cooperative games: a way to modify aggressive and cooperative behaviors in young children. *Journal of Applied Behavior Analysis*, 27(3), pp. 435–446.

Behne, T. et al., 2005. Unwilling versus unable: infants' understanding of intentional action. *Developmental Psychology*, 41(2), pp. 328–337.

Bekoff, M., 1972. The development of social interaction, play, and metacommunication in mammals: an ethological perspective. *The Quarterly Review of Biology*, 47(4), pp. 412–434.

Bekoff, M. & Allen, C., 1998. Intentional communication and social play: how and why animals negotiate and agree to play. *Animal Play*, pp. 97–114. Available at: http://dx.doi.org/10.1017/cbo9780511608575.006.

Bennett, M. & Yeeles, C., 1990. Children's understanding of showing off. *The Journal of Social Psychology*, 130(5), pp. 591–596.

Bentivoglio, M. & Grassi-Zucconi, G., 1997. The pioneering experimental studies on sleep deprivation. *Sleep*, 20(7), pp. 570–576.

Bentley, A., 2006. Booming baby food: infant food and feeding in post-World War II America. *The Michigan Historical Review*, 32(2), pp. 63–87.

Bertenthal, B.I., Rose, J.L. & Bai, D.L., 1997. Perception–action coupling in the development of visual control of posture. *Journal of Experimental Psychology: Human Perception and Performance*, 23(6), p.1631.

Blair, P.S. et al., 2009. Hazardous cosleeping environments and risk factors amenable to change: case-control study of SIDS in South West England. *BMJ*, 339, p.b3666.

Blasi, A. et al., 2011. Early specialization for voice and emotion processing in the infant brain. *Current Biology*, 21(14), pp. 1220–1224.

Bos, P. A. et al. 2010. Testosterone administration modulates neural responses to crying infants in young females. *Psychoneuroendocrinology*, 35(1), 114–121.

Botvin, G.J. & Sutton-Smith, B., 1977. The development of structural complexity in children's fantasy narratives. *Developmental Psychology*, 13(4), pp. 377–388.

Braddick, O. et al., 1983. The onset of binocular function in human infants. *Human Neurobiology*, 2(2), pp. 65–69.

Brandt, C. et al., 2013. Development of vocalization and hearing in American mink (*Neovison vison*). *The Journal of Experimental Biology*, 216 (Pt 18), pp. 3542–3550.

Bratis, D. et al., 2010. Sleep disturbance symptoms and their associations with alexithymia, depression and anxiety. *Annals of General Psychiatry*, 9(1), p. S163.

Brooker, E., Blaise, M. & Edwards, S., 2014. *SAGE Handbook of Play and Learning in Early Childhood*, SAGE Publishing.

Brown, A., 2018. No difference in self-reported frequency of choking between infants introduced to solid foods using a baby-led weaning or traditional spoon-feeding approach. *Journal of Human Nutrition and Dietetics: the official journal of the British Dietetic Association*, 31(4), pp. 496–504.

Brown, J.R. & Dunn, J., 1991. 'You can cry, Mum': The social and developmental implications of talk about internal states. *The British Journal of Developmental Psychology*, 9(2), pp. 237–256.

Bruckman, A., 1999. Can educational be fun? Game Developers Conference, San Jose, California; pp. 75–79. Available at https://www.cc.gatech.edu/~asb/papers/bruckman_gdc99.html

Buchsbaum, D. et al., 2012. The power of possibility: causal learning, counterfactual reasoning, and pretend play. *Philosophical Transactions of the Royal Society of London. Series B, Biological Sciences*, 367(1599), pp. 2202–2212.

Burghardt, G.M., 2010. Defining and Recognizing Play. In A.D. Pellegrini, ed., *The Oxford Handbook of the Development of Play*, Oxford University Press.

Bushdid, C. et al., 2014. Humans can discriminate more than 1 trillion olfactory stimuli. *Science*, 343(6177), pp. 1370–1372.

Butte, N.F. et al., 1992. Sleep organization and energy expenditure of breast-fed and formula-fed infants. *Pediatric Research*, 32(5), pp. 514–519.

Byrne, E.L., Corney, D.P.A. & Lotto, R.B., 2011. An Ecology-based approach to Perceptual Modelling. In E.J. Davelaar, ed., *Proceedings of the Twelfth Neural Computation and Psychology Workshop*, World Scientific Publishing.

Cain, N. & Gradisar, M., 2010. Electronic media use and sleep in school-aged children and adolescents: a review. *Sleep Medicine*, 11(8), pp. 735–742.

Call, J. et al., 2004. 'Unwilling' versus 'unable': chimpanzees' understanding of human intentional action. *Developmental Science*, 7(4), pp. 488–498.

Cameron, S.L., Heath, A.-L.M. & Taylor, R.W., 2012. How feasible is baby-led weaning as an approach to infant feeding? A review of the evidence. *Nutrients*, 4(11), pp. 1575–1609.

Carey, S.E., Diamond, R. & Woods, B., 1980. Development of face recognition: a maturational component? *Developmental Psychology*. Available at: https://dash.harvard.edu/handle/1/33010397 [accessed 14 December 2018].

Carlson, F.M., 2011. *Big Body Play: Why Boisterous, Vigorous, and Very Physical Play Is Essential to Children's Development and Learning*, National Association for the Education of Young Children.

Carno, M.-A. et al., 2003. Developmental stages of sleep from birth to adolescence, common childhood sleep disorders: overview and nursing implications. *Journal of Pediatric Nursing*, 18(4), pp. 274–283.

Carpenter, M., Akhtar, N. & Tomasello, M., 1998. Fourteen- through 18-month-old infants differentially imitate intentional and accidental actions. *Infant Behavior & Development*, 21(2), pp. 315–330.

Carpenter, M., Nagell, K. & Tomasello, M., 1998. Social cognition, joint attention, and communicative competence from 9 to 15 months of age. *Monographs of the Society for Research in Child Development*, 63(4), pp. i–vi, 1–143.

Cartmill, E.A. & Byrne, R.W., 2010. Semantics of primate gestures: intentional meanings of orangutan gestures. *Animal Cognition*, 13(6), pp. 793–804.

de Carvalho, A., Dautriche, I. & Christophe, A., 2016. Preschoolers use phrasal prosody online to constrain syntactic analysis. *Developmental Science*, 19(2), pp. 235–250.

Casey, B.J., Giedd, J.N. & Thomas, K.M., 2000. Structural and functional brain development and its relation to cognitive development. *Biological Psychology*, 54(1–3), pp. 241–257. Available at: http://dx.doi.org/10.1016/s0301-0511(00)00058-2.

Chalmers, N.R. & Locke-Haydon, J., 1984. Correlations among measures of playfulness and skillfulness in captive common marmosets (*Callithrix jacchus jacchus*). *Developmental Psychobiology*, 17(2), pp. 191–208.

Chance, S.A. & Crow, T.J., 2007. Distinctively human: cerebral lateralisation and language in *Homo sapiens*. *Journal of Anthropological Sciences*, 85, pp. 83–100.

Chomsky, N., 1975. *Reflections on Language*, Random House USA Inc.

Chomsky, N., 2006. *Language and Mind*, Cambridge University Press.

Chomsky, N., 2010. Some simple evo devo theses: how true might they be for language? *The Evolution of Human Language: Biolinguistic Perspectives*, 62, pp. 54–62.

Coplan, R.J., Arbeau, K.A. & Armer, M., 2008. Don't fret, be supportive! Maternal characteristics linking child shyness to psychosocial and school adjustment in kindergarten. *Journal of Abnormal Child Psychology*, 36(3), pp. 359–371.

Corballis, M.C., 2014. Left brain, right brain: facts and fantasies. *PLOS Biology*, 12(1), p.e1001767.

Corballis, M.C., 2017. A Word in the Hand: The Gestural Origins of Language. In M. Mody, ed., *Neural Mechanisms of Language*, Springer US, pp. 199–218.

Cordes, C., & Miller, E., eds, 2000. Fool's gold: a critical look at computers in childhood. *Alliance for Childhood*. Available at: http://files.eric.ed.gov/fulltext/ED445803.pdf

Corfe, S., 2018. *What are the Barriers to Eating Healthily in the UK?* Social Market Foundation. Available at: http://www.smf.co.uk/publications/barriers-eating-healthily-uk/ [accessed 22 May 2019].

Corney, D. & Lotto, R.B., 2007. What are lightness illusions and why do we see them? *PLOS Computational Biology*, 3(9), pp. 1790–1800.

Covington, L.B. et al., 2019. Toddler bedtime routines and associations with nighttime sleep duration and maternal and household factors. *Journal of Clinical Sleep Medicine: Official Publication of the American Academy of Sleep Medicine*, 15(6), pp. 865–871.

Crago, M.B., Allen, S.E.M. & Hough-Eyamie, W.P., 1997. Exploring Innateness through Cultural and Linguistic Variation. In M. Gopnik, ed., *The Inheritance and Innateness of Grammars*, Oxford University Press, pp. 70–90.

Crawford, C.J., 1994. Parenting practices in the Basque Country: implications of infant and childhood sleeping location for personality development. *Ethos*, 22(1), pp. 42–82.

Creel, S.C. et al., 2018. Speaking a tone language enhances musical pitch perception in 3–5-year-olds. *Developmental Science*, 21(1). Available at: http://dx.doi.org/10.1111/desc.12503.

Cross, T.G., 1979. Mothers' speech adjustments and child language learning: some methodological considerations. *Language Sciences*, 1(1), pp. 3–25.

Crowley, S.J., Acebo, C. & Carskadon, M.A., 2007. Sleep, circadian rhythms, and delayed phase in adolescence. *Sleep Medicine*, 8(6), pp. 602–612.

Crystal, S.R. & Bernstein, I.L., 1998. Infant salt preference and mother's morning sickness. *Appetite*, 30(3), pp. 297–307.

DeCasper, A.J. & Spence, M.J., 1986. Prenatal maternal speech influences newborns' perception of speech sounds. *Infant Behavior & Development*, 9(2), pp. 133–150.

Decety, J. et al., 2004. The neural bases of cooperation and competition: an fMRI investigation. *NeuroImage*, 23(2), pp. 744–751.

Deković, M. & Janssens, J.M., 1992. Parents' child-rearing style and child's sociometric status. *Developmental Psychology*, 28(5), pp. 925–932.

Delhikar, N. et al., 2019. Autobiographical memory from different life stages in individuals with obstructive sleep apnea. *Journal of the International Neuropsychological Society*, 25(3), pp. 266–274.

DeLoache, J.S., Uttal, D.H. & Rosengren, K.S., 2004. Scale errors offer evidence for a perception-action dissociation early in life. *Science*, 304(5673), pp. 1027–1029.

Dimitrov, S. et al., 2019. Gαs-coupled receptor signaling and sleep regulate integrin activation of human antigen-specific T cells. *The Journal of Experimental Medicine*, 216(3), pp. 517–526.

Dixson, H.G.W. et al., 2017. Scaling Theory of Mind in a Small-scale Society: A Case Study From Vanuatu. *Child Development*, 89(6), pp. 2157–2175. Available at: http://doi.org/10.1111/cdev.12919.

Doan, T. et al., 2007. Breast-feeding increases sleep duration of new parents. *The Journal of Perinatal & Neonatal Nursing*, 21(3), pp. 200–206.

Doi, T., 2014. *The Anatomy of Dependence*, reprint edition, Kodansha International.

Donahue, M. & Mitchell, S., 2019. Report: Dollar stores are targeting struggling urban neighborhoods and small towns. One community is showing how to fight back. ILRS (Institute for Local Self-Reliance). Available at: https://ilsr.org/dollar-stores-target-cities-towns-one-fights-back/ [accessed 22 May 2019].

Dougherty, K. & Silver, C., 2007. Chef-nutritionist teams spark

enjoyment and learning in cooking education series for 8- to 12-year-olds. *Journal of Nutrition Education and Behavior*, 39(4), pp. 237–238.
Drummond, J.D.K. et al., 2017. Helping the one you hurt: toddlers' rudimentary guilt, shame, and prosocial behavior after harming another. *Child Development*, 88(4), pp. 1382–1397.
Dubois, L. et al., 2007. Preschool children's eating behaviours are related to dietary adequacy and body weight. *European Journal of Clinical Nutrition*, 61(7), pp. 846–855.
Dumontheil, I., Apperly, I.A. & Blakemore, S.-J., 2010. Online usage of theory of mind continues to develop in late adolescence. *Developmental Science*, 13(2), pp. 331–338.
Dunn, E.W. et al., 2010. On the costs of self-interested economic behavior: how does stinginess get under the skin? *Journal of Health Psychology*, 15(4), pp. 627–633.
Dunn, J., Bretherton, I. & Munn, P., 1987. Conversations about feeling states between mothers and their young children. *Developmental Psychology*, 23(1), pp. 132–139.
Dunn, J., Brown, J. & Beardsall, L., 1991. Family talk about feeling states and children's later understanding of others' emotions. *Developmental Psychology*, 27(3), pp. 448–455.
Dunne, J. et al., 2019. Milk of ruminants in ceramic baby bottles from prehistoric child graves. *Nature*, 574(7777), pp. 246–248.
Dunphy-Lelii, S. & Wellman, H.M., 2004. Infants' understanding of occlusion of others' line-of-sight: implications for an emerging theory of mind. *The European Journal of Developmental Psychology*, 1(1), pp. 49–66.
Dye, M.W.G. & Bavelier, D., 2010. Differential development of visual attention skills in school-age children. *Vision Research*, 50(4), pp. 452–459.
Ehret, G., 1987. Left hemisphere advantage in the mouse brain for recognizing ultrasonic communication calls. *Nature*, 325(6101), pp. 249–251.
Ehrsson, H.H., Spence, C. & Passingham, R.E., 2004. That's my

hand! Activity in premotor cortex reflects feeling of ownership of a limb. *Science*, 305(5685), pp. 875–877.

Eisenberger, N.I., Lieberman, M.D. & Williams, K.D., 2003. Does rejection hurt? An fMRI study of social exclusion. *Science*, 302(5643), pp. 290–292.

Ekirch, A.R., 2001. Sleep we have lost: pre-industrial slumber in the British Isles. *The American Historical Review*, 106(2), pp. 343–386.

Elkind, D., 2007. *The Power of Play: Learning What Comes Naturally*, Da Capo Press.

Erard, M., 2019. A cultural history of first words. *The Paris Review*. Available at: https://www.theparisreview.org/blog/2019/07/26/a-cultural-history-of-first-words/ [accessed 28 November 2019].

Ervin-Tripp, S., 1971. An overview of theories of grammatical development. *The Ontogenesis of Grammar*, 189–212.

Ervin-Tripp, S., 1996. Context in Language. In D.I. Slobin et al., eds, *Social interaction, social context, and language*, Psychology Press, pp. 39–54.

Everett, D., 2010. *Don't Sleep, There are Snakes: Life and Language in the Amazonian Jungle*, Profile Books.

Exelmans, L. & Van den Bulck, J., 2016. Bedtime mobile phone use and sleep in adults. *Social Science & Medicine*, 148, pp. 93–101.

Fabes, R.A. et al., 2001. Preschoolers' spontaneous use of emotion language: relations to social status. *Journal of Early Education and Development*, 12, pp. 11–17.

Falciglia, G.A. et al., 2000. Food neophobia in childhood affects dietary variety. *Journal of the American Dietetic Association*, 100(12), pp. 1474–1481.

Fassbender, W., 2011. Grauen in der Dose. *Neue Zürcher Zeitung*, Switzerland. Available at: https://web.archive.org/web/20111124044024/http://nachgewuerzt.blog.nzz.ch/2011/08/22/grauen-in-der-dose/ [accessed 20 October 2020].

Ferber, R., 2006. *Solve Your Child's Sleep Problems: New, Revised, and Expanded Edition*, Simon and Schuster.

Fernandez, D.C. et al., 2018. Light affects mood and learning through distinct retina-brain pathways. *Cell*, 175(1), pp. 34–35.

Fiese, B.H. & Schwartz, M., 2008. Reclaiming the family table: mealtimes and child health and wellbeing. *Social Policy Report*, 22(4). Society for Research in Child Development. Available at: http://files.eric.ed.gov/fulltext/ED521697.pdf [accessed 4 December 2019].

Fisher, C. & Inch, S., 1996. Nipple confusion – who is confused? *The Journal of Pediatrics*, 129(1), pp. 174–175.

Fisher, J.O. & Birch, L.L., 1999. Restricting access to palatable foods affects children's behavioral response, food selection, and intake. *The American Journal of Clinical Nutrition*, 69(6), pp. 1264–1272.

Flinker, A. et al., 2015. Redefining the role of Broca's area in speech. *Proceedings of the National Academy of Sciences of the United States of America*, 112(9), pp. 2871–2875.

Floden, D. et al., 2008. Impulsivity and risk-taking behavior in focal frontal lobe lesions. *Neuropsychologia*, 46(1), pp. 213–223.

Fodor, J.A., 1966. How to Learn to Talk: Some Simple Ways. In F. Smith and G.A. Miller, eds, *The Genesis of Language*, MIT Press, pp. 105–122.

Forbes, J.F., Weiss, D.S. & Folen, R.A., 1992. The cosleeping habits of military children. *Military Medicine*, 157(4), pp. 196–200.

Forestell, C.A. & Mennella, J.A., 2007. Early determinants of fruit and vegetable acceptance. *Pediatrics*, 120(6), pp. 1247–1254.

Frank, G., Plunkett, S.W. & Otten, M.P., 2010. Perceived parenting, self-esteem, and general self-efficacy of Iranian American adolescents. *Journal of Child and Family Studies*, 19(6), pp. 738–746.

Frith, U. & Frith, C.D., 2003. Development and neurophysiology of mentalizing. *Philosophical Transactions of the Royal Society of London. Series B, Biological Sciences*, 358(1431), pp. 459–473.

Fu, G. et al., 2016. Learning to be unsung heroes: development of reputation management in two cultures. *Child Development*, 87(3), pp. 689–699.

Galloway, A.T. et al., 2006. 'Finish your soup': counterproductive effects of pressuring children to eat on intake and affect. *Appetite*, 46(3), pp. 318–323.

Gardner, M., & Steinberg, L., 2005. Peer influence on risk taking, risk preference, and risky decision making in adolescence and adulthood: an experimental study. *Developmental Psychology*, 41(4), 625–635.

Gay, C.L., Lee, K.A. & Lee, S.-Y., 2004. Sleep patterns and fatigue in new mothers and fathers. *Biological Research for Nursing*, 5(4), pp. 311–318.

Gessner, B.D., Ives, G.C. & Perham-Hester, K.A., 2001. Association between sudden infant death syndrome and prone sleep position, bed sharing, and sleeping outside an infant crib in Alaska. *Pediatrics*, 108(4), pp. 923–927.

Gilkerson, J. et al., 2017. Mapping the early language environment using all-day recordings and automated analysis. *American Journal of Speech-Language Pathology / American Speech-Language-Hearing Association*, 26(2), pp. 248–265.

Glendinning, J.I., 1994. Is the bitter rejection response always adaptive? *Physiology & Behavior*, 56(6), pp. 1217–1227.

Godoi, D. & Barela, J.A., 2008. Body sway and sensory motor coupling adaptation in children: effects of distance manipulation. *Developmental Psychobiology*, 50(1), pp. 77–87.

Goldin-Meadow, S., 2005. *The Resilience of Language: What Gesture Creation in Deaf Children Can Tell Us About How All Children Learn Language*, Psychology Press.

Goldstein, J. H., 2013. Technology and play. *Scholarpedia Journal*, 8(2), 30434.

Golinkoff, R.M. & Alioto, A., 1995. Infant-directed speech facilitates lexical learning in adults hearing Chinese: implications for language acquisition. *Journal of Child Language*, 22(3), pp. 703–726.

Golinkoff, R.M. & Ames, G.J., 1979. A comparison of fathers' and mothers' speech with their young children. *Child Development*, 50(1), pp. 28–32.

Göncü, A. & Gaskins, S., 2010. Comparing and Extending Piaget's and Vygotsky's Understandings of Play: Symbolic Play as Individual, Sociocultural, and Educational Interpretation. In *Oxford Handbooks Online*. Accessible at: https://doi.org/10.1093/oxfordhb/9780195393002.013.0005.

Göncü, A., Mistry, J. & Mosier, C., 2000. Cultural variations in the play of toddlers. *International Journal of Behavioral Development*, 24(3), pp. 321–329.

Goyal, D., Gay, C. & Lee, K., 2009. Fragmented maternal sleep is more strongly correlated with depressive symptoms than infant temperament at three months postpartum. *Archives of Women's Mental Health*, 12(4), pp. 229–237.

Grasso, D. J. et al., 2009. ERP correlates of attention allocation in mothers processing faces of their children. *Biological Psychology*, 81(2), 95–102.

Graziano, M.S., Cooke, D.F. & Taylor, C.S., 2000. Coding the location of the arm by sight. *Science*, 290(5497), pp. 1782–1786.

Gustafsson, E. et al., 2013. Fathers are just as good as mothers at recognizing the cries of their baby. *Nature Communications*, 4, p.1698.

Gustafsson, M.-L. et al., 2019. Changes in the amount of sleep and daytime sleepiness: A follow-up study of schoolchildren from ages 10 to 15 years. *International Journal of Nursing Practice*, 25(1), p.e12689.

Häberling, I.S., Corballis, P.M. & Corballis, M.C., 2016. Language, gesture, and handedness: evidence for independent lateralized networks. *Cortex*, 82, pp. 72–85.

Haggan, M., 2002. Self-reports and self-delusion regarding the use of Motherese: implications from Kuwaiti adults. *Language Sciences*, 24(1), 17–28.

Hale, L. & Guan, S., 2015. Screen time and sleep among school-aged children and adolescents: a systematic literature review. *Sleep Medicine Reviews*, 21, pp. 50–58.

Hall, W. A. et al., 2006. Effects of an intervention aimed at reducing night waking and signaling in 6- to 12-month-old infants. *Behavioral Sleep Medicine*, 4(4), 242–261.

Hammons, A.J. & Fiese, B.H., 2011. Is frequency of shared family meals related to the nutritional health of children and adolescents? *Pediatrics*, 127(6), pp. e1565–74.

Harlow, M., 2013. Toys, Dolls and the Material Culture of Childhood. In J.E. Grubbs and T. Parkin, eds, *The Oxford Handbook of Childhood and Education in the Classical World*, Oxford University Press, pp. 322–340.

Harris, P.L. et al., 1986. Children's understanding of the distinction between real and apparent emotion. *Child Development*, 57(4), pp. 895–909.

Hart, B. & Risley, T.R., 2003. The early catastrophe: The 30 million word gap by age 3. *American Educator*, 27(1), pp. 4–9.

Hartanto, A., Toh, W.X. & Yang, H., 2018. Bilingualism narrows socioeconomic disparities in executive functions and self-regulatory behaviors during early childhood: evidence from the early childhood longitudinal study. *Child Development*. Available at: http://dx.doi.org/10.1111/cdev.13032.

Heath, S.B., 1983. *Ways with Words: Language, Life and Work in Communities and Classrooms*, Cambridge University Press.

Heider, F. & Simmel, M., 1944. An experimental study of apparent behavior. *The American Journal of Psychology*, 57(2), pp. 243–259.

Hepach, R., Vaish, A., & Tomasello, M., 2013. Young children sympathize less in response to unjustified emotional distress. *Developmental Psychology*, 49(6), 1132–1138.

Hepach, R. et al., 2016. Young children want to see others get the help they need. *Child Development*, 87(6), pp. 1703–1714.

Hepper, P.G., 1993. In utero release from a single transient hypoxic episode: a positive reinforcer? *Physiology & Behavior*, 53(2), pp. 309–311.

Hoff, E., 2003. The specificity of environmental influence: socioeconomic status affects early vocabulary development via maternal speech. *Child Development*, 74(5), pp. 1368–1378.

Hoff, E., 2006. How social contexts support and shape language development. *Developmental Review: DR*, 26(1), pp. 55–88.

Hoff, E., 2013. *Language Development*, Cengage Learning.

Hoff-Ginsberg, E., 1998. The relation of birth order and socioeconomic status to children's language experience and language development. *Applied Psycholinguistics*, 19(4), pp. 603–629.

Horne, JA & Reyner, Louise, 1995. Sleep related vehicle accidents. *BMJ* (Clinical research ed.). 310. 565–7. 10.1136/bmj.310.6979.565.

van der Horst, K., 2012. Overcoming picky eating. Eating enjoyment as a central aspect of children's eating behaviors. *Appetite*, 58(2), pp. 567–574.

van der Horst, K. et al., 2016. Picky eating: associations with child eating characteristics and food intake. *Appetite*, 103, pp. 286–293.

van der Horst, K., Ferrage, A. & Rytz, A., 2014. Involving children in meal preparation. Effects on food intake. *Appetite*, 79, pp. 18–24.

Howard, J., 2018. How parents set their kids bedtimes around the world. Available at: https://edition.cnn.com/2018/01/05/health/baby-bedtimes-parenting-without-borders-explainer-intl/index.html [accessed 7 February 2021].

Hughes, A.M., 2015. *Developing Play for the Under 3s: The Treasure Basket and Heuristic Play*, Routledge.

Hughes, C. & Devine, R.T., 2017. For better or for worse? Positive and negative parental influences on young children's executive function. *Child Development*. Available at: http://dx.doi.org/10.1111/cdev.12915.

Hughes, F.P., 2009. *Children, Play, and Development*, SAGE Publishing.

Huttenlocher, J. et al., 2010. Sources of variability in children's language growth. *Cognitive Psychology*, 61(4), pp. 343–365.

Hyland, R. et al., 2006. Nutrition-related health promotion through an after-school project: the responses of children and their families. *Social Science & Medicine*, 62(3), pp. 758–768.

Hysing, M. et al., 2015. Sleep and use of electronic devices in adolescence: results from a large population-based study. *BMJ Open*, 5(1), p.e006748.

Jaafar, S.H. et al., 2016. Effect of restricted pacifier use in breastfeeding term infants for increasing duration of breastfeeding. *Cochrane Database of Systematic Reviews*, (8), p.CD007202.

Jago, R. et al., 2012. Parent and child screen-viewing time and home media environment. *American Journal of Preventive Medicine*, 43(2), pp. 150–158.

James, W., 2007. *The Principles of Psychology*, volume 1, Cosimo, Inc.

Jandó, G. et al., 2012. Early-onset binocularity in preterm infants reveals experience-dependent visual development in humans. *Proceedings of the National Academy of Sciences of the United States of America*, 109(27), pp. 11049–11052.

Jasińska, K.K. & Petitto, L.-A., 2018. Age of bilingual exposure is related to the contribution of phonological and semantic knowledge to successful reading development. *Child Development*, 89(1), pp. 310–331.

Jay, M. et al., 2008. Iron Age breastfeeding practices in Britain: isotopic evidence from Wetwang Slack, East Yorkshire. *American Journal of Physical Anthropology*, 136(3), pp. 327–337.

Jenni, O.G. & O'Connor, B.B., 2005. Children's sleep: an interplay between culture and biology. *Pediatrics*, 115 (suppl 1), pp. 204–216.

Kauer, J. et al., 2015. Adult picky eating. Phenomenology, taste sensitivity, and psychological correlates. *Appetite*, 90, pp. 219–228.

Kavanaugh, R.D., 2010. Origins and Consequences of Social

Pretend Play. In A.D. Pellegrini, ed., *The Oxford Handbook of the Development of Play*, Oxford University Press.
Keller, M.A. & Goldberg, W.A., 2004. Co-sleeping: help or hindrance for young children's independence? *Infant and Child Development*, 13(5), pp. 369–388.
Khan, K.S. et al., 2016. Age-related progressions in story structure in young children's narratives. *Journal of Speech, Language, and Hearing Research*, 59(6), pp. 1395–1408.
Kim, P. et al., 2010. The plasticity of human maternal brain: longitudinal changes in brain anatomy during the early postpartum period. *Behavioral Neuroscience*, 124(5), 695–700.
Kirkorian, H.L. & Anderson, D.R., 2017. Anticipatory eye movements while watching continuous action across shots in video sequences: a developmental study. *Child Development*, 88(4), pp. 1284–1301.
Kitamura, A. et al., 2010. Role played by afferent signals from olfactory, gustatory and gastrointestinal sensors in regulation of autonomic nerve activity. *Biological & Pharmaceutical Bulletin*, 33(11), pp. 1778–1782.
Köymen, B., Mammen, M. & Tomasello, M., 2016. Preschoolers use common ground in their justificatory reasoning with peers. *Developmental Psychology*, 52(3), pp. 423–429.
Krause, A.J. et al., 2019. The pain of sleep loss: a brain characterization in humans. *The Journal of Neuroscience*, 39(12), pp. 2291–2300.
Krupenye, C. et al., 2016. Great apes anticipate that other individuals will act according to false beliefs. *Science*, 354(6308), pp. 110–114.
Laakso, M.-L. et al., 1999. Early intentional communication as a predictor of language development in young toddlers. *First Language*, 19(56), pp. 207–231.
Lasky, R.E. & Williams, A.L., 2005. The development of the auditory system from conception to term. *NeoReviews*, 6(3), pp. e141–e152.
Lattner, S., Meyer, M.E. & Friederici, A.D., 2005. Voice

perception: sex, pitch, and the right hemisphere. *Human Brain Mapping*, 24(1), pp. 11–20.

Leat, S.J., Yadav, N.K. & Irving, E.L., 2009. Development of visual acuity and contrast sensitivity in children. *Journal of Optometry*, 2(1), pp. 19–26.

Lee, D.N. & Aronson, E., 1974. Visual proprioceptive control of standing in human infants. *Perception & Psychophysics*, 15(3), pp. 529–532.

Lee, S. et al., 2019. Longitudinal associations of childhood bedtime and sleep routines with adolescent body mass index. *Sleep*, 42(1). Available at: http://dx.doi.org/10.1093/sleep/zsy202.

Lempers, J.D., Flavell, E.R. & Flavell, J.H., 1977. The development in very young children of tacit knowledge concerning visual perception. *Genetic Psychology Monographs*, 95(1), pp. 3–53.

Lévy, F., Gheusi, G., & Keller, M., 2011. Plasticity of the parental brain: a case for neurogenesis. *Journal of Neuroendocrinology*, 23(11), 984–993.

Lewis, R.J. & Janda, L.H., 1988. The relationship between adult sexual adjustment and childhood experiences regarding exposure to nudity, sleeping in the parental bed, and parental attitudes toward sexuality. *Archives of Sexual Behavior*, 17(4), pp. 349–362.

Liem, D.G. & Mennella, J.A., 2002. Sweet and sour preferences during childhood: role of early experiences. *Developmental Psychobiology*, 41(4), pp. 388–395.

Li, L. et al., 2009. Observations on increased accidental asphyxia deaths in infancy while cosleeping in the state of Maryland. *The American Journal of Forensic Medicine and Pathology*, 30(4), pp. 318–321.

Liu, L. & Kager, R., 2015. Bilingual exposure influences infant VOT perception. *Infant Behavior & Development*, 38, pp. 27–36.

Lozada, M., D'Adamo, P. & Carro, N., 2014. Plasticity of altruistic behavior in children. *Journal of Moral Education*, 43(1), pp. 75–88.

Lynch, C. et al., 2014. Fruit and vegetable consumption in a sample of 11-year-old children in ten European countries – the PRO GREENS cross-sectional survey. *Public Health Nutrition*, 17(11), pp. 2436–2444.

Machin, A., 2018. *The Life of Dad: The Making of a Modern Father*. Simon and Schuster.

Mamassian, P., 2015. Sensory development: late integration of multiple cues. *Current Biology: CB*, 25(21), pp. R1044–R1046.

Marsh, J., 2010. Young children's play in online virtual worlds. *Journal of Early Childhood Research*, 8(1), pp. 23–39.

Martin, A. & Olson, K.R., 2013. When kids know better: paternalistic helping in 3-year-old children. *Developmental Psychology*, 49(11), pp. 2071–2081.

Martin-Biggers, J. et al., 2014. Come and get it! A discussion of family mealtime literature and factors affecting obesity risk. *Advances in Nutrition* , 5(3), pp. 235–247.

Maßberg, D. & Hatt, H., 2018. Human olfactory receptors: novel cellular functions outside of the nose. *Physiological Reviews*, 98(3), pp. 1739–1763.

Masten, C.L. et al., 2009. Neural correlates of social exclusion during adolescence: understanding the distress of peer rejection. *Social Cognitive and Affective Neuroscience*, 4(2), pp. 143–157.

McCoy, R.C. et al., 2004. Frequency of bed sharing and its relationship to breastfeeding. *Journal of Developmental and Behavioral Pediatrics: JDBP*, 25(3), pp. 141–149.

McGivern, R.F. et al., 2002. Cognitive efficiency on a match to sample task decreases at the onset of puberty in children. *Brain and Cognition*, 50(1), pp. 73–89.

McHale, S.M., Crouter, A.C. & Tucker, C.J., 2001. Free-time activities in middle childhood: links with adjustment in early adolescence. *Child Development*, 72(6), pp. 1764–1778.

McInnes, K. et al., 2009. Behavioural differences exhibited by children when practising a task under formal and playful conditions. *Educational and Child Psychology*, 26(2), pp. 31–39.

McKenna, J.J. et al., 1993. Infant–parent co-sleeping in an evolutionary perspective: implications for understanding infant sleep development and the sudden infant death syndrome. *Sleep*, 16(3), pp. 263–282.

McKenna, J.J. & McDade, T., 2005. Why babies should never sleep alone: a review of the co-sleeping controversy in relation to SIDS, bedsharing and breast feeding. *Paediatric Respiratory Reviews*, 6(2), pp. 134–152.

McMillan, B.T.M. & Saffran, J.R., 2016. Learning in complex environments: the effects of background speech on early word learning. *Child Development*, 87(6), pp. 1841–1855.

Mead, M. & Macgregor, F.C., 1951. Growth and culture: a photographic study of Balinese childhood. Available at: https://psycnet.apa.org/fulltext/1952-03326-000.pdf.

Meguerditchian, A., Vauclair, J. & Hopkins, W.D., 2013. On the origins of human handedness and language: a comparative review of hand preferences for bimanual coordinated actions and gestural communication in nonhuman primates. *Developmental Psychobiology*, 55(6), pp. 637–650.

Meltzoff, A.N. & Moore, M.K., 1977. Imitation of facial and manual gestures by human neonates. *Science*, 198(4312), pp. 75–78.

Mennella, J.A. & Beauchamp, G.K., 1991. Maternal diet alters the sensory qualities of human milk and the nursling's behavior. *Pediatrics*, 88(4), pp. 737–744.

Mennella, J.A. & Beauchamp, G.K., 2002. Flavor experiences during formula feeding are related to preferences during childhood. *Early Human Development*, 68(2), pp. 71–82.

Mennella, J.A., Johnson, A. & Beauchamp, G.K., 1995. Garlic ingestion by pregnant women alters the odor of amniotic fluid. *Chemical Senses*, 20(2), pp. 207–209.

Mikkilä, V. et al., 2004. Longitudinal changes in diet from childhood into adulthood with respect to risk of cardiovascular diseases: The Cardiovascular Risk in Young

Finns Study. *European Journal of Clinical Nutrition*, 58(7), pp. 1038–1045.

Miller, H. E., Vlach, H. A., & Simmering, V. R., 2017. Producing spatial words is not enough: understanding the relation between language and spatial cognition. *Child Development*, 88(6), 1966–1982.

Miller, J.G., Kahle, S. & Hastings, P.D., 2015. Roots and benefits of costly giving: children who are more altruistic have greater autonomic flexibility and less family wealth. *Psychological Science*, 26(7), pp. 1038–1045.

Milligan, K., Astington, J.W. & Dack, L.A., 2007. Language and theory of mind: meta-analysis of the relation between language ability and false-belief understanding. *Child Development*. Available at: https://doi.org/10.1111/j.1467-8624.2007.01018.x.

Mindell, J.A. et al., 2015. Bedtime routines for young children: a dose-dependent association with sleep outcomes. *Sleep*, 38(5), pp. 717–722.

Mindell, J.A., 1993. Sleep disorders in children. *Health Psychology* (American Psychological Association), 12(2), pp. 151–162.

Mireku, M.O. et al., 2019. Night-time screen-based media device use and adolescents' sleep and health-related quality of life. *Environment International*, 124, pp. 66–78.

Mischel, W. & Ebbesen, E.B., 1970. Attention in delay of gratification. *Journal of Personality and Social Psychology*, 16(2), pp. 329–337.

Moll, H., Khalulyan, A. & Moffett, L., 2017. 2.5-year-olds express suspense when others approach reality with false expectations. *Child Development*, 88(1), pp. 114–122.

Montoya, J. L. et al., 2012. Regional brain responses in nulliparous women to emotional infant stimuli. *PloS One*, 7(5), e36270.

Moon, R.Y. et al., 2012. Pacifier use and SIDS: evidence for a consistently reduced risk. *Maternal and Child Health Journal*, 16(3), pp. 609–614.

Morelli, G.A. et al., 1992. Cultural variation in infants' sleeping arrangements: questions of independence. *Developmental Psychology*, 28(4), p.604.

Morgan, P.J. et al., 2010. The impact of nutrition education with and without a school garden on knowledge, vegetable intake and preferences and quality of school life among primary-school students. *Public Health Nutrition*, 13(11), pp. 1931–1940.

Morris, S. et al., 2001. Economic evaluation of strategies for managing crying and sleeping problems. *Archives of Disease in Childhood*, 84(1), pp. 15–19.

Mosko, S. et al., 1997. Maternal proximity and infant CO_2 environment during bedsharing and possible implications for SIDS research. *American Journal of Physical Anthropology*, 103(3), pp. 315–328.

Mueller, V., Sepulveda, A., & Rodriguez, S., 2014. The effects of baby sign training on child development. *Early Child Development and Care*, 184(8), 1178–1191.

Nardini, M. et al., 2006. Differential developmental trajectories for egocentric, environmental and intrinsic frames of reference in spatial memory. *Cognition*, 101(1), pp. 153–172.

NCSDR/NHTSA Expert Panel on Driver Fatigue and Sleepiness, 1999. *Drowsy Driving and Automobile Crashes*, Available at: https://patentimages.storage.googleapis.com/04/97/4c/4a2103019ac838/US7301465.pdf [accessed 25 September 2019].

Nederkoorn, C., Jansen, A. & Havermans, R.C., 2015. Feel your food. The influence of tactile sensitivity on picky eating in children. *Appetite*, 84, pp. 7–10.

Neifert, M., Lawrence, R. & Seacat, J., 1995. Nipple confusion: toward a formal definition. *The Journal of Pediatrics*, 126(6), pp. S125–S129. Available at: http://dx.doi.org/10.1016/s0022-3476(95)90252-x.

Nelson, K., 1985. *Making Sense: The Acquisition of Shared Meaning (Developmental Psychology Series)* 1st edition, Academic Press.

Nelson, P.B., Adamson, L.B. & Bakeman, R., 2008. Toddlers' joint engagement experience facilitates preschoolers' acquisition of theory of mind. *Developmental Science*, 11(6), pp. 847–852.

Neumark-Sztainer, D. et al., 2014. What's for dinner? Types of food served at family dinner differ across parent and family characteristics. *Public Health Nutrition*, 17(1), pp. 145–155.

New, R.S. & Richman, A.L., 1996. Maternal Beliefs and Infant Care Practices in Italy and the United States. In S. Harkness and C.M. Super, eds, *Parents' Cultural Belief Systems: Their Origins, Expressions, and Consequences*, The Guilford Press, pp. 385–404.

Newman, R.S., 2005. The cocktail party effect in infants revisited: listening to one's name in noise. *Developmental Psychology*, 41(2), pp. 352–362.

Nippold, M.A., 1993. Developmental markers in adolescent language: syntax, semantics, and pragmatics. *Language, Speech, and Hearing Services in Schools*, 24(1), pp. 21–28.

Ochs, E., 1982. Talking to children in Western Samoa. *Language In Society*, 11(1), pp. 77–104.

Okami, P., Weisner, T. & Olmstead, R., 2002. Outcome correlates of parent–child bedsharing: an eighteen-year longitudinal study. *Journal of Developmental and Behavioral Pediatrics*, 23(4), pp. 244–253.

Panksepp, J. et al., 1994. Effects of neonatal decortication on the social play of juvenile rats. *Physiology & Behavior*, 56(3), pp. 429–443. Available at: http://dx.doi.org/10.1016/0031-9384(94)90285-2.

Parga, J.J. et al., 2018. A description of externally recorded womb sounds in human subjects during gestation. *PLOS ONE*, 13(5), p.e0197045.

Patrick, J. et al., 1980. Patterns of human fetal breathing during the last 10 weeks of pregnancy. *Obstetrics and Gynecology*, 56(1), pp. 24–30.

Pellegrini, A.D., Dupuis, D. & Smith, P.K., 2007. Play in evolution and development. *Developmental Review*, 27(2), pp. 261–276.

Pellegrini, A.D. & Smith, P.K., 1998. Physical activity play: the nature and function of a neglected aspect of playing. *Child Development*, 69(3), pp. 577–598.

Pellis, S.M. & Pellis, V.C., 1987. Play-fighting differs from serious fighting in both target of attack and tactics of fighting in the laboratory rat *Rattus norvegicus*. *Aggressive Behavior*, 13(4), pp. 227–242.

Pellis, S.M. & Pellis, V.C., 1990. Differential rates of attack, defense, and counterattack during the developmental decrease in play fighting by male and female rats. *Developmental Psychobiology*, 23(3), pp. 215–231.

Peterson, C.C., 2000. Kindred spirits: influences of siblings' perspectives on theory of mind. *Cognitive Development*, 15(4), pp. 435–455.

Peterson, C.C. & Siegal, M., 2002. Mindreading and moral awareness in popular and rejected preschoolers. *The British Journal of Developmental Psychology*, 20(2), pp. 205–224.

Phillips, A.T. & Wellman, H.M., 2005. Infants' understanding of object-directed action. *Cognition*, 98(2), pp. 137–155.

Pika, S. et al., 2005. The gestural communication of apes. *Gesture*, 5(1–1), pp. 41–56.

Pinker, S., 1995. *The Language Instinct: The New Science of Language and Mind*, Penguin Press.

Plessow, F. et al., 2011. Chronic sleep curtailment impairs the flexible implementation of task goals in new parents. *Journal of Sleep Research*, 20(2), pp. 279–287.

Plester, B.A. & Sayers, J.G., 2007. Taking the piss: the functions of banter in three IT companies. *Humor: International Journal of Humor Research*, 20(2), pp. 157–187.

Porges, S.W., 2011. *The Polyvagal Theory: Neurophysiological Foundations of Emotions, Attachment, Communication, and Self-regulation* (Norton Series on Interpersonal Neurobiology), W. W. Norton.

Potegal, M. & Einon, D., 1989. Aggressive behaviors in adult rats deprived of playfighting experience as juveniles. *Developmental Psychobiology*, 22(2), pp. 159–172.

Power, T.G., 1999. *Play and Exploration in Children and Animals*, Psychology Press.

Putnam., F.W., 1997. *Dissociation in Children and Adolescents: A Developmental Perspective*, 1st edition, Guilford Press.

Quatman-Yates, C.C. et al., 2012. A systematic review of sensorimotor function during adolescence: a developmental stage of increased motor awkwardness? *British Journal of Sports Medicine*, 46(9), pp. 649–655.

Quintilian & Butler, H.E., 1920. *'The Institutio Oratoria' of Quintilian: With an English Translation*, W. Heinemann.

Rasmussen, C.E. & Jiang, Y.V., 2019. Judging social interaction in the Heider and Simmel movie. *Quarterly Journal of Experimental Psychology*, 72(9), pp. 2350–2361.

Rasmussen, M. et al., 2008. Secular trends in fruit intake among Danish schoolchildren, 1988 to 2006: changing habits or methodological artefacts? *The International Journal of Behavioral Nutrition and Physical Activity*, 5, p. 6.

Reid, M.J., Walter, A.L. & O'Leary, S.G., 1999. Treatment of young children's bedtime refusal and nighttime wakings: a comparison of 'standard' and graduated ignoring procedures. *Journal of Abnormal Child Psychology*, 27(1), pp. 5–16.

Ribot, K.M., Hoff, E. & Burridge, A., 2018. Language use contributes to expressive language growth: evidence from bilingual children. *Child Development*, 89(3), pp. 929–940.

Rigda, R.S., McMillen, I.C. & Buckley, P., 2000. Bed sharing patterns in a cohort of Australian infants during the first six months after birth. *Journal of Paediatrics and Child Health*, 36(2), pp. 117–121.

Robinson, C.C. et al., 2003. Sequential transition patterns of preschoolers' social interactions during child-initiated play: is parallel-aware play a bidirectional bridge to other play states? *Early Childhood Research Quarterly*, 18(1), pp. 3–21.

Robinson, C.W. & Zajicek, J.M., 2005. Growing minds: the effects of a one-year school garden program on six constructs of life skills of elementary school children. *HortTechnology*, 15(3), pp. 453–457.

Robinson-O'Brien, R., Story, M., & Heim, S., 2009. Impact of garden-based youth nutrition intervention programs: a review. *Journal of the American Dietetic Association*, 109(2), 273–280.

Roopnarine, J.L. 2010. Cultural Variations in Beliefs about Play, Parent–Child Play, and Children's Play. In *Oxford Handbooks Online*. https://doi.org/10.1093/oxfordhb/9780195393002.013.0003

Rosen, M., 2019. *Michael Rosen's Book of Play: Why Play Really Matters, and 101 Ways to Get More of it in Your Life*, Profile Books.

Rosenstein, D. & Oster, H., 1988. Differential facial responses to four basic tastes in newborns. *Child Development*, 59(6), pp. 1555–1568.

de Rosnay, M. & Hughes, C., 2006. Conversation and theory of mind: do children talk their way to socio-cognitive understanding? *The British Journal of Developmental Psychology*, 24(1), pp. 7–37.

Roth-Hanania, R., Davidov, M. & Zahn-Waxler, C., 2011. Empathy development from 8 to 16 months: early signs of concern for others. *Infant Behavior & Development*, 34(3), pp. 447–458.

Rowe, M.L., 2008. Child-directed speech: relation to socioeconomic status, knowledge of child development and child vocabulary skill. *Journal of Child Language*, 35(1), pp. 185–205.

Rucas, S.L. & Miller, A.A., 2013. Sleep and risk-taking propensity in life history and evolutionary perspectives. Available at: https://www.semanticscholar.org/paper/f8ef1e0b94d72144bce83241677cbce1713554ed [accessed 19 September 2019].

Rupp, A.C. et al., 2018. Distinct ipRGC subpopulations mediate light's acute and circadian effects on body temperature and sleep. Available at: http://dx.doi.org/10.1101/496323.

Sabbagh, M.A. et al., 2006. Executive functioning and theory-of-mind in preschool children from Beijing, China: comparisons with US preschoolers. *Psychological Science*, 17, pp. 74–81.

Sachs, J., Bard, B. & Johnson, M.L., 1981. Language learning with restricted input: case studies of two hearing children of deaf parents. *Applied Psycholinguistics*, 2(1), pp. 33–54.

Sadeh, A. et al., 2007. Infant sleep and parental sleep-related cognitions. *Journal of Family Psychology* (American Psychological Association), 21(1), pp. 74–87.

Sadeh, A.V.I. et al., 2009. Sleep and sleep ecology in the first 3 years: a web-based study. *Journal of Sleep Research*, 18(1), pp. 60–73.

Saxton, M., 2017. *Child Language: Acquisition and Development*, SAGE Publishing.

Schaal, B., Marlier, L. & Soussignan, R., 1998. Olfactory function in the human fetus: evidence from selective neonatal responsiveness to the odor of amniotic fluid. *Behavioral Neuroscience*, 112(6), pp. 1438–1449.

Schousboe, I. & Winther-Lindqvist, D., 2013. *Children's Play and Development: Cultural-Historical Perspectives*, Springer Science & Business Media.

Schwab, J.F. et al., 2018. Fathers' repetition of words is coupled with children's vocabularies. *Journal of Experimental Child Psychology*, 166, pp. 437–450. Available at: http://dx.doi.org/10.1016/j.jecp.2017.09.012.

Senghas, A. & Coppola, M., 2001. Children creating language: how Nicaraguan sign language acquired a spatial grammar. *Psychological Science*, 12(4), pp. 323–328.

Shahaeian, A. et al., 2011. Culture and the sequence of steps in theory of mind development. *Developmental Psychology*, 47(5), pp. 1239–1247.

Simon, A., 1987. Emotional stability pertaining to the game of Dungeons & Dragons. *Psychology in the Schools*, 24(4), pp. 329–332.

Singer, J.L. & Singer, D.G., 1998. Barney & Friends as entertainment and education: evaluating the quality and effectiveness of a television series for preschool children. Available at: https://psycnet.apa.org/record/1997-36540-007.

Singh, L. et al., 2018. Novel word learning in bilingual and monolingual infants: evidence for a bilingual advantage. *Child Development*, 89(3), pp. e183–e198.

Smith, T.J., Levin, D. & Cutting, J.E., 2012. A window on reality: perceiving edited moving images. *Current Directions in Psychological Science*, 21(2), pp. 107–113.

Smotherman, W.P., 1982. Odor aversion learning by the rat fetus. *Physiology & Behavior*, 29(5), pp. 769–771.

Snow, C.E., 1972. Mothers' speech to children learning language. *Child Development*, 43(2), pp. 549–565.

Snow, C.E., 2013. Social Perspectives on the Emergence of Language. In B. MacWhinney, ed, *The Emergence of Language*, Psychology Press, pp. 275–294.

Snow, C.E. et al., 1976. Mothers' speech in three social classes. *Journal of Psycholinguistic Research*, 5(1), pp. 1–20.

Soderstrom, M., 2007. Beyond babytalk: Re-evaluating the nature and content of speech input to preverbal infants. *Developmental Review*, 27(4), pp. 501–532.

Sperry, D. E., Sperry, L. L., & Miller, P. J., 2018. Language does matter: but there is more to language than vocabulary and directed speech. *Child Development*. Available at: https://doi.org/10.1111/cdev.13125.

Steger, B., 2004. Negotiating Sleep Patterns in Japan. In B. Steger and L. Brunt, eds, *Night-time and Sleep in Asia and the West*, Routledge, pp. 77–98.

Stephenson, R., Caron, A.M. & Famina, S., 2015. Behavioral sleep–wake homeostasis and EEG delta power are decoupled by chronic sleep restriction in the rat. *Sleep*, 38(5), pp. 685–697.

Stevens, E.E., Patrick, T.E. & Pickler, R., 2009. A history of infant feeding. *The Journal of Perinatal Education*, 18(2), pp. 32–39.

Stiles, A., 2006. Robert Louis Stevenson's 'Jekyll and Hyde' and the double brain. *Studies in English literature*, 46(4), pp. 879–900.

Storr, W., 2020. *The Science of Storytelling: Why Stories Make Us Human, and How to Tell Them Better*. William Collins.

Stremler, R. et al., 2006. A behavioral-educational intervention to promote maternal and infant sleep: a pilot randomized, controlled trial. *Sleep*, 29(12), pp. 1609–1615.

Sumner, E. et al., 2019. Cake or broccoli? Recency biases children's verbal responses. *PLOS ONE*, 14(6), p.e0217207.

Swain, J. E. et al. Parenting and beyond: common neurocircuits underlying parental and altruistic caregiving. *Parenting, Science and Practice*, 12(2–3), 115–123.

Taguchi, H.L., 2014. New Materialisms and Play. In L. Brooker et al., eds, *The SAGE Handbook of Play and Learning in Early Childhood*, SAGE Publishing, pp. 79–90.

Tamis-LeMonda, C.S. et al., 1996. Responsive parenting in the second year: specific influences on children's language and play. *Infant and Child Development*, 5(4), pp. 173–183.

Tamis-LeMonda, C.S. et al., 2004. Fathers and mothers at play with their 2- and 3-year-olds: contributions to language and cognitive development. *Child Development*, 75(6), pp. 1806–1820.

Tamis-LeMonda, C.S. et al., 2018. Routine language: speech directed to infants during home activities. *Child Development*. Available at: http://dx.doi.org/10.1111/cdev.13089.

Telzer, E.H. et al., 2013. The effects of poor quality sleep on brain function and risk taking in adolescence. *NeuroImage*, 71, pp. 275–283.

Thomas, A., 2006. Fan fiction online: Engagement, critical response and affective play through writing. *Australian Journal of Language & Literacy*, 29(3).

Tom, M.S., Fischbeck, P.S. & Hendrickson, C.T., 2016. Energy use, blue water footprint, and greenhouse gas emissions for current food consumption patterns and dietary recommendations in the US. *Environment Systems and Decisions*, 36(1), pp. 92–103.

Tomasello, M. & Haberl, K., 2003. Understanding attention: 12- and 18-month-olds know what is new for other persons. *Developmental Psychology*, 39(5), pp. 906–912.

Townsend, E. & Pitchford, N.J., 2012. Baby knows best? The impact of weaning style on food preferences and body mass index in early childhood in a case-controlled sample. *BMJ Open*, 2(1), p.e000298.

Ulber, J., Hamann, K. & Tomasello, M., 2016. Extrinsic rewards diminish costly sharing in 3-year-olds. *Child Development*, 87(4), pp. 1192–1203.

Vaish, A., Carpenter, M. & Tomasello, M., 2010. Young children selectively avoid helping people with harmful intentions. *Child Development*, 81(6), pp. 1661–1669.

Vanderheyden, W.M. et al., 2018. Astrocyte expression of the *Drosophila* TNF-alpha homologue, Eiger, regulates sleep in flies. *PLOS Genetics*, 14(10), p.e1007724.

Van Lancker, D. & Cummings, J.L., 1999. Expletives: neurolinguistic and neurobehavioral perspectives on swearing. *Brain Research Reviews*, 31(1), pp. 83–104.

Verheijen, G.P. et al., 2019. The influence of competitive and cooperative video games on behavior during play and friendship quality in adolescence. *Computers in Human Behavior*, 91, pp. 297–304.

Vickers, Z., 1991. Sound perception and food quality. *Journal of Food Quality*, 14(1), pp. 87–96.

Viner, R.M. et al., 2019. Roles of cyberbullying, sleep, and physical activity in mediating the effects of social media use on mental health and well-being among young people in England: a secondary analysis of longitudinal data. *The Lancet: Child & Adolescent Health*. Available at: http://dx.doi.org/10.1016/S2352-4642(19)30186-5.

Wang, A. T. et al. 2006. Developmental changes in the neural basis of interpreting communicative intent. *Social Cognitive and Affective Neuroscience*, 1(2), 107–121

Warneken, F. & Tomasello, M., 2006. Altruistic helping in human infants and young chimpanzees. *Science*, 311(5765), pp. 1301–1303.

Warneken, F. & Tomasello, M., 2013a. Parental presence and encouragement do not influence helping in young children: parental influence on helping in young children. *Infancy* (International Society on Infant Studies), 18(3), pp. 345–368.

Warneken, F. & Tomasello, M., 2013b. The emergence of contingent reciprocity in young children. *Journal of Experimental Child Psychology*, 116(2), pp. 338–350.

Webb, A.R. et al., 2015. Mother's voice and heartbeat sounds elicit auditory plasticity in the human brain before full gestation. *Proceedings of the National Academy of Sciences of the United States of America*, 112(10), pp. 3152–3157.

Webber, L. et al., 2010. Associations between children's appetitive traits and maternal feeding practices. *Journal of the American Dietetic Association*, 110(11), pp. 1718–1722.

Wehr, T.A. et al., 1993. Conservation of photoperiod-responsive mechanisms in humans. *The American Journal of Physiology*, 265(4 Pt 2), pp. R846–57.

Weisberg, D. S. et al., 2013. Talking it up: play, language development, and the role of adult support. *American Journal of Play*, 6(1), 39–54.

Welles-Nystrom, B. (2005). Co-sleeping as a window into Swedish culture: considerations of gender and health care. *Scandinavian Journal of Caring Sciences*, 19(4), 354–360.

Wellman, H.M., 2011. Developing a theory of mind. In U. Goswami, ed, *The Wiley-Blackwell Handbook of Childhood Cognitive Development*, 2nd edition, pp. 258–284.

Wellman, H.M. & Liu, D., 2004. Scaling of Theory-of-Mind tasks. *Child Development*, 75(2), pp. 523–541.

Werker, J.F., 1986. The development of cross-language speech perception. *The Journal of the Acoustical Society of*

America, 79(S1). Available at: https://www.researchgate.net/publication/253530647_The_development_of_cross-language_speech_perception [accessed 8 October 2019].

Werker, J.F. et al., 1981. Developmental aspects of cross-language speech perception. *Child Development*, 52(1), pp. 349–355.

Werker, J.F. & Tees, R.C., 1983. Developmental changes across childhood in the perception of non-native speech sounds. *Canadian Journal of Psychology*, 37(2), pp. 278–286.

Werker, J.F. & Tees, R.C., 1984. Cross-language speech perception: evidence for perceptual reorganization during the first year of life. *Infant Behavior & Development*, 7(1), pp. 49–63.

Werthmann, J. et al., 2015. Bits and pieces. Food texture influences food acceptance in young children. *Appetite*, 84, pp. 181–187.

Whitebread, D. et al., 2009. Play, cognition and self-regulation: what exactly are children learning when they learn through play? *Educational and Child Psychology*, 26(2), p. 40.

Wong, R.S. et al., 2020. Parent technology use, parent–child interaction, child screen time, and child psychosocial problems among disadvantaged families. *The Journal of Pediatrics*. Available at: http://dx.doi.org/10.1016/j.jpeds.2020.07.006.

Woodruff, S.J. & Kirby, A.R., 2013. The associations among family meal frequency, food preparation frequency, self-efficacy for cooking, and food preparation techniques in children and adolescents. *Journal of Nutrition Education and Behavior*, 45(4), pp. 296–303.

Woollacott, M., Debu, B. & Mowatt, M., 1987. Neuromuscular control of posture in the infant and child: is vision dominant? *Journal of Motor Behavior*, 19(2), pp. 167–186.

Wright, P., MacLeod, H.A. & Cooper, M.J., 1983. Waking at night: the effect of early feeding experience. *Child: Care, Health and Development*, 9(6), pp. 309–319.

Xie, W. et al., 2019. Poor sleep quality and compromised

visual working memory capacity. *Journal of the International Neuropsychological Society*, 25(6), pp. 583–594.

Yang, J. et al., 2015. Pre-constancy vision in infants. *Current Biology*, 25(24), pp. 3209–3212.

Yip, M., 2002. *Tone*, Cambridge University Press.

Yovsi, R.D. & Keller, H., 2007. The architecture of cosleeping among wage-earning and subsistence farming Cameroonian Nso families. *Ethos*, 35(1), pp. 65–84.

Yow, W.Q. & Markman, E.M., 2011. Bilingualism and children's use of paralinguistic cues to interpret emotion in speech. *Bilingualism: Language and Cognition*, 14(04), pp. 562–569.

Yow, W.Q. & Markman, E.M., 2016. Children increase their sensitivity to a speaker's nonlinguistic cues following a communicative breakdown. *Child Development*, 87(2), pp. 385–394.

Yu, Q. & Kitayama, S., 2019. Does facial action modulate neural responses of emotion? An examination with the late positive potential (LPP). *Emotion*. Available at: http://dx.doi.org/10.1037/emo0000717.

Zeidler, H. et al., 2016. Taking turns or not? Children's approach to limited resource problems in three different cultures. *Child Development*, 87(3), pp. 677–688.

Zimmerman, E. & Thompson, K., 2015. Clarifying nipple confusion. *Journal of Perinatology* (California Perinatal Association), 35(11), pp. 895–899.

Zwart, R. et al., 2005. The affordance of gap crossing in toddlers. *Infant Behavior & Development*, 28(2), pp. 145–154.

Notes

Introduction: The Only Advice You Need

1. Mischel & Ebbesen 1970
2. Machin 2018
3. Grasso et al. 2009
4. Swain et al. 2012
5. Kim et al. 2010
6. Lévy et al. 2011
7. Montoya et al. 2012
8. Bos et al. 2010
9. Panksepp et al. 1994

1: Little Aliens

1. James 2007
2. Smith et al. 2012
3. Storr 2020
4. Newman 2005
5. Leat et al. 2009
6. Braddick et al. 1983
7. Jandó et al. 2012
8. Mamassian 2015
9. Byrne et al. 2011; Corney & Lotto 2007

10. Yang et al. 2015
12. Kirkorian & Anderson 2017
12. Nardini et al. 2006
13. Dye & Bavelier 2010
14. Anbuhl et al. 2016
15. Brandt et al. 2013
16. Lasky & Williams 2005
17. Parga et al. 2018
18. Webb et al. 2015
19. DeCasper & Spence 1986
20. Blasi et al. 2011
21. Anbuhl et al. 2016
22. DeLoache et al. 2004
23. Ehrsson et al. 2004
24. Graziano et al. 2000
25. Quatman-Yates et al. 2012
26. Bertenthal et al. 1997
27. Godoi & Barela 2008
28. Woollacott et al. 1987
29. Zwart et al. 2005

2: Learning to Eat – From Bump to Broccoli

1. Kitamura et al. 2010
2. Bushdid et al. 2014
3. Maßberg & Hatt 2018
4. Smotherman 1982
5. Hepper 1993
6. Patrick et al. 1980
7. Patrick et al. 1980
8. Mennella et al. 1995
9. Schaal et al. 1998
10. Crystal & Bernstein 1998
11. Stevens et al. 2009
12. Jay et al. 2008
13. Dunne et al. 2019

14. Neifert et al. 1995
15. Fisher & Inch 1996
16. Zimmerman & Thompson 2015
17. Jaafar et al. 2016
18. Moon et al. 2012
19. Keller & Goldberg 2004
20. Mennella & Beauchamp 1991
21. Mennella & Beauchamp 2002
22. Liem & Mennella 2002
23. Rosenstein & Oster 1988
24. Glendinning 1994
25. Barbehenn & Peter Constabel 2011
26. Bentley 2006
27. Brown 2018
28. Townsend & Pitchford 2012
29. Cameron et al. 2012
30. Forestell & Mennella 2007

3: Food Fights

1. Fiese & Schwartz 2008
2. Werthmann et al. 2015
3. Fassbender 2011
4. Werthmann et al. 2015; Van der Horst et al. 2016
5. Lynch et al. 2014
6. Rasmussen et al. 2008
7. Mikkilä et al. 2004
8. Van der Horst et al. 2016
9. Falciglia et al. 2000
10. Dubois et al. 2007; Van der Horst 2012
11. Nederkoorn et al. 2015
12. Kauer et al. 2015
13. Kauer et al. 2015
14. American Psychiatric Association 2013
15. Webber et al. 2010
16. Van der Horst 2012

17. Galloway et al. 2006
18. Batsell et al. 2002
19. Anam 2019
20. Fisher & Birch 1999
21. Robinson-O'Brien et al. 2009
22. Morgan et al. 2010
23. Robinson & Zajicek 2005
24. Van der Horst 2012
25. Van der Horst et al. 2014
26. Dougherty & Silver 2007
27. Hyland et al. 2006
28. Woodruff & Kirby 2013
29. Martin-Biggers et al. 2014
30. Neumark-Sztainer et al. 2014
31. Donahue & Mitchell 2019
32. Corfe 2018
33. Van der Horst 2012
34. Hammons & Fiese 2011
35. Fiese & Schwartz 2008

4: From 'Go the F*ck to Sleep' to 'Why Are You Still in Bed?' Why Sleep Is Never Simple

1. Vanderheyden et al. 2018
2. Crowley et al. 2007
3. Stephenson et al. 2015
4. Carno et al. 2003
5. Bentivoglio & Grassi-Zucconi 1997
6. Jenni & O'Connor 2005
7. Horne & Reyner 1995
8. Plessow et al. 2011
9. Gay et al. 2004
10. Bratis et al. 2010
11. Goyal et al. 2009
12. Delhikar et al. 2019; Xie et al. 2019
13. Krause et al. 2019

14. Dimitrov et al. 2019
15. Stremler et al. 2006
16. McKenna & McDade 2005
17. McKenna et al. 1993
18. Doi 2014
19. Anders & Taylor 1994
20. Welles-Nystrom 2005
21. Keller & Goldberg 2004
22. McKenna & McDade 2005
23. Gessner et al. 2001; Li et al. 2009
24. Blair et al. 2009
25. McKenna & McDade 2005
26. Doan et al. 2007
27. McKenna & McDade 2005
28. Blair et al. 2009
29. McCoy et al. 2004; Rigda et al. 2000
30. McKenna & McDade 2005
31. Mosko et al. 1997
32. Keller & Goldberg 2004
33. Forbes et al. 1992
34. Lewis & Janda 1988; Okami et al. 2002
35. Crawford 1994
36. Ferber 2006
37. Mindell 1993
38. Jenni & O'Connor 2005
39. New & Richman 1996
40. Steger 2004
41. Mead & Macgregor 1951
42. Morelli et al. 1992
43. Jenni & O'Connor 2005
44. Yovsi & Keller 2007
45. Ekirch 2001
46. Wehr et al. 1993
47. Mindell 1993
48. Sadeh et al. 2007

49. Ball 2003
50. Wright et al. 1983; Butte et al. 1992
51. Morris et al. 2001
52. Ball 2003
53. Sadeh et al. 2007
54. Sadeh et al. 2007
55. Reid et al. 1999
56. Hall et al. 2006
57. Sadeh et al. 2009
58. Lee et al. 2019
59. Mindell et al. 2015
60. Covington et al. 2019
61. Howard 2018
62. Gustafsson et al. 2019
63. Hysing et al. 2015; Hale & Guan 2015
64. Cain & Gradisar 2010
65. Alter 2017
66. Viner et al. 2019
67. Exelmans & Van den Bulck 2016
68. Mireku et al. 2019
69. Fernandez et al. 2018
70. Rupp et al. 2018
71. Mireku et al. 2019
72. Telzer et al. 2013
73. Rucas & Miller 2013

5: Listening Ears On, Please! How to Communicate with Babies

1. Gustafsson et al. 2013
2. Mueller et al. 2014
3. Hoff 2013
4. Lattner et al. 2005
5. Hoff 2013
6. Hoff 2013
7. Van Lancker & Cummings 1999

8. Corballis 2014
9. Stiles 2006
10. Chance & Crow 2007
11. Bauer 1993; Ehret 1987
12. Chomsky 2010
13. Meguerditchian et al. 2013; Corballis 2017; Cartmill & Byrne 2010; Häberling et al. 2016; Pika et al. 2005; Flinker et al. 2015; Arbib 2005
14. Corballis 2014
15. Fodor 1966
16. Chomsky 2006; Chomsky 1975
17. Ervin-Tripp 1971
18. Cross 1979
19. Ochs 1982
20. Cross 1979
21. Hoff 2006
22. Cross 1979
23. Golinkoff & Ames 1979; Schwab et al. 2018
24. Snow 1972
25. Pinker 1995, p. 94
26. Annie Mae as quoted in Heath 1983, p. 84
27. Haggan 2002
28. Soderstrom 2007
29. Carpenter, Nagell & Tomasello 1998; Laakso et al. 1999
30. Tamis-LeMonda et al. 1996
31. Barnes et al. 1983
32. Hoff 2006
33. Nelson 1985
34. Liu & Kager 2015
35. Singh et al. 2018
36. Jasińska & Petitto 2018
37. Hartanto et al. 2018; Barac et al. 2016
38. Yow & Markman 2016; Yow & Markman 2011
39. Ribot et al. 2018
40. Werker & Tees 1984; Werker & Tees 1983; Werker et al. 1981

41. Werker 1986
42. Creel et al. 2018
43. Sumner et al. 2019
44. McMillan & Saffran 2016
45. Erard 2019

6: From Speaking to Reading: How Kids Learn to Express Themselves

1. Saxton 2017
2. De Carvalho et al. 2016
3. Ambridge et al. 2013
4. Golinkoff & Alioto 1995
5. Banasik 2013
6. Frith & Frith 2003
7. Crago et al. 1997
8. Goldin-Meadow 2005; Senghas & Coppola 2001
9. Tamis-LeMonda et al. 2018
10. Sperry et al. 2018
11. Hart & Risley 2003
12. Gilkerson et al. 2017; Hoff 2003; Hoff-Ginsberg 1998; Huttenlocher et al. 2010; Rowe 2008
13. Snow 2013
14. Hoff 2006
15. Snow et al. 1976; Sachs et al. 1981
16. Hoff 2006
17. Singer & Singer 1998
18. Rowe 2008
19. Tamis-LeMonda et al. 2004
20. Ervin-Tripp 1996
21. Ervin-Tripp 1996
22. Köymen et al. 2016
23. Miller et al. 2017
24. Botvin & Sutton-Smith 1977
25. Khan et al. 2016
26. Nippold 1993

7: Unicorn-Robot-Firefighter-Princesses: Why Stories and Play Are the Best Thing You Can Share with Kids

1. Hughes 2015, p. 2
2. Taguchi 2014
3. Quintilian & Butler 1920, p. 33
4. Harlow 2013
5. Brooker et al. 2014
6. Schousboe & Winther-Lindqvist 2013
7. Carlson 2011
8. McInnes et al. 2009
9. Burghardt 2010, p. 9
10. Burghardt 2010
11. Bruckman 1999
12. Elkind 2007
13. McInnes et al. 2009
14. Burghardt 2010, pp. 13–16
15. Bateson 2010
16. Bateson 2010, p. 46
17. Kavanaugh 2010
18. Power 1999
19. Rosen 2019, p. 20
20. Kavanaugh 2010
21. McInnes et al. 2009
22. Göncü et al. 2000
23. Everett 2010, p. 88
24. Göncü & Gaskins 2010
25. Roopnarine 2010
26. Weisberg et al. 2013
27. Buchsbaum et al. 2012
28. Fabes et al. 2001
29. De Rosnay & Hughes 2006; Sabbagh et al. 2006; Whitebread et al. 2009; Milligan et al. 2007
30. Decety et al. 2004
31. Floden et al. 2008
32. Eisenberger et al. 2003

33. Masten et al. 2009
34. Coplan et al. 2008
35. Robinson et al. 2003
36. McHale et al. 2001
37. Thomas 2006
38. Simon 1987
39. Adams 2013
40. Chalmers & Locke-Haydon 1984
41. Potegal & Einon 1989
42. Pellis & Pellis 1990; Pellis & Pellis 1987
43. Pellegrini et al. 2007
44. Panksepp et al. 1994
45. Hughes 2009
46. Bekoff 1972
47. Plester & Sayers 2007
48. Pellegrini & Smith 1998
49. Bekoff & Allen 1998
50. Hughes 2009
51. Putnam 1997, p. 211
52. Cordes & Miller 2000
53. Goldstein 2013
54. Verheijen et al. 2019
55. Jago et al. 2012
56. Wong et al. 2020
57. Marsh 2010

8: What's On Your Mind: Learning to Understand Other People's Thoughts – and Our Own

1. Heider & Simmel 1944
2. Rasmussen & Jiang 2019
3. Wellman 2011
4. Wellman 2011
5. Krupenye et al. 2016
6. Wellman & Liu 2004
7. Shahaeian et al. 2011; Frank et al. 2010

8. Dixson et al. 2017
9. Meltzoff & Moore 1977
10. Yu & Kitayama 2019
11. Nelson et al. 2008
12. Hughes & Devine 2017
13. Peterson 2000
14. Brown & Dunn 1991
15. Dunn et al. 1991; Dunn et al. 1987
16. Harris et al. 1986
17. Moll et al. 2017
18. Peterson & Siegal 2002
19. Tomasello & Haberl 2003
20. Dunphy-Lelii & Wellman 2004
21. Lempers et al. 1977
22. Dumontheil et al. 2010
23. Phillips & Wellman 2005
24. Behne et al. 2005
25. Call et al. 2004
26. Carpenter, Akhtar & Tomasello 1998
27. Casey et al. 2000

9: The Kids Are All Right

1. Roth-Hanania et al. 2011
2. Warneken & Tomasello 2013a
3. Warneken & Tomasello 2013b
4. Email interview with Dr Julia Ulber February 2019
5. Drummond et al. 2017
6. Dunn et al. 2010
7. Aknin et al. 2012
8. Hepach et al. 2016
9. Interview by email with Dr Amrisha Vaish February 2019
10. Warneken & Tomasello 2006
11. Bay-Hinitz et al. 1994
12. Email exchange with Dr Alia Martin February 2019

13. Martin & Olson 2013
14. Email exchange with Dr Alia Martin February 2019
15. Vaish et al. 2010
16. Interview by email with Dr Amrisha Vaish February 2019
17. Hepach et al. 2013
18. Interview by email with Dr Amrisha Vaish February 2019
19. McGivern et al. 2002; Carey et al. 1980
20. Wang et al. 2006
21. Gardner & Steinberg 2005
22. Zeidler et al. 2016
23. Aknin et al. 2015
24. Email exchange with Dr Alia Martin February 2019
25. Fu et al. 2016
26. Phone call with Dr Kang Lee February 2019
27. Email exchange with Dr Gail Heyman February 2019
28. Phone call with Dr Kang Lee February 2019
29. Banerjee 2002
30. Bennett & Yeeles 1990
31. Phone call with Dr Kang Lee February 2019
32. Email exchange with Dr Gail Heyman February 2019
33. Phone call with Dr Kang Lee February 2019
34. Warneken & Tomasello 2013a
35. Ulber et al. 2016
36. Email exchange with Dr Julia Ulber February 2019
37. Email exchange with Dr Julia Ulber February 2019
38. Porges 2011
39. Miller et al. 2015
40. Lozada et al. 2014
41. Deković & Janssens 1992
42. Hepach et al. 2016
43. Email exchange with Dr Julia Ulber February 2019

Index